SAGE was founded in 1965 by Sara Miller McCune to support the dissemination of usable knowledge by publishing innovative and high-quality research and teaching content. Today, we publish over 900 journals, including those of more than 400 learned societies, more than 800 new books per year, and a growing range of library products including archives, data, case studies, reports, and video. SAGE remains majority-owned by our founder, and after Sara's lifetime will become owned by a charitable trust that secures our continued independence.

Los Angeles | London | New Delhi | Singapore | Washington DC | Melbourne

DEMYSTIFYING CRIMINAL JUSTICE SOCIAL WORK IN INDIA

DEMYSTIFYING CRIMINAL JUSTICE SOCIAL WORK IN INDIA

EDITED BY

MARK DAVID CHONG
ABRAHAM P. FRANCIS

Los Angeles | London | New Delhi
Singapore | Washington DC | Melbourne

First published in 2017 by

 SAGE Publications India Pvt Ltd
B1/I-1 Mohan Cooperative Industrial Area
Mathura Road, New Delhi 110 044, India
www.sagepub.in

SAGE Publications Inc
2455 Teller Road
Thousand Oaks, California 91320, USA

SAGE Publications Ltd
1 Oliver's Yard, 55 City Road
London EC1Y 1SP, United Kingdom

SAGE Publications Asia-Pacific Pte Ltd
3 Church Street
#10-04 Samsung Hub
Singapore 049483

Published by Vivek Mehra for SAGE Publications India Pvt Ltd, typeset in 10.5/12.5pt Cambria by Diligent Typesetter India Pvt Ltd, Delhi and printed at Chaman Enterprises, New Delhi.

Library of Congress Cataloging-in-Publication Data Available

ISBN: 978-93-860-6247-5 (HB)

SAGE Team: Supriya Das, Sandhya Gola and Ritu Chopra

We dedicate this book to all those social workers/ practitioners who believe in constantly improving our practice of social work and for their engagement in the field of criminal justice system.

As editors of this book, we dedicate our combined efforts to all the chapter authors and their communities of practice.

We dedicate this book to all those who allowed us to gain practice wisdom from them—our clients, colleagues, students, groups and communities, whose support and critical review have helped us to produce this collection of writings.

Bulk Sales

SAGE India offers special discounts
for purchase of books in bulk.
We also make available special imprints
and excerpts from our books on demand.

For orders and enquiries, write to us at

Marketing Department
SAGE Publications India Pvt Ltd
B1/I-1, Mohan Cooperative Industrial Area
Mathura Road, Post Bag 7
New Delhi 110044, India

E-mail us at **marketing@sagepub.in**

Get to know more about SAGE

Be invited to SAGE events, get on our mailing list.
Write today to **marketing@sagepub.in**

This book is also available as an e-book.

Contents

Section III
Way Forward

List of Illustrations

Tables

Figures

List of Abbreviations

BPR	business process re-engineering
BPR&D	Bureau of Police Research and Development
CCA	criminology and correctional administration
CCL	child in conflict with law
CHRI	Commonwealth Human Rights Initiative
CJIs	criminal justice institutions
CJS	criminal justice system
CJSW	criminal justice social work
CNCP	Child in Need of Care and Protection
CPO	Central Police Organisations
CRC	Convention on the Rights of the Child
CRF	Central Paramilitary Forces
CrPC	Criminal Procedure Code
CSWCJS	Certificate Social Work and Criminal Justice System
CWC	Child Welfare Committee
DCB	Digital Communication Technology
DGP	Director General of Police
DPSP	Directive Principles of State Policy
Dy IGP	Deputy Inspector General of Police
EIS	East India Company
EPCG	European Probation Curriculum Group
FAPs	field action projects
FIR	First Information Report
ICDS	Integrated Child Development Scheme
ICT	Internet Communication Technology
IGNOU	Indira Gandhi National Open University
IPC	Indian Penal Code
IPS	Indian Police Service
ITPA	Immoral Traffic (Prevention) Act
JCL	Juveniles in Conflict with Law
JDS	Justice Delivery System
JJ Act	Juvenile Justice (Care and Protection of Children) Act

JJB	Juvenile Justice Board
JJS	juvenile justice system
LGBT	lesbian, gay, bisexual and transgender
MSU	Maharaja Sayajirao University of Baroda
MSW	Master of Social Work
NCRB	National Crime Records Bureau
NCW	National Commission for Women
NGO	non-governmental organisation
NICFS	National Institute of Criminology & Forensic Science
NHRC	National Human Rights Commission
NPC	National Police Commission
NISD	National Institute of Social Defence
OCD	obsessive–compulsive disorder
PADC	Police Act Drafting Committee
PIL	Public Interest Litigation
PM	Principal Magistrate
PO	probation officer
PTSD	post-traumatic stress disorder
PSW	police social work
RC	Ribeiro Committee
RCJJ	Resource Cell for Juvenile Justice
SARC	Second Administrative Reforms Commission
SAARC	South Asian Association of Regional Cooperation
SBP	strengths-based practice
SCW	State Commission for Women
SHRC	State Human Rights Commission
SOSW	School of Social Work
SP	Superintendent of Police
SLL	Special and Local Laws
SSP	Senior Superintendent of Police
TANDA	Towards Advocacy, Networking and Developmental Action
TISS	Tata Institute of Social Sciences
UGC	University Grants Commission
UN	United Nations
UNESCO	United Nations Educational, Scientific and Cultural Organization
WHO	World Health Organization

Foreword

I am delighted indeed to write a foreword for the book edited by Dr Mark David Chong and Associate Professor Abraham P. Francis titled *Demystifying Criminal Justice Social Work in India*. This book is the result of a collaboration between two scholars (the former being a criminologist and a lawyer, and the latter, a social work academic) which will help social work students, practitioners, researchers and educators in their various endeavours with the criminal justice system (CJS) in India. In doing so, they have attracted scholars from various universities, colleges and non-governmental organisations (NGOs) in India to contribute and share their experiences and expertise with the readers. Thus, this book offers a critical insight into criminal justice social work (CJSW) based on their research, practice, reflections and clinical expertise.

As we know, the application of social work in the CJS is an important area of practice in India. It is one that requires culturally appropriate research, innovation and relevant practice frameworks. The academic discourses, debates and ideas presented in this book reveal an excellent academic rigour and showcase robust thinking in this field. It demands serious thinking, prompts the reader to revisit the often taken-for-granted concepts and supports them to develop a practice framework that is grounded in research. This will hopefully inspire the readers to advocate for changes in their own practice contexts.

The book additionally initiates some relevant contemporary and evidence-based discussions on various matters related to the Indian CJS. I find the title *Demystifying Criminal Justice Social Work in India* particularly interesting and fascinating as it talks about demystifying some of the often misunderstood or mistaken notions around this subject, thereby bringing greater clarity to this important theme. In fact, it is a path-breaking research project that will not only inspire social work students in shaping the way they perceive the world, but will also be an impetus to further research, collaboration and publications to enrich the field of CJSW in India.

What do social workers do? This is a question very often asked by people from both practice and the academia. Social workers are employed in a variety of contexts and work towards promoting social justice and human rights. In July 2014, the International Federation of Social Workers (IFSW) as well as the International Association of Schools of Social Work defined 'social work' as:

> [A] practice-based profession and an academic discipline that promotes social change and development, social cohesion, and the empowerment and liberation of people. Principles of social justice, human rights, collective responsibility and respect for diversities are central to social work. Underpinned by theories of social work, social sciences, humanities and indigenous knowledge, social work engages people and structures to address life challenges and enhance wellbeing. (IFSW, n.d.)

Rapp and Sullivan (2014) stated that '[t]he importance of recognizing and exploiting strengths in the natural environment is vitally important to social work, and is one clear area that distinguishes this discipline from others in the helping professions' (p. 137). Not content with the critical analysis of the existing issues that plague the CJS, this book offers a glimpse of how criminal justice social workers can address these challenges in new and exciting ways. Here, the editors extol the virtues of utilising a strengths-based practice to mitigate the coercive and stigmatising elements of the CJS. That said, this approach does not simply discount the obvious problems or weaknesses of the offenders or of the victims of crime, but rather concentrates on offering possibilities, promises and hope to those who often lack such optimism in life (Francis, 2014, p. 27). To that end, Francis and Chong (2015) proposed the embedding of three 'C's into the CJS that represent a strengths-based practice (SBP), which can be utilised alongside the existing and necessary fundamental aims of control and compliance. These three 'C's are as follows: climate, compassion and commitment (Francis & Chong, 2015, p. 95). Without going into detail here, suffice it to say that social workers employing such a perspective will view their clients (whether offenders or victims), not just as problems or symptoms of some social malaise but as human beings—imperfect but not without redeemable qualities that can be leveraged upon to encourage reformation. Such an approach would dovetail ideally into the social workers' existing professional principles of recovery, social justice and fight against stigmatisation, discrimination and violations of human rights (AASW Code of Ethics, 2010, p. 12; AASW Practice Standards, 2013, p. 7; AASW Practice Standards for Mental Health Social Workers, 2014, pp. 6, 8). The SBP will certainly bolster a criminal justice social worker's efforts to address powerlessness, marginality, stigma and socio-economic disadvantage at a time when a punitive and custodial approach is gaining an upper hand over the reformative, humane and rehabilitative approach in the legislatures, bureaucracies and the public after the Nirbhaya case in India. This has led to the amendment of law for trying juveniles as adults in cases of grievous crimes, which is regressive in my view.

There is no doubt that social work practice in the CJS can be challenging (Patterson 2012, p. 129). Sadly, institutional support for CJSW in India has not progressed as much as it has in the United States, Scotland or Canada. While social workers undergo a rigorous training both in the field and in class rooms, there has always been much debate around specialisations in social work education, particularly at the undergraduate level. Unfortunately, CJSW modules do not feature very prominently in most undergraduate social work programmes in the country. This is something that should be reviewed as social workers definitely require specialised training to practice in the CJS as it requires significant knowledge and skills in other disciplines/subjects such as criminology, criminal law and procedure, as well as criminal psychology, to name just a few. As Patterson argued, '[e]fforts to challenge social injustice and racial disparities will require that social work collaborate with other disciplines' (2012, p. 175). Consequently, developing relevant interdisciplinary expertise is essential to social work practice in the CJS. It is indeed unfortunate that institutions such as National Institute of Social Defence and Directorates of Social Welfare/Corrections have over the years been headed by administrators rather than professional social workers who preceded them.

Given the rapid social changes occurring in India, as well as the ever-changing landscape of professional practice, we cannot remain silent spectators but need to adequately respond to the challenges confronting society with conviction, determination and sensitivity. Social workers are called upon to respond to or intervene in these contexts not only by demonstrating their competence and confidence in practice but also by being compassionate and innovative in their approach (Francis, 2015). This book offers readers an opportunity to not only analyse these challenges from a critical point of view, but also provides guidance on how to meet them head-on with research-based knowledge, robust practical experience and hope.

I, therefore, congratulate the editors and chapter authors for making a significant contribution to the social work literature in this challenging field and wish the readers that they will engage as practitioners in the CJS. I hope this book will inspire them to become involved in more research, to build collaborative ventures and to move beyond the contents of this book to positively touch the lives of offenders and victims of crime, and thereby become messengers of possibility, promise and hope to those who are often the most socially marginalised groups.

Delhi   **Professor R. R. Singh**
30 June 2016   Former Head, Department of Social Work,
                            University of Delhi and Director, Tata
                            Institute of Social Sciences, Mumbai

References

Australian Association of Social Workers. (2010). Code of ethics. Retrieved from http://www.aasw.asn.au/document/item/1201
———. (2013). *Practice standards*. Retrieved from http://www.aasw.asn.au/document/item/4551
———. (2014). *Practice standards for mental health social workers*. Retrieved from https://www.aasw.asn.au/document/item/6739

International Federation of Social Workers (IFSW). (n.d.). *Global definition of social work*. Retrieved from http://ifsw.org/

Francis, A., & Chong, M. D. (2015). Application of strengths-based principles in addressing mental health issues in the criminal justice system. In A. Francis, P. L. Rosa, L. Sankaran, & S. P. Rajeev (Eds), *Social work practice in mental health: Cross-cultural perspectives* (pp. 90–102). New Delhi: Allied Publishers.

Francis, A. P. (2014). Strengths-based practice: 'Not about discounting problems but offering possibilities, promises and hope'. *Adelaide Journal of Social Work, 1*(1), 27–44.

Francis, A. (2015). *The social worker as a multidisciplinary team member: Embedding the 3 C's (competence, confidence and compassion) in social work education in mental health.* SWSD 2015. Conference paper presented at East London, South Africa.

Patterson, G. (2012). *Social work practice in the criminal justice system.* New York: Routledge.

Rapp, C., & Sullivan, W. P. (2014).The strengths model: Birth to toddlerhood. *Advances in Social Work*, *15*(1), 129–42.

Acknowledgements

The publishing of this edited book has been a long and arduous process, beginning sometime in 2013, and only now finding its way to completion in 2017. Throughout this trying period, our chapter contributors have never wavered in their support for this worthwhile endeavour, and for that, Associate Professor Abraham and I, as editors of this book, are most grateful. On our side, this manuscript has gone through four rounds of peer review (two internal and two external), before undergoing another two rounds by reviewers from the publisher, SAGE. This has been an exacting quality control process, and while it is arguable that this manuscript is not perfect, we nevertheless hope that our readers will still recognise and appreciate the quality, breadth and depth of analysis that is on offer here. Our chapter contributors have not only provided the readers with their expert academic insights into this exciting area of criminal justice social work (CJSW), but also shared with them their personal experiences as professional social workers, criminologists and counsellors, their empirical research endeavours as well as their policy reform aspirations.

Let us not mince our words here—this book is clearly seminal in nature! It represents a near comprehensive treatise on how CJSW can be used to address the plight suffered by offenders and victims of crime in India today. It is a manuscript that we believe, through God's grace, will act as an intellectual wellspring for social work and criminology students, researchers and professionals, for years to come. This, of course, would not have been possible without the expertise and generosity of spirit exhibited by our chapter contributors, namely, Professor Vijay Raghavan; Ms Sashwati Mishra; Professor K. Jaishankar; Amit Gopal Thakre; Jamie Fellows; Associate Professor Sonny Jose; Ms Kelly-Ann Williams; Associate Professor Ruchi Sinha; Professor Ilango Ponnuswami; Praveen Varghese Thomas;

Assistant Professor Roshni Nair; Assistant Professor K. P. Asha Mukundan; S. Khandpasole Pravin; Mrs P. Khandpasole Jyoti; Ms Katherine Hoffensetz; Professor Sanjai Bhatt; Dr Atul Pratap Singh; Assistant Professor Digvijoy Phukan; Dr Venkat Pulla; Ms Margaret Henni and Dr Debarati Halder.

Additionally, this endeavour has received some financial support through a grant amounting to AUS$4957.10, awarded by the Faculty of Arts, Education and Social Sciences, James Cook University, in 2013, for sessional marking support and research assistance.

We are also deeply grateful to our internal and external peer reviewers, including the two blind peer reviewers from SAGE, as well as Professor Vishanthie Sewpaul from the University of KwaZulu-Natal (South Africa); Professor R. Srinivasa Murthy, Professor of Psychiatry (Retd), from the Association for the Mentally Challenged, Bengaluru; Dr Selwyn Stanley from Plymouth University; Dr Vimla V. Nadkarni, the President of the International Association of Schools of Social Work (India); Dr Venkat Pulla from Australian Catholic University; Dr R. Nalini from Pondicherry University; Professor Gracious Thomas from Indira Gandhi National Open University; Professor Sanjai Bhatt from the University of Delhi; Professor Pallassana R. Balgopal from the University of Illinois; Associate Professor Archana Dassi from Jamia Millia Islamia University (New Delhi) and Professor Lambert Engelbrecht from Stellenbosch University (South Africa).

And, having the eminent Professor R. R. Singh to write the Foreword for us was simply icing on the cake! As many of you will know, Professor Singh was not only the former Head of the Social Work Department at the University of Delhi, but he was also the Director of Tata Institute of Social Sciences in Mumbai. In his Foreword, Professor Singh expressed his hope that our book would ultimately inspire readers

> to become involved in more research, to build collaborative ventures, and to move beyond the contents of this book to positively touch the lives of offenders and victims of crime, and thereby become messengers of possibility, promise and hope to those who are often the most socially marginalised groups.

This truly encapsulates the essence of what we hope this manuscript will achieve in the future, God willing.

Associate Professor Abraham and I are likewise deeply appreciative of the guidance and patience of SAGE, and, in particular, the efforts of Ms Aditi Chopra, Ms Elina Majumdar (Mukherjee), Mr Shambhu Sahu, Ms Supriya Das and Ms Sandhya Gola, among many others. Where would we be without you!

On a more personal note, I would like to share with you some of my thoughts about this book. This edited book represents a significant milestone in my collaborative partnership with Associate Professor Abraham. In addition to this text, we have already published two book chapters together and are in the process of co-authoring two journal articles on CJSW. He was also instrumental in my applying for three grants and has introduced me to numerous social work academics and practitioners who have enriched my intellectual life considerably. I am pleased to say that Associate Professor Abraham is not just a valued colleague of mine, but also a trusted friend and mentor. I thank God for his friendship and constant encouragement, particularly in the face of personal and professional disappointments. May God always bless him and the fruits of his labour. Indeed, I would not have been privileged to make his acquaintance all those years ago but for Dr Wendy Li who very kindly introduced me to him at a tea organised by the School of Arts and Social Sciences. It was Dr Li who thought that it would be a good idea for me to collaborate with Associate Professor Abraham on a project that she was then involved in as well. Thank you so much, Dr Li!

I would also like to thank

- my beautiful wife, Sharon Lim; my wonderful parents, Dr Chong Seng Kong and Cynthia Mark; my loving sisters, Mellisa Rebecca Chong and Michelle Chong; my maternal grandparents, Anayat Ulla Mark and Grace Mark; my paternal grandparents and step-grandmother, Chong Yoke Cheong, Low Lian Thai and Chan Yook Lean; my parents-in-law, Richard and Lydia Lim;
- my extended family, Uncle Patrick Mark; the MacDonald Family (Uncle John, Auntie Jo, Andrew, Nicole, Dylan, Jason

and Sacha); the Ahmed Family (Uncle Nasir, Auntie Veena, Zainab, Daniel, Zia and Fakhteh); my baptismal Godparents, Uncle Bunny and Auntie Yvonne Gomez (including my God-siblings, Anne, Ian, Jackie, Denis and Bertie); my confirmation Ninong, Consul General Henry Bensurto Jr. (and his lovely wife, Mariza and son, Matthew); my God-children (Jeanne Marie, her husband, Heng Boon Ngee, and sons, Matthew and Mark); my talented cousin, Julian Cheong, and David Ho; Uncle Pierre and Auntie Christine Cheong; Dr Chong Seng Fook and Dr Agnes Tan; Uncle Chong Sing You and Auntie Polly; Meiling and David Blackburn; Jimmy and Conny Chong; the Tan Family (Uncle Meng Kwan, Auntie Kim Choo, my dear jiejie Chen, Alvin, Grace, Rick, Ting, Dr Ken Sutin, Tyan, Nick, Min and Steve); the Ooi Family (Auntie Ah Eng, Dr Ooi Yoon Phaik, Dr Stefan Seiler, Dr Ooi Yoon Lim, Dr Lau Shyan Ling, Yoon Teik, Michelle, Dr Ricky Ooi and Auntie Kooi See); Uncle Chok Kuan; Uncle Eddie Loh and Loh Sau Lai;

- as well as my dear friends, and supportive colleagues, Dr Mark Hon and Dr Yeo Su-Jan; Dr Tracy Loh; Khairul Lokman; Ratner Vellu and Sharayne Fong; Suseela Pillay; Vinit Chhabra; Daniel, Amy, Dylan and Ryan Tan; Krishnan Nadarajan; Sherain Tan; the Solomon Family (Uncle Das, Auntie Inbam; John, Dianne, Helina and Selina); Louis Lim PBM; Dinir Salvador Rios da Rocha; Alan Koh; Sheila de Niro and Nick; James Chan; Serene Lee; Dr Katijah Dawood; Her Honour, Judge Wong Choon Ning; Emberlin Chong; Joseph John PB, PBS; Lashman Singh and Mrs Singh; Glenfield De Souza P. Kepujian PBS; Nabi ha Malim; Anne Durray; Pandiyan Vellasami PBM, PB, PBS; Rita Anthony PB; Angeline Kwah; Sharon Ng; Father Kevin Muldoon; Father Sean Finnegan; Father Joshy Kunnel; His Honour Judge Brian Donovan QC and Brenda Donovan; Cheah Kuan Tatt and Chew Suen Yee; Dr Erwin Lobo and Olivia Nguy-Lobo; Jee Leong; John and Fiona Ting; Kevin Curley; Patricia Rowling; Glenn Chu; Dr Joshua Chang; Looi Kwok Peng; Andrew Chia; The Honourable Sylvia Lim MP; Vinod Sabnani; Associate Professor Narayanan Ganapathy; Prasanna Devi and Murali Nair; Regina and Charles Vincent; Jason Lim; Auntie

Vasantha and Anura Neysadurai; Dr Glenn Marinas; Chua Siew Whoon and Christopher Chua; Cheryl Lim; Auntie Margaret and Dennis Khng; Audrey Goh; Dr James Tan; Dean Ashley Rudge Rudnev; Dr Rachel Shee Wei Leng; the Kurniawan Sisters (Natalia, Dina and Dr Margareth); Cindy Lay; Dr Claire Koh; Uncle and Auntie Lim, Danie and Daniel Lim; Teresa Foong; Harold Ignatius Tan; Abang Azahar; Ellain Tan; Andrew Yeo; Qui Ren Hua; Jeffrey Chen Guanghui; Dr Seto Sai Wang and Iris Ko; Koh Chin Chin; Ong Chin Heng PPA(G); Her Honour, Judge Ong Chin Rhu; Her Honour, Justice Valerie Thean; Sharon Ong; Chong Kah Wei, P. Kepujian; His Honour, Judge Christopher Goh; Dalbir Kaur; Foo Chai Hong; Associate Professor Hayden Lesbirel; Dr Surin Maisrikrod; Dr David Mitchell; Dr Shelley Greer; Dr Nigel Chang; Dr Allison Craven; Associate Professor Garry Kidd; the Ruddick Family (Uncle David, Auntie Kerry, Christopher, Edward, James and Joanna); Rakesh Singh; David Leow; Brian Chew; Sahabuddin; K.V. Grisan; Allister and Jackie Crocker; Superintendent (V) (Retired) Stephen Chee; the Koh Brothers (Kelvin, Eugene and Gaven); David Chew Siong Tai; Mark Tay; Ms Babette Doherty; Dr Theresa Petray; Dr Simon Foale; Dr Claire Brennan; Dr Nick Osbaldiston; Dr Janice Wegner; Dr Robin Rodd; Dr Michael Wood; Associate Professor Anita Lundberg; Dr Victoria Kuttainen; Professor Stephen Graw; Professor Sean Ulm; Professor Russell McGregor; Distinguished Professor Alexandra Aikhenvald; Professor Robert Dixon; Dr Mervyn Bendle; Associate Professor Stephen Moston; Dr Terry Engelberg-Moston; Associate Professor Nonie Harris; Associate Professor Debra Miles; Peter Jones; Dr Narayan Gopalkrishnan; Dr Amanda Nickson; Dr Marcus Barber; Dr Ines Zuchowski; Professor Michael Ackland; Dr Anna Hayes; Associate Professor Douglas Hunt; Dr Christian Reepmeyer; Ms Florence Boulard; Dr George Kutash; Associate Professor Richard Lansdown; Associate Professor Stephen Torre; Associate Professor Nerina Caltabiano; Associate Professor Marie Caltabiano; Associate Professor Susan Gair; Dr Kerry McBain; Dr Marie M'Balla-Ndi; Dr Maxine Newlands; Dr Ariella Van Luyn; Dr James Coughlan; Dr Roger

Wilkinson; Dr Garry Coventry; Dr Eduardo de la Fuente; Dr Beryl Buckby; Dr Leh Woon Mok; Associate Professor Deborah Graham; Dr Peter Raggatt; Dr Lindsay Simpson; Associate Professor Wendy Earles; Lynette Rooke; Rochelle Doherty; Renee Feather; Renee Joyce; Graham Aspinall; Paulene Curcuruto; Deborah Cavanagh; Leona Murray; Natalia Veles; Christine Bird; Robina McDermott; Belinda Wilson; Vicki Matthews; Helen Jusseaume; Alaina Jones; Helen Jackson; Kate Palmer; Wayne Morris; Margaret Smith; Dominique Sandilant; Richa Dixit; Debbie Buckley; Charmaine Hayes-Jonkers; Adrian van Rossum; Michelle Dooley; Sharyn Harrington; Louise Lennon; Michelle McClure; Louise Veitch; Sheryl Giles; Mary O'Donnell; Ruth Millar; Kaeli Mee; Lauren Littler; Stian Andreassen; Ginny Hall; Jodie Wilson; Barbara Pannach; Christopher Ende; Shannon Hogan; Dr Liz Tynan; Dr Julie Funnell; Matthew, Nicole and Logan Fox; Pragathesvaran Letchmanan; Grace Lee Hui Ling; Steven Chiang; Marilyn Lee; Melissa San-Pho; Carmen Seah; Jaliah Mohammed Arif; Lilian Lee Tang Ling; Lum Wai Ling; Marilyn Soh; Srila Kurup; Rudy Gunaratnam; Cynthia Goh-Lim; Darshan Sandhu; Johnny Tan; Ai Ling; Pok Cheng Sim; Mathavan Devadas; Lim Poh Bee; Albert Toh; Teo Yuan Ching; Eileen Ng; Her Honour, Judge Nicole Isabel Loh; Meilina Ong; Caris Tay; Annie Gomez; Her Honour, Judge Wendy Yu; Ferlin Jayatissa; Chng Lye Beng; His Honour, Judge Lim Keng Yeow; Azlina Ahmad; Shok Ling Lee; Wong Thim Chun; Violet Phung; Carol Chen; Lim Siew Lin; His Honour, Judge Eddy Tham; Her Honour, Ms Salina Ishak; Her Honour, Judge Cornie Ng; Eric Tin; His Honour, Judge Shawn Ho; His Honour, Judge Zainol Abeedin; Chan Wai Yin; Kamissah Mahmud; Tham Yeong Shin; Abdul Ghani Majid; Mok-Goh Kit Soon; and Donald Koh.

I am likewise deeply indebted to my teachers and/or mentors, and, in particular, would like to mention how much I appreciate the guidance and efforts taken by Cikgu Tijah; Madam Anne; Ms Kim Leng; Mr Anbu Nathan; Coach Zolkifly; Mr Harold E. Mathieu; Mr Thevanthiran (Mr Dave); Mr Thomas Tan Thian Poh; Ms Lucy Yeo; Mrs Lalitha Perera; Mr Allan Au Yong; Mrs Sivaprasad;

Mrs Fernandez; Ms Lim Siew Lian; Mr Tan Bock Cheng; Mrs Rosalind Koh; Mrs Ong Seok Cheang; Dr Alexander Kerr; Mr Olusoji Elias; Professor Wayne Morrison; Professor Emeritus Rob Reiner; Professor Emeritus Ivan Shearer; Professor Don Rothwell; Professor Emeritus Terry Carney; Ms Sue Ng; His Honour, Senior District Judge Richard Magnus; His Honour, Judge Hamzah Moosa; Mr Lee Choon Yip; Mr Richard Lau; Colonel Lim Chin; Lieutenant (as he then was) Chow Kin Seng; Colonel Tay Ee Learn; Warrant Officer Madam Lim; Corporal M. Y. Lim; Sergeant Mike; Corporal David; Corporal Rahim; Professor Colin Ryan; Professor Janet Greeley; Professor Nola Alloway; Professor Rosita Henry; Professor Robbie Robertson; Professor Sue McGinty; Professor Iain Gordon; Associate Professor Glenn Dawes; Dr Amy Forbes; Dr Anne Swinbourne; Associate Professor Cecily Knight; Associate Professor Kay Martinez; Professor Rob White; Associate Professor Robert Beckman; Professor Ann Brooks; Dr Selina Lim; Dr Greg Manning; Mr Andrew Gowens; Shihan David Chew; Sensei Shannon Bell; Commodore (Retired) Seshadri Vasan; Dr Xin Chen; Professor Helene Marsh; Mr Yeo Li Pheow and Mr Jerry Chen.

My accomplishments would not have been possible without their loving encouragement, guidance and assistance. I am, in very significant ways, a product of their effort and kindness, and I just hope that my meagre contribution to this equation has not left them too disappointed in terms of its outcomes. I also hope that I have not overly disappointed my Lord and God, for without His tender mercy and forgiveness, I would be an absolute shadow of the man that I am now—*Kýrie, eléison*.

To my beloved 'kids'—my students from when I was pursuing my PhD at Sydney Law; my students when I was teaching at Temasek Polytechnic (both police and non-police alike) and my students at James Cook University—this book is for you. Be enthused. Have fun. And work hard. You will always be in my prayers, and may God continue to bless you exceedingly.

Mark David Chong FRSA
PhD (Law), LLM (Merit), LLB (Hons)

Introduction: Demystifying Criminal Justice Social Work—Filling the Void

Mark David Chong and Abraham P. Francis

Introduction*

The valuable role that a professional social worker can play in the criminal justice system (CJS) is indisputable, and this has been the case for a very long time. As highlighted by Treger and Allen (2007), the establishment of a separate juvenile court in the United States in 1899 was a watershed event, not only for youth justice advocates but also for those who were most involved in the day-to-day delivery of social work and welfare services to neglected and delinquent children in Cook County, Illinois. Given their immense contribution to the care and rehabilitation of such challenging youth, social workers would from then on become essential actors within the US CJS more generally as well. Since at least the mid-1980s, the importance of social workers has been

---

*This publication has been produced by the editors only with the aim of enhancing the development of the literature on criminal justice social work. Every effort has been made in preparing this book to provide accurate, up-to-date and relevant information that is in accordance with the accepted standards of practice at the time of publication. The authors of the chapters are solely responsible for the opinions, criticisms and factual information presented by them. As editors, we have carefully reviewed, formatted and made necessary changes to the chapters, and disclaim liabilities, direct or consequential, as a result of any errors or conclusions that may have arisen due to the individual efforts of the authors of this collection.

ostensibly mirrored in the Indian juvenile justice system (JJS) (Kakar, 2015, p. 52). The Juvenile Justice Board (JJB) (what is essentially a children's criminal court in India) was created to adjudicate upon, and to dispose of, cases involving youth who were in conflict with the criminal law. What is so special about this tribunal, however, lies in its composition of members. Each sitting board must have a magistrate, and *two social workers*, for it to be properly constituted (Kakar, 2015, p. 61). Yet, despite this apparently significant role, professional social workers in India who have long been involved in criminal justice practice have not really seen the type of development and prominence experienced and enjoyed by their fellow colleagues elsewhere in the world,[1] for example, in Canada (Champagne & Felizardo, n.d.) and Scotland (Scottish Government, 2010) where the *profession* is actively and institutionally encouraged and financially supported by the State to provide specialist services to offenders and victims of crime. The provision of such bio-psychosocial assistance, often termed as 'criminal justice, correctional or forensic' social work (Wilson, 2010, p. 1), is considered to be an indispensable scaffold sorely needed by offender populations and crime victims alike, with many professional social workers performing substantive roles in community-based non-governmental or non-profit organisations servicing at-risk-of-crime youth, faith-based agencies with similar functions, government-run/funded primary healthcare and behavioural facilities that assist in the monitoring and rehabilitating of ex-convicts, the courts and correctional institutions (both for adults and juveniles) (Wilson, 2010, p. 1).

---

[1] For example, the appointment of 'social workers' to the JJB is not preconditioned on the appointees' professional social work credentials or even their disciplinary-specific academic qualifications, but is primarily based on their relevant life experiences, in this case being their participation in educational, health or welfare activities involving children for at least seven years (Konar, 2005, p. 2). Furthermore, the person appointed as a social worker member of the JJB need only possess a bachelor's degree from a recognised university, with preference being given to applicants having a qualification in 'any one of the social sciences such as criminology, psychology, sociology, social work, economics, home science, education, political science, and studies pertaining to women, rural development, law or medicine' (*The Hindu*, 2015).

Sadly, that same level of institutional support is not seen in India—and to be clear, this is not because the need for such professional expertise is unnecessary. The number of people affected by crime, whether as offenders or victims, is not insignificant by any measure. It should be noted that in 2013 alone, 2,647,722 cognizable crimes[2] under the Indian Penal Code (IPC) were reported to, and registered as First Information Reports (FIRs), by the police across the country (National Crime Records Bureau, 2015a, p. 1). In 2014, this figure had risen to 2,851,563 offences under the same legislation[3] (National Crime Records Bureau, 2015a, p. 1). Of these crimes reported in 2014, 11.6 per cent were of a violent nature,[4] primarily committed in the states of Uttar Pradesh (330,754 cases), Bihar (34,277 cases) and Maharashtra (32,574 cases) (National Crime Records Bureau, 2015a, p. 2). As for crimes committed against women,[5] such offences represented 9.6 per cent of the total number of IPC crimes reported in 2010. By 2014, however, this proportion had increased to 11.8 per cent nationwide (National Crime Records Bureau, 2015a, p. 2). Furthermore, in 2014, a total of 13,833 children had been reported to have been sexually assaulted under the IPC, as well as 4,930 children pursuant to the Protection of Children from Sexual Offences Act (National Crime Records Bureau, 2015a, p. 3). Human trafficking offences under the IPC likewise saw a 38.7 per cent jump in incidences between 2013 and 2014[6] (National Crime Records Bureau, 2015a, p. 3). Juvenile delinquents (also referred to as 'juveniles in conflict with law') were heavily represented in the crime statistics, with the police registering a 5.7 per cent increase of cases brought under the IPC, and a 21.8 per cent surge in cases

---

[2] These are usually the more serious offences that when registered as a First Information Report by the police, empower them to investigate and/or make arrests without the need for a warrant or other sanction from the courts.

[3] These statistics do not, however, include offences committed under special and local Indian laws.

[4] For example, offences against the body, property, women and public safety.

[5] For example, rape, cruelty by a relative, outraging/insulting of modesty, immoral trafficking, kidnapping and abduction, dowry deaths and so on.

[6] For example, slavery and exploitation of a trafficked person.

under other relevant special and local Indian laws (National Crime Records Bureau, 2015a, p. 4).

In response to these reported offences, the police investigated 3,793,771 cases under the IPC, and thereafter, 3,790,812 suspects were arrested in connection with 2,851,563 cases in 2014[7] (National Crime Records Bureau, 2015a, p. 5). Of the 48,230 juveniles apprehended in the same year, while most of them were residing with their parents at the material time (80.2%), over half were from low socio-economic backgrounds (55.6%), most were arrested for the first time (94.6%), slightly more than a fifth were illiterate (21.8%) and only a third had primary level education (31.1%) (National Crime Records Bureau, 2015a, p. 4).

As for those who had been successfully prosecuted and punished by the courts, many of them would find themselves incarcerated in severely draconian conditions. By way of illustration, the occupancy rate[8] of prisons[9] across the country highlighted significant levels of overcrowding.[10] In 2012, the occupancy rate was at 112.2 per cent (National Crime Records Bureau, 2015b, p. i). In 2013, the extent of overcrowding was higher at 118.4 per cent, although in 2014, there was a slight improvement with a 117.4 per cent occupancy rate (National Crime Records Bureau, 2015b, p. i). Such overcrowding was highest in Dadra and Nagar Haveli (331.7%), Chhattisgarh (258.9%) and Delhi (221.6%) (National Crime Records Bureau, 2015b, p. i). Many of these inmates were illiterate or poorly educated (National Crime Records Bureau, 2015b, p. ii), and slightly more than 1 per cent were suffering from mental illness[11] (National Crime Records Bureau, 2015b, p. i).

---

[7] Please note that the number of investigation cases opened by the police in any given year need not necessarily tally with the number of offences reported to them during that same period.

[8] This is defined as the 'number of inmates accommodated in jail against the authorized capacity of 100 inmates'.

[9] This would include jails such as Central, district, sub, women and open, as well as Borstal schools and other special incarcerative facilities.

[10] This occurs when the occupancy rate is more than 100 per cent.

[11] Please note that statistics garnered from other, albeit smaller cohort studies, show a higher incidence of mental illness/disorder among inmates from Indian prisons (Ayirolimeethal, Ragesh, Ramanujam, & George, 2014, p. 152).

Worse still, statistics showed that at the end of 2014, a total of 457 children who were the offspring of 390 convicted female inmates were likewise housed with their mothers in these depressing surroundings (National Crime Records Bureau, 2015b, p. i). Even more egregious, 1,320 children were similarly 'incarcerated' with their mothers in such penal conditions—Women who were, for one reason or another, not granted bail, and consequently, had to remain in the custody of the State (a category of accused persons who are also known as 'undertrials') while awaiting their 'day in court' (National Crime Records Bureau, 2015b, p. i). What made this particularly distressing was the fact that these were the children of women who had not yet been proven guilty in any court of law.

Given these dismal facts and figures, it is obvious that there is indeed an acute need for more professional social workers to become criminal justice practitioners and researchers in this field. Unfortunately, two significant hurdles immediately present themselves. Firstly, there is a strong stigma attached to criminal justice social work (CJSW) given its potentially coercive enforcement and social control roles vis-à-vis the traditional social work objectives of achieving social justice and protecting human rights through the services the profession provides to its clients. In July 2014, the International Federation of Social Workers as well as the International Association of Schools of Social Work (IFSW) defined 'social work' as

> a practice-based profession and an academic discipline that promotes social change and development, social cohesion, and the empowerment and liberation of people. Principles of social justice, human rights, collective responsibility and respect for diversities are central to social work. Underpinned by theories of social work, social sciences, humanities and indigenous knowledge, social work engages people and structures to address life challenges and enhance wellbeing. (IFSW, 2014)

This therefore raises the troubling question as '[t]o whom is the social worker in the justice system obligated, the offender or the community' (Treger & Allen, 2007, p. 46). This is a significant issue because the interests of these two parties may often be poles apart, with a social worker having conflicting roles of 'protecting offender rights, providing social support, and conducting ... rehabilitation', on the one hand, and surveillance, '[implementing] sanctions, and [initiating] breach action when the offender has not complied with a court order', on the other (Moore, 2005, p. 220). Thus, social workers might well be reluctant to seek employment in the CJS as

> [s]ome [of them] may be ideologically opposed to working in the correctional system, wary of losing their professional identity and fearful of complicity with coercive, diagnostic treatment models. Some may be wary of the ethical tensions between the offender and the criminal justice, organisation and societal systems, not to mention the tensions between offender and victim. (Agllias, 2004, p. 332)

Secondly, there is a relative dearth of relevant text and research-based reference books concerning this subject matter, that is, criminal forensic, correctional or CJSW, in India. By way of illustration, a recent publication in 2011 on the state of CJSW in the country did not even cite one book that dealt with such matters from an exclusively Indian perspective (Vadiraj, Gopal, SDTT, & Sahni, 2011). It is arguable that this was because of the lack of books that exclusively covered such a topic in the market. For example, searching through a range of online Indian bookshops and publishing houses, c. 2013, only led to the discovery of the following items:

- William and Christopher (2004) and
- general Indian social work textbooks that have chapter/s on particular aspects of criminal justice practice, for example,

  - Jha (2002)—one chapter on 'social work and delinquents and criminals';
  - Sarkar (2011)—one chapter on 'social work with young offenders';
  - Sachdev (2012)—one chapter on 'the problem of deviance' and
  - Chaudhary (2012)—three chapters on 'laws and drug abuse', 'laws and child trafficking' and 'women, crime and laws'.

Such texts, though excellent, were not at all comprehensive in this regard, at least to the extent that they could be used as a *holistic one-stop research resource* or *textbook* for students and professionals wanting to read about Indian CJSW in greater detail. There were, however, exceptional texts from other jurisdictions, including, for example, the following:

United Kingdom:

- McIvor and Raynor (2007)
- Pickford and Dugmore (2012)

United States:

- Roberts and Springer (2007)
- Patterson (2012)

South Africa:

- Holtzhausen (2012)

Given the concerns aforementioned, there is clearly an urgent need for a local text that will engage more fully with this fascinating area of social work practice in India. In order to address the twin challenges highlighted earlier, such a manuscript would have two primary aims. The first would be to demystify CJSW so as to reassure students and early career practitioners that practising forensic or correctional social work will not inevitably lead to the relinquishing of a social workers' core principles of 'social justice, human rights, collective responsibility and respect for diversities' (IFSW, 2014). Consequently, the present book will attempt to open up a vista of opportunity to engage and challenge social work students and practitioners in India to consider CJSW as not only a worthwhile endeavour of study, but also as a desirable professional calling.

The second objective of the manuscript would be to fill the apparent paucity or void of the relevant *local* academic and professional literature in this area. The chapters of this book would not only include a technical overview of the key issues concerning this specialty but also examples of empirical work and/or rigorous theoretical analysis so as to provide its readers with a template upon which to emulate such scholarly pursuits.

The Structure of the Book and an Outline of the Indian Criminal Justice System

To achieve these laudable aims in a systematic way, the first part of this manuscript will provide its readers with a firm foundational grasp of the key theoretical concepts, paradigms and problems that underpin CJSW in India. Thereafter, the second section will offer concrete 'social work in action' chapters that highlight how these fundamental frameworks can be or have been applied in practice. The final portion of the text will then go on to challenge and push the readers to consider three major areas that require particular attention: encouraging education and training in this area, protecting the human rights of offenders and victims of crime, and addressing an emerging trend of cyber victimisation. The concluding chapter will finally tie up all the loose ends and offer the reader glimpses of what the future could hold for criminal justice social workers. It will hopefully inspire students, scholars and social workers alike to aspire to become an integral and indispensable part of the CJS. In fact, this whole book is designed to help achieve that end by demystifying the day-to-day concerns and practices of criminal justice social workers as they go about servicing and serving their clients, most of whom will be adult offenders, juvenile delinquents and victims of crime.

This simple framework was adopted because it will provide the reader with a relatively easy way of deciphering what is in reality quite complicated ideas, theories and processes. Unfortunately, the Indian CJS is a complex labyrinth of: (a) formal agencies of social control (the most important being, the police, the courts and the prison administration), (b) legislation (for example, the Police Act, Prison Act, IPC, Criminal Procedure Code and Indian Evidence Act) and (c) departmental policies whose lines of jurisdiction and authority often overlap (an outline of the criminal procedural processes will be provided as each chapter in this manuscript is introduced below).

Thus, social workers who are interested in criminal justice practice must develop a keen insight into the workings of the relevant criminal legislative regimes, law enforcement services, judicial system and correctional institutions. As India is a country governed by the rule of law (i.e., that everyone is equal under the law, and that no person, group or even the government is above the law), this becomes an especially important skill to acquire if one hopes to be able to successfully navigate the CJS, particularly because its primary aim may well be contradictory inter se. For example, Thilagaraj noted that the most important objectives of India's CJS are, among others, the 'protection of the rights of victims as well as persons in conflict with law, [and] punishment and rehabilitation of those adjudged guilty of committing of crimes...' (2013, p. 119). Knowing why these incongruities occur, and perhaps more importantly, being aware of how to avoid the pitfalls associated with these contradictions, will require an exploration of the underlying value paradigms and problems that dominate the system.

Section I: Foundational Frameworks, Theories, Concepts and Problems

In this regard, Professor Vijay Raghavan and Sashwati Mishra (Chapter 1) identified for the reader these very pitfalls, and more importantly, the profound influence social work has exerted over the Indian CJS. In the United States, social workers have long been involved in the CJS (Patterson, 2012, p. 14). While not as early as that, social workers in India have also played an important role in their own CJS. From the profession's humble roots in the 1930s to a more concerted and organized effort in the 1950s, this chapter will outline the important achievements of Indian social workers (whether as prison, social welfare and/or probation officers, within the CJS), the underlying social forces, the events that spurred this positive development (Sriranjinin & Gopal, 2011, p. 6), as well as the future challenges the profession will encounter in the face of rampant globalization, increasing income disparity and the withdrawal/reduction of government social services as a result of tighter fiscal budgets (Raghavan, 2013, p. 286).

But to better understand how social workers can make a difference in the lives of offenders, they must be acutely aware of the drivers of human behaviour, particularly the deviant kind. Here, Professor K. Jaishankar and Amit Gopal Thakre (Chapter 2) explain to the reader why understanding the causes of criminal behaviour is critical to any intervention that seeks to deter, rehabilitate, reform and/or reintegrate the offender back into the community. With those ends in mind, criminology assists social workers in identifying and highlighting the various criminogenic factors that significantly increase the likelihood of such offending conduct. Depending upon the school of thought that one appeals to, the roots of deviancy may lie in, for example, the misguided/mistaken exercise of rational free will, weaknesses in our biology (for example, genetic mutations, hormonal/biochemical imbalances, neurotransmitter deficiencies and so on), psychiatric/psychological disorders, dysfunctional social structures/culture/environments, inequitable distribution and oppressive use of power (political/economic/social) and poor/inadequate processes of socialization, just to name a few. However, according to Patterson (2012, p. 10), '[t]he most relevant theories for social work practice are those that consider the influence of both environmental and psychological factors, or biological, psychological, and social environmental influences'. Consequently, while this chapter will provide the reader with an overview of the criminological enterprise, more emphasis will, however, be placed on the theories most used by social workers in this context, that is, those that are bio-social or psycho-social in nature.

This then leads nicely to the next chapter (Chapter 3) where Mark David Chong, Jamie Fellows, Sonny Jose, Abraham P. Francis and Kelly-Ann Williams highlight how the prevalence of mental illness or disorders raises quite distinct challenges for social work practice. To that extent, this chapter will critically examine the nature and incidence of the types of mental illnesses commonly suffered by offenders and victims of crime, the justification for social work intervention, the benefits that would accrue from such involvement, the specific non-psychiatric mental health services that social workers may offer to mentally ill prison inmates and victims of crime and, finally, some of the challenges faced by criminal justice social workers and the potential solutions thereto.

Section II: Criminal Justice Social Work Practice

The next segment of this book will deal primarily with the 'nuts and bolts' of professional social work practice within the CJS.

As the police are the 'gatekeepers' of this institution, it is fitting that we should begin with them. In India, there are key enforcement bodies both at the federal[12] and state[13] levels (Thilagaraj, 2013, p. 200). Specifically empowered to investigate and arrest suspects for cognizable offences,[14] the police are also generally tasked, among other duties, to maintain law and order as well as to prevent crime within the community (Thilagaraj, 2013, p. 201). Ruchi Sinha (Chapter 4) will show how the role of the police officer as the custodian of the CJS makes this formal agent of social control one of the most important actors within society. Given how significant this task is, an active collaboration between social workers and the police should be encouraged. Patterson (2012, p. 51) noted that

> police social work [was identified] as a new area of social work practice in which social workers provide assessment and crisis intervention to persons experiencing delinquency, mental health issues, alcohol and substance use and abuse, family and neighbour conflicts. Additional tasks include providing services to crime victims, counselling police officers and their families, and providing training and consultation.

---

[12] For example, the Central Bureau of Investigation, the Central Intelligence Bureau and the Central Police Reserve.

[13] Which, in turn, is divided jurisdictionally into zones, ranges and districts all under the overall leadership of a Director General of Police.

[14] It should be noted that where the offence reported is not cognizable, the police may still lay that information before a Judicial Magistrate in order to obtain a summons, warrant of arrest, search warrant or any other relevant legal instrument so as to take appropriate action against a suspected offender (Thilagaraj, 2013, pp. 200–01).

These duties can be performed by dedicated civilian social workers or by police officers who have social work qualifications. This chapter will attempt to chart such joint endeavours in India, outlining, in particular, challenges involved in developing collaborative practices (which may be due to the differing cultures, roles and philosophies of the police and the social work profession) and how these obstacles may be overcome, particularly when the

> root cause of the conflict may lie within structural inequalities, a power imbalance in society, or lack of effective and timely psycho-social or socio-legal inputs. Over time, the problem/conflict may erupt again, or may assume a more serious or violent nature. It is here that trained social workers can play an important role. (Raghavan, 2012, p. 10)

Social workers may likewise act as robust scaffolding structures not just for offenders, but likewise for victims who are socially marginalised or disadvantaged because they are unemployed, uneducated, young, suffering from mental illness and/or without familial support. Thus, it will be argued here that social workers are ideally positioned to be able to get to

> the 'bottom of the matter' with the skill sets available to them—the knowledge and the knowhow to work effectively with the police, individuals, groups and communities. Their intervention in the situation can help in addressing the underlying causes and begin a process of realignment of forces towards peace building. (Raghavan, 2012, p. 10)

Achieving such an outcome is, of course, no mean feat, and this chapter will critically explore the role and problems associated with police social work in India, ultimately offering recommendations that will hopefully improve and facilitate greater and more meaningful cooperation between the police and the social work profession.

It should be noted that once a criminal case has been investigated by the police, a number of possible dispositions may occur. First, the police may find that the case was false, it was based on a mistake of fact or law, or a non-cognizable offence was involved or disclosed (National Crime Records Bureau, 2015a, p. 67). Usually, once a closure report to that effect is filed in court, no further action can be taken by the police. If the police, however, are convinced that a true case was disclosed, one of two dispositions become available, that is, the police can either issue a charge sheet that contains the basic information of the suspect's alleged crime/s or the police may decline, for whatever reason, to have any charge sheet filed, but will still submit a final report disclosing a true case to the court (National Crime Records Bureau, 2015a, p. 67). If the former option is selected, the final investigation report (including the relevant evidence) together with the charge sheet will be submitted to the public prosecutor who will thereafter take the matter to the Judicial Magistrate Court for an initial enquiry. If that tribunal is of the opinion that the case is not ill founded and hence should continue to proceed (also called 'taking cognizance of an offence') (Pillai, 2008, p. 254), the matter will then, at some point in the future, be tried in the Judicial Magistrate Court, Session Court or High Court, as the case may be, so as to determine the innocence or guilt of the accused person (Thilagaraj, 2013, p. 205).

While awaiting trial, he/she may apply for permission from the tribunal to be released until their next court appearance.[15] This is called a bail application, and it is premised on the fact that the accused is legally presumed to be innocent until proven guilty beyond reasonable doubt by a court of law (Pillai, 2008, p. 282). This may be done as a matter of right, if the crime is a bailable one,[16] or through an application to ask the court to exercise its discretion to grant bail, if a non-bailable offence[17] is involved (Pillai, 2008, p. 283). If successful, the accused person will thereafter be released on his/her own recognizance/surety (i.e., without posting security) or on the condition that he/she must furnish

---

[15] It should be noted that the police, at the investigation stage, can also grant bail to a suspect if the offence is a bailable one. If a non-bailable offence is suspected to have been committed, the Criminal Procedure Code requires the police to bring the suspect before the court within 24 hours of his/her arrest, at which time, they may, at that point, make a bail application to the presiding Judicial Magistrate.

[16] For example, please refer to the First Schedule of the Criminal Procedure Code.

[17] For example, this refers to offences not listed in the First Schedule of the Criminal Procedure Code.

sufficient security, bond or acceptable bailors (sureties),[18] failing which the accused person will have to be remanded in prison (and hence becomes an 'undertrial' accused) until their next court appearance and/or bail application hearing. The court may, of course, refuse to grant bail, but this is usually only done if, for example, there is a significant likelihood that he/she will abscond, commit other crimes while out on bail, destroy evidence and/or tamper with prosecution witnesses (Pillai, 2008, p. 282).

When the matter finally goes to trial, an adversarial approach is generally adopted in order to determine the innocence or guilt of the accused person. This basically means that such a criminal trial is premised on the assumption that 'the State using its investigative resources and employing competent counsel [i.e. a public prosecutor] will prosecute the accused who, in turn, will employ equally competent legal services [i.e. a defence lawyer] to challenge the evidence of the prosecution' (Pillai, 2008, p. 336). The court (whether the Judicial Magistrate, Session or High Court), while acting as an 'umpire' between the two opposing sides, will nevertheless retain overall control over the proceedings so as to ensure a fair trial, and one that protects not only the public interest but also 'the individual interests of the accused person' (Pillai, 2008, p. 337). Furthermore, where the accused person is indigent and too poor to employ a competent defence counsel, the State will provide him/her with legal aid, paid out of the country's coffers (Pillai, 2008, p. 336).

If the accused person pleads guilty or at the end of the trial is found to be guilty by the court, he/she will then be sentenced by the judge.[19] Punishment meted out (depending upon whether

---

[18] This security or bond may be forfeited at the discretion of the court, if the accused person absconds or jumps bail in order to avoid either the trial or the sentence hearing, if already convicted.

[19] It, of course, goes without saying that if the accused person is acquitted (i.e., found not guilty) by the court, he/she will usually be released immediately. Even if the accused person has been convicted, he/she may still appeal against the conviction and/or the sentence to a superior court. The public prosecutor may, likewise, appeal against an acquittal and/or a sentence, as the case may be.

the case was subject to a warrant, summons or summary trial) may include, among others, admonishment and release, release on probation of good conduct[20] (under Section 360 of the Criminal Procedure Code as opposed to the provisions contained in the Probation of Offenders Act), probation pursuant to the Probation of Offenders Act, a fine (i.e., a financial penalty), forfeiture of property, a term of imprisonment (rigorous or simple), imprisonment for life or the death penalty (Pillai, 2008, pp. 588–89, 598–99).

By far, imprisonment is one of the most common punishments imposed by the court, whether as part of its discretion to do so or because it has been made mandatory by law (Pillai, 2008, p. 607). Nevertheless, there is a

> real risk involved in sending persons, particularly young offenders or first offenders, to prison, because such persons, instead of being reformed there in jail, are more likely to become obdurate criminals as a result of their association with hardened criminals of mature age. (Pillai, 2008, p. 607)

Furthermore,

> it should also be noted that short-term imprisonment does not serve a useful purpose. A short stay in jail sometimes proves more harmful to the accused. It brands a person as a previous convict without affording him the advantage of living a disciplined life in jail for a sufficiently long time. (Pillai, 2008, p. 608)

These are just some of the reasons why the next chapter is so important to this discourse. It will show how correctional social work potentially represents one of the most important contributions that the profession can make to improve the CJS. It would include, for example, its ability and capacity to effectively and empathetically provide a 'wide variety of rehabilitation services related to alcohol and substance abuse, and ... mental health assessments in correctional facilities' (Patterson, 2012, p. 84) in state homes and probation hostels, remand/observation homes,

---

[20] This disposal is rarely used.

reception centres and protective homes, borstal/certified schools, sub-jails, district prisons (Class I and Class II), as well as central prisons, across India. In this context, correctional social workers are engaged in clinical practice by administering treatment suitability assessments, offering individual/group counselling sessions and delivering appropriate rehabilitation programmes. Other specialised expertise, for example, advocacy, case and crisis management, and infrastructural capacity building, are also often called upon by social workers in order to achieve the goals of rehabilitation, re-integration and community safety. Unfortunately, while this may be the case in the developed world, the state of correctional social work in India has lagged behind quite considerably. Professor Ilango Ponnuswami, Sonny Jose and Praveen Varghese Thomas (Chapter 5) argue that social workers should be more involved in such tasks (but are not), even though there is a growing realisation among prison administrators that there is an acute need to evolve from the age-old tradition of rigorous isolation and mere custodial measures to a more reformative and rehabilitative model of intervention. In the earlier days, correctional social work was more vibrant. But owing to the lack of patronage, this specialization did not see as much growth and progression as the years went by. As such, this chapter will outline the problems afflicting the system, as well as what can be done to ameliorate the situation through the revision of prison programme content, as well as social work education and training curriculums.

In addition to the use of penal institutions, as stated earlier, non-incarcerative measures are also employed against convicted offenders. Indeed, social workers often find themselves involved in recommending and/or enforcing community-based punishments like probation and parole/furlough. Probation, as a disposition of court, is usually made pursuant to the Probation of Offenders Act[21] in favour of youth offenders or criminals who have committed less serious offences in lieu of a prison sentence (Thilagaraj, 2013, pp. 208–09). This disposition is designed to facilitate the reformation and rehabilitation of a

---

[21] Or Section 360 of the Criminal Procedure Code, as the case may be.

convicted person through the imposition of certain conditions by the court, and supervised/enforced by a district probation officer.[22] Putting into effect such community-based punishments, like probation, may encompass 'conducting investigations and enforcement, conducting field visits in dangerous neighborhoods, executing warrants and taking [the offenders] into custody who are wanted by law enforcement officials' (Patterson, 2012, p. 91). It is no wonder that such positions are not normally considered to be enviable employment opportunities for social workers. More specifically in an Indian context, probation officers face a range of other challenges as well, including primary role dilution (in contrast with tasks clearly set out in the relevant legislation), disadvantageous power differentials between probation officers and other agents of the CJS, and lack of resources (Nair & Raghavan, 2011). Roshni Nair and Professor Vijay Raghavan (Chapter 6) explore these matters more fully in a case study pertaining to the probation system in the state of Maharashtra, India, in an attempt to better understand the problems associated with the system, and hopefully recommend ways in which improvements can be made to revive probation as a viable means of diversion and rehabilitation.

While the chapters outlined above primarily deal with adult offenders, the following chapter (Chapter 7), however, exclusively examines the role social workers play in the JJS. In the United States, social workers in the late nineteenth century proved to be instrumental in establishing the first juvenile court in Chicago, Illinois (Patterson, 2012, p. 14). Their role in this regard was significant and life-changing to say the least,

---

[22] From a conceptual point of view, however, parole is quite different from probation. It is generally administered to a convicted criminal who has been punished with a term of imprisonment but, thereafter, undergoes his/her punishment in an exemplary fashion, and hence becomes deserving of early release because of their 'good behaviour' (Thilagaraj, 2013, p. 209). That said, parole is not normally granted for that reason in India, and is instead ordered as a 'conditional supervision of sentence for a short duration to enable the prisoners to attend to certain problems' (Thilagaraj, 2013, p. 209). This is, in effect, a furlough and is provided for under the Criminal Procedure Code.

particularly because children are generally considered to be most amenable to reformation and rehabilitation, provided, of course, the intervention (whatever it may be) was timely and appropriate (i.e., taking into account the key characteristics and needs of the delinquent, as well as the criminogenic factors at play in relation to him/her). In India, the now repealed Juvenile Justice (Care and Protection of Children) Act 2000 sought to care for, protect, treat and rehabilitate not only 'children in need of care and protection' but also 'juveniles in conflict with law' who were, at least before 2015, under the age of 18. Social workers are thus ideally located to achieve the objectives of this legislation (Thilagaraj, 2013, p. 209).[23] Criminal justice social workers are specifically tasked to assist competent authorities (i.e., JJBs/courts and child welfare committees) to reduce recidivism and increase the likelihood of reintegrating troubled youth back into the community (Thilagaraj, 2013, p. 209). K. P. Asha Mukundan (Chapter 7) will interrogate these matters through her discussion of a field action project called the 'Resource Cell for Juvenile Justice', highlighting, in particular, the challenges of social work intervention within the JJS from a socio-legal perspective. The efficacy of such rehabilitative initiatives are particularly important given the recent Juvenile Justice (Care and Protection of Children) Act 2015 which repealed the *2000 Act* so as to allow for juveniles aged between 16 and 18 years who are accused of a heinous offence (i.e., that which carries a punishment of a prison sentence of at least seven years or more) to be now tried as an adult if the JJB is of the opinion that the crime was perpetrated with their full knowledge and understanding of the consequences of their actions (Anand, 2015; Gupta, 2015).

The next chapter, however, does not deal with offenders at all, whether adult or juvenile, but instead focuses on investigating the extent to which the CJS supports and assists victims of crime.

---

[23] In formulating those aims, the 2000 Act specifically took into account certain relevant provisions contained in the Indian Constitution, as well as various instruments from the United Nations, including, for example, the Standard Minimum Rules for the Administration of Juvenile Justice 1985, the Convention on the Rights of the Child 1989 and the Rules for the Protection of Juveniles Deprived of their Liberty 1990.

Sadly, Khandpasole Pravin S., Khandpasole Jyoti P., Mark David Chong and Katherine Hoffensetz (Chapter 8) note how victims of crime are not only vulnerable to being re-victimised by criminals; they are also often recipients of a secondary form of victimisation. In regard to the latter, this phenomenon refers to a process whereby victims of crime are marginalised or 'victimised' by the CJS itself. For example, they may be side-lined by the police, the prosecution and/or the courts once their statements/testimonies have been given at the police station and/or at trial; they are not entitled to any additional social welfare services on account of their victimisation; financial compensation for the injury or the loss suffered by the victim may have to be sought from the criminal (as opposed to the State) through the civil rather than the criminal courts;[24] and their families will have to fend for themselves when the victims have been severely injured or killed (Khandpasole, 2011). This gap in welfare services and assistance is a significant shortcoming of any CJS that espouses to act in the best interests of the victims, and consequently social workers can play a significant role in ameliorating this sorry predicament. This chapter will examine the current weaknesses of the Indian CJS when it concerns victims, the social work interventions already place, as well as what still needs to be done in order to address any outstanding deficiencies.

Section III: Way Forward

This third section of the book concentrates on issues that are highly relevant in relation to the direction that Indian CJSW should take, as well as the emerging challenges and opportunities that such social workers will face in the future. Despite the dire need for social workers to be substantively involved in

---

[24] Please take note though of section 357 of the Criminal Procedure Code. This provision 'empowers the [criminal] court to grant compensation to the victim' from the convicted person; although this amount will be taken into account by a civil court if the latter later orders the defendant (i.e., the convicted person) to pay damages to the plaintiff (i.e., the victim) as well (Pillai, 2008, p. 614).

helping offenders and victims of crime, lamentably, not many have heeded the call. As mentioned previously, there are, of course, a number of very good reasons for this, for example, not wanting to be a part of a coercive system of social control; enforcement functions are contradictory to core social work values of caring, empathy and empowerment; and clients are primarily mandated rather than voluntary.

That said, another significant cause could be the lack of understanding of what CJSW entails, the intellectually stimulating expertise one needs to do such work and the exciting, albeit challenging, employment opportunities it offers. The latter problem, however, can be addressed through education and professional course development. Professor Sanjai Bhatt, Atul Pratap Singh and Digvijoy Phukan (Chapter 9) will attempt to critically examine the tertiary educational and professional frameworks employed in India (and how these relate to the country's CJS), as well as the trials and tribulations associated with the task of ensuring quality control in the curriculum, teaching and placement training of future criminal justice social workers in India.

The next chapter reviews the state of human rights protection and violation within the CJS, and how social workers can play an important role in ameliorating the situation. Too many offenders and their victims are themselves marginalised or stigmatised for reasons other than their involvement in the CJS. Many are already socially excluded, discriminated against and abused because of their age, ethnicity, religion, caste, socio-economic status, gender, lack of education and/or unemployment. Using the plight of women and children as a case study, Venkat Pulla, Mark David Chong, Abraham P. Francis and Margaret Henni (Chapter 10) will elaborate upon these key issues by outlining the nature and scope of the relevant human rights regimes, uncovering the extent to which such human rights abuses in the CJS have occurred against them, the role social workers may play in protecting the human rights of these clients (whether criminals or victims of crime), as well as their families, and finally canvassing possible solutions that may be implemented so as to prevent future violations or at least remedy some of its more deleterious effects.

With the advent of technology, victims of cybercrimes are sadly increasing in number. For example, the official crime statistics reveal that the occurrence of cybercrimes has increased by 69 per cent in 2014 as compared to the previous year (National Crime Records Bureau, 2015a, p. 4). This growing problem requires urgent attention as the victims of such offences require special treatment that is different from conventional procedures meted out for victims of more run-of-the-mill types of crimes. Debarati Halder and Professor K. Jaishankar (Chapter 11) explore the plight of private individuals who have been victimised by such offences, as well as the challenges associated with adequately addressing their needs by criminal justice social workers.

Conclusion

As the preceding paragraphs amply illustrate, this project is an exciting endeavour, showcasing ideas, arguments, opinions and recommendations concerning CJSW from some of the best minds in India. The relatively wide coverage of the book has not been at the expense of its substance or depth, and as the reader will quickly realise, the chapters not only provide a good foundational overview of fundamental tenets, but they also challenge the status quo, as none of the authors are content to simply describe 'what is' but rather go on to demonstrate how things 'ought to be'. CJSW is admittedly not for everyone. It is demanding, and full of contradictions. It will require of you courage but discretion, empathy but discernment. It will not be for the faint-hearted. And yet, the intangible rewards are great indeed. You will bring hope to those who have been victimised, to help them overcome the effects of their traumatic experience, acting as it were a conduit for reparation and healing. You will also bring hope to the offender, leading them back onto the path of redemption and restoration. What could be nobler than that, a calling to serve both the sinner and those sinned against? This manuscript will hopefully guide you on this journey, and to help you navigate safely the Indian CJS.

References

Agllias, K. (2004). Women in corrections: A call to social work. *Australian Social Work, 57*(4), 331–42.

Anand, U. (2015, December 24). In fact: Supreme Court ruling window to challenge new juvenile law. *The Indian Express.* Retrieved from http://indianexpress.com/article/explained/in-fact-suprme-court-ruling-window-to-challenge-new-juvenile-law/

The Hindu. (2015, March 17). Applications invited for Juvenile Justice Board member posts. (2015, March 17). *The Hindu.* Retrieved from http://www.thehindu.com/news/national/tamil-nadu/applications-invited-for-juvenile-justice-board-member-posts/article7002037.ece

Ayirolimeethal, A., Ragesh, G., Ramanujam, J. M., & George, B. (2014). Psychiatric morbidity among prisoners. *Indian Journal of Psychiatry, 56*(2), 150–53.

Champagne, D., & Felizardo, V. (n.d.). *Social work practice in corrections.* Retrieved from http://www.casw-acts.ca/en/social-work-practice-corrections

Chaudhary, G. (2012). *Law and social work.* New Delhi: Anmol Publications Pvt. Limited.

Chong, M. D., & Francis, A. P. (2014). Social justice and human rights issues in mental health practice. In A. P. Francis (Ed.), *Social work in mental health: Areas of practice, challenges and ways forward* (pp. 244–64). New Delhi: SAGE Publications.

Gupta, S. (2015, May 7). Adult laws will cover 16–18 year olds. *The Hindu.* Retrieved from http://www.thehindu.com/todays-paper/adult-laws-will-cover-1618-year-olds/article7182511.ece

Holtzhausen, L. (Ed.). (2012). *Criminal justice social work: A South African practice framework.* Cape Town: Juta and Company Ltd.

International Federation of Social Workers (IFSW). (2014). *Global definition of social work.* Retrieved from http://ifsw.org/policies/definition-of-social-work/

Jha, J. K. (Ed.). (2002). *Social work and community development.* New Delhi: Anmol Publications Pvt. Limited.

Kakar, S. (2015). Juvenile justice and juvenile delinquency in India. In M. D. Krohn & J. Lane (Eds), *The handbook of juvenile delinquency and juvenile justice* (pp. 49–64). Chichester: Wiley Blackwell.

Khandpasole, P. (2011). Victims' rehabilitation: Mirage in the desert. *Dialogues in Criminal Justice and Rehabilitation, 2,* 4–5.

Konar, D. (2005). Juvenile justice as a part of child and adolescent care. *Journal of Indian Association for Child and Adolescent Mental Health, 1*(3), 1–6.

McIvor, G., & Raynor, P. (2007). *Developments in social work with offenders.* London: Jessica Kinglsey Publishers.

Moore, E. (2005). Criminal justice: Extending the social work focus. In M. Alston & J. McKinnon (Eds.), *Social work: Fields of practice* (2nd ed., pp. 207–21). South Melbourne: Oxford University Press.

Nair, R., & Raghavan, V. (2011). A study in the probation system in Maharashtra. *Dialogues in Criminal Justice and Rehabilitation*, 3, 11–14.

National Crime Records Bureau (NCRB). (2015a). *Crime in India 2014: Compendium*. New Delhi: Ministry of Home Affairs, Government of India.

———. (2015b). *Prison statistics in India*. New Delhi: Ministry of Home Affairs, Government of India.

Patterson, G. T. (2012). *Social work practice in the criminal justice system*. New York, NY: Routledge.

Pickford, J., & Dugmore, P. (2012). *Youth justice and social work* (2nd ed.). London: SAGE Publications.

Pillai, K. N. C. (2008). *R. V. Kelkar's criminal procedure* (5th ed.). Lucknow: Eastern Book Company.

Raghavan, V. (2013). Social work intervention in criminal justice. In S. Singh (Ed.), *Social work and social development* (pp. 265–89). Chicago, IL: Lyceum Books Inc.

———. (Ed.). (2012). *Social work interventions at police stations*. Mumbai: Prayas.

Roberts, A. R., & Springer, D. W. (Eds). (2007). *Social work in juvenile and criminal justice settings* (3rd ed.). Springfield, IL: Charles C. Thomas Publisher Ltd.

Sachdev, S. (2012). *A textbook of social work*. New Delhi: Dominant Publishers.

Sarkar, S. (2011). *Direct social work practice: Theory and skills*. Jaipur: Y King Books.

Scottish Government. (2010). *National outcomes and standards for social work services in the criminal justice system*. Edinburgh, Scotland: Author.

Thilagaraj, R. (2013). Criminal justice system in India. In J. Liu, S. Jou, & B. Hebenton (Eds), *Handbook of Asian criminology* (pp. 199–211). New York: Springer.

Treger, H., & Allen, G. F. (2007). Social work in the justice system: An overview. In A.R. Roberts & D.W. Springer (Eds), *Social work in juvenile and criminal justice settings* (3rd ed., pp. 44–52). Springfield, IL: Charles C Thomas.

Vadiraj, S., Gopal, A., SDTT, & Sahni, S. (2011). *Social work in India's criminal justice institutions: Need, experiences and challenges*. Mumbai: Sir Dorabji Tata Trust and the Allied Trusts (SDTT).

William, A. T., & Christopher, A. J. (2004). *Women criminals in India: Sociological and social work perspective*. New Delhi: Anmol Publications Pvt. Limited.

SECTION I

Foundational Frameworks, Theories, Concepts and Problems

1

The Influence of Social Work within the Indian Criminal Justice System: A Critical Overview

Vijay Raghavan and Sashwati Mishra

Introduction

The involvement of social workers in the criminal justice system (CJS) in the United States, United Kingdom and other parts of Europe dates back to more than two centuries. The first juvenile court was set up in Chicago, Illinois, in 1899, where the social worker's role was incorporated keeping in mind the rehabilitative objective (Patterson, 2012, p. 14). With the growth and development of the juvenile justice system (JJS), an institutional space for the social worker was created in the form of the child welfare officer, the probation officer and the aftercare officer, in response to the needs of the neglected child, at-risk child, the child in 'moral danger' and the child in conflict with the law (Government of India, 1960). The role of the social worker in the CJS was also strengthened with the introduction of probation as an alternative to imprisonment in the American CJS. The probation officer who was mandated to file the social investigation report of the offender at the post-conviction stage later also played the role of rehabilitation agent during the supervision period, if the probationer was released on supervision (Nieto, 1996; Stohr & Walsh, 2008).

The movement of criminological thought away from biological determinism towards the disciplines of psychology, sociology and social psychology also contributed to the placement of social workers, among other professionals, within the CJS. For example, the development of the ecological, the subcultural, the social learning and the strain theories led to locating crime in psycho-social and environmental factors. This in turn resulted in the possibility of, and the need to, work with the individual offender with a focus on behavioural change, through counselling, therapy and influencing the socio-economic and environmental factors, which may have led to the criminal behaviour in the first place. This shift required a different breed of professionals to intervene in the system, instead of the earlier heavy reliance on personnel who were trained to ensure safety, security and discipline amongst the offending population. The CJS began to increasingly hire psychologists, psychiatrists, counsellors, therapists and social workers as its fifth wing, apart from the existing wings of the police, the prosecution, the judiciary and custodial staff. By the middle of the twentieth century, social workers were firmly ensconced in the CJS, especially in the West, in tune with the changing thrust of punishment that focused on retribution and deterrence to the inclusion of rehabilitative and correctional goals (Brownell & Roberts, 2002; Wilson, 2010).

The Indian CJS, as it exists today, draws its origins from colonial rule. The '1857 Sepoy Mutiny' against the East India Company (EIC) was a result of a combination of years of misrule by the EIC and precipitating social, political, economic and religious factors (Streets, 2001). It led to the establishment of 'direct rule' by the British Crown in the Indian-occupied territory, followed by legal and administrative reforms to correct the impression of 'misrule' that the EIC had come to represent in the minds of the Indian population and the British public back home. Prominent among the reforms carried out by the British was the establishment of a uniform legal and criminal justice system, with the passing of the Indian Penal Code (IPC) and the Criminal Procedure Code (CrPC) in 1861, and the Indian Evidence Act in 1872. The mechanism to enforce these pieces of legislation was put in place with the passing of the Police Act (1861), the Indian High Courts Act (1861) and the Prisons Act (1894).

These laws continue to form the backbone of the CJS in post-Independence India, with some cosmetic changes introduced from time to time based on pressures from below or on top in a changing socio-political context. The system, however, remains opaque to the rapid changes in criminological and penological thought over the last century or so. One sees very little evidence of correctional or rehabilitative undercurrents seeping into the system, which largely continues to be based on punitive and deterrent philosophies. Traces of correctional social work, however, can be found in two areas: JJS and provisions relating to the release of convicted offenders on probation and parole. The latter, in particular, finds its place in the system as an afterthought rather than as a shareholder amongst competing philosophies.

With this brief overview, the following sections will attempt to trace the history of social work intervention in juvenile and adult CJSs.

Emergence of Social Work Intervention in Juvenile Justice Institutions

The first steps towards providing social work services in the field of juvenile corrections were taken with the setting up of reformatory schools under the Reformatory Schools Act, 1897. The staff appointed to work in these institutions did not have formal training to work with children, which was in conflict with the law. They mostly involved the children in educational and vocational training programmes. Prior to 1936, there were no formal training opportunities for personnel working with offenders, and the workers learnt skills on the job. Some of the workers were very committed. They developed an understanding of children's problems through experience, made use of libraries, lectures and study groups, and ultimately became excellent youth workers (Panakal, 1967). The first batch of social workers graduated in 1938, after the establishment of Sir Dorabji Tata Graduate School of Social Work, later renamed as the Tata Institute of Social

Sciences (TISS), a premier university in the field of social work and social sciences in the country, in 1936 and later one of them was appointed as a probation officer in Bombay (The Association for Moral and Social Hygiene in India, 1939). The Annual Report of the Children's Aid Society, Bombay, 1938, stated that, having realised the need for trained professional workers to work in the field of corrections, it would send one of their probation officers to Sir Dorabji Tata Graduate School of Social Work for two years (Children's Aid Society, 1938, p. 23). However, most of the staff working in children's institutions actually learnt as apprentices of those who had devoted long years of service in correctional institutions (Panakal, 1967).

Probation officers were employed in the Bombay Presidency in the 1930s in the Children's Aid Society[1] and the Aftercare Associations[2] in the erstwhile Bombay state. The probation officers were supported in their work by voluntary supervisors who were concerned individuals drawn from the public. These voluntary supervisors would assist the probation officers in their day-to-day responsibilities and would dedicate an hour or two every week after their work hours to perform this task. There were about 42 voluntary supervisors out of which 18 were women in the Children's Aid Society in Bombay. The Annual Report of the Children's Aid Society[3] in 1938 specifically acknowledged and

---

[1] The Children's Aid Society was set up in 1927 as a voluntary organisation, fully funded by the Government of Bombay, and as a model of public–private partnership. It undertook the responsibility of running all institutions set up under the newly legislated Bombay Children's Act, 1924, including the Remand Home (now Observation Home) at Umerkhadi (Dongri), Bombay (now Mumbai). For more details, please visit http://www.casmumbai.org/.

[2] The Aftercare Associations were set up in all districts of Bombay, as branches of the Bombay Aftercare Association, under the same public–private partnership model, that is, set up as a voluntary organisation but fully funded by the government to run its activities.

[3] The Annual Report of the Children's Aid Society, Bombay, 1938, stated that having released the need for trained professional workers to work in the fields of corrections, the Children's Aid Society would be sending one of their probation officers to Sir Dorabji Tata Graduate School of Social Work for two years. There was a growing recognition of need of workers with specialised knowledge and skills in the field of corrections.

thanked these voluntary supervisors for their contribution to the cause of child welfare. There seems to have been an atmosphere of active partnership between concerned members of the public and the juvenile justice functionaries, especially when it came to guiding and releasing children on license as per the provisions of the Children's Act (The Association for Moral and Social Hygiene in India, 1939).

The juvenile justice legislation in the early part of the twentieth century was aimed at protecting and not punishing the child. The motive of the magistrates attached to the juvenile courts gradually shifted towards child welfare. In the same spirit, the Bombay government took 'a desirable and effective step by appointing a lady stipendiary magistrate skilled in social welfare work and possessing very good knowledge of psychology' (Sethna, 1952, p. 352). The first lady stipendiary magistrate was Miss Budden, followed by Dr Katayun Cama (PhD). Under the heading '*raison d'etre* of the juvenile court', it is stated that these ladies as stipendiary magistrates were 'a doctor in philosophy or a master of arts skilled in sociology and in the treatment of deficient and delinquent children—very good protective and preventive work is done. She allows treatment only after due deliberations' (Sethna, 1952, p. 354). There was a growing realisation that skilled staff with education in sociology, philosophy and/or welfare, as well as an inter-disciplinary orientation would be effective youth workers in the JJS. The JJS grew as there was support for this kind of work, and the focus on child welfare not only strengthened the system, but also created space for greater absorption of youth workers through its expansion.

It was realised that aftercare homes for children and adult prisoners would aid in checking recidivism and the prevention of crime. Many concerned organisations and individuals shouldered this responsibility. There were homes for children at Hubli, Poona and Bombay, and some of these included the aftercare hostels run by David Sasoon Industrial School, Byramjee Jeejeebhoy Home, Shraddhanand Anath Mahila Ashram (Home for Orphan Girls and Women), Salvation Army's Home and the Bombay Probation and Aftercare Association Homes. It was also recognised that it was important to create sufficient infrastructure to support released prisoners and children and at the same time, build capacities and skills of those workers running these institutions. It was further concluded that 'if probation and supervision work is to be successfully rendered, probation officers must be trained in their line. There are special courses for training probation officers at TISS, Bombay and the University of Calcutta' (Sethna, 1952, p. 360).

Emergence of Social Work Intervention in Prison Settings

Prisons and correctional institutions have undergone many changes from time to time, based on the recommendations made by various reform committees appointed by the government during the period 1836–2000.[4] The earliest moves towards social work intervention with adult populations in criminal justice were made through citizen participation in humanising prisons and creating structures for the rehabilitation of prisoners. It was recognised that the State efforts alone could not achieve the goal of reducing crime in society, and steps were taken to ensure that persons who had fallen into crime owing to their derelict circumstances were brought back into the mainstream. It required what was then known as 'public participation in social defence', and what we today call public–private or State–civil society partnership. Prisons were one of the earliest structures to set an example of this partnership with the introduction of the system of prison visitors. These visitors were drawn from members of the public and included members from state legislatures, social workers and other concerned citizens. Many of these individuals were driven by compassion and commitment and made sincere efforts

---

[4] The details of historical review of prison reforms and correctional institutions in India could be read in Part I of 'Draft National Policy on Prison Reform and Correctional Administration' on Bureau of Police Research and Development (BPR&D) website. The details could be found on http://bprd. nic.in/writereaddata/linkimages/0534473971-National%20Policy%20 on%20Prison%20Reform%20and%20Correctional%20Administration%20 Part%201.pdf.

to provide support to correctional institutions. They enquired about the living condition of the inmates inside the prison, listened to the grievances of the prisoners and worked towards their rehabilitation (Sethna, 1952).

Over time, the need for social work intervention in prisons was gradually acknowledged. The Indian Jail Committee, 1919–20, stated that prison officers should be skilled in social welfare work. The Bombay government decided to introduce trained staff, psychologists and psychiatrists in all prisons in 1949.[5] The main aim of this decision was to provide trained and sympathetic staff that could ease stress and support the prisoners by providing psychological support. This approach also marked a shift in attempts to transform the nature of punishment to one that was reformative and constructive instead of being merely retributive. The need for the specialised work performed by social workers was beginning to be recognised in prisons as 'social welfare workers educate the prisoners and help in bringing about their reformation. There should be sufficient number of social workers both for the female and male prisoners' (Sethna, 1952, p. 286).

The work of providing aid and aftercare services[6] to discharged prisoners was first developed in Bengal, Uttar Pradesh, Madras and Bombay, followed by Madhya Pradesh, Delhi and Hyderabad. The main agency that emerged in all these states to provide aid and aftercare to released prisoners was the Discharged Prisoners' Aid Societies and the Aftercare Associations. In the Bombay Presidency, a committee was formed in 1913 based on the suggestions made by the then Inspector General of Prisons, Lt. Col.

---

[5] During the same time, members of Salvation Army, Chaplains of the Church of England and Roman Catholic Church would deliver religious and moral lectures at Yerawada Central Prison. In jails, in Bombay, the same provision to deliver moral lectures by members of society for both male and female prisoners was made.

[6] Some of the aspects which a released prisoner needed help include employment, accommodation, money grants for vocational training and studies, monetary assistance for petty trade, railway fare, reinstatement in service, loans, vehicle license, legal assistance, clothes and medical attention, subsistence allowance, recommendations for job and establishing contacts with relatives and families. The workers at the Discharged Prisoners' Aid Societies and Aftercare Association undertook all this work.

Jackson. The committee, which had members from the Bombay Legislative Council, strongly recommended that, 'help must come from the public and that a Released Prisoners Aid Society should be established' (Sethna, 1952, p. 302). The Bombay Presidency Released Prisoners Aid Society[7] came into existence on 18 March 1914.[8] Much before the Home for Released Prisoners was set up by the Bombay Presidency Released Prisoners Aid Society,[9] other members of the Society had made attempts to set up homes for released prisoners in their individual capacities. Such efforts surfaced around the late nineteenth and early twentieth centuries. Many concerned and socially conscious women understood the need for establishing more homes for released prisoners, including Lady Leonora John Scott, wife of Lord Sydenham, the then Governor of Bombay. Over time, homes for released prisoners were started in the Bombay state by the Salvation Army, Poona Released Prisoners' Aid Society and Ahmedabad Released Prisoners' Aid Society.

The administrative staff of the Discharged Prisoners' Aid Societies comprised the superintendent, probation officer, welfare officer, weaving instructor, peon, sweeper and cook. As stated by the Advisory Committee on Aftercare Programmes (1954), the workers in these associations faced many difficulties in carrying

---

[7] The probation officers from Bombay Presidency Released Prisoners Aid Society visited the prisons in Bombay regularly and would obtain details of the prisoners to be released to understand the help needed by the prisoner to become a functional and contributing member of the society. The Society assisted the prisoners to find employment and until the employment was found, supported the prisoners by providing accommodation at the Society's home at Agripada, Bombay.

[8] The meeting for setting up the Bombay Presidency Released Prisoners Aid Society was held at University Hall. Those present and supported the formation of Released Prisoners Aid Society included the then Governor, Lord Willingdon; Sir Jamsetjee Jeejeebhoy, Bart; Fazalbhoy M. Chinoy; Sir Pherozshah M. Mehta and others. It was realized that it was the duty of the Society to ensure the rehabilitation of the prisoner.

[9] Bombay Presidency Released Prisoners Aid Society did the much needed work for supporting the released prisoners over the next 30 years. In 1946, a resolution was passed for the dissolution of the Released Prisoners Aid Society and it was amalgamated with Bombay Province Probation and Aftercare Association.

out their work. Some of these difficulties included high caseloads, inability to follow up on cases, the social stigma faced, lack of employment for released prisoners, as well as the overall lack of government support, infrastructure and finances to carry out correctional duties and aftercare programmes. These gaps were filled, to some extent, by volunteers visiting the prisons and engaged with the young offenders and provided support to the staff of the Discharged Prisoners' Aid Societies and Aftercare Associations to carry out their day-to-day activities.[10] They sometimes also helped young offenders find jobs and get settled in the community. These voluntary workers in the Discharged Prisoners' Aid Societies and Probation and Aftercare Associations not only assisted the staff of various correctional institutions, but also undertook an important role in the education and raising of critical consciousness of their needs and difficulties to the public, thereby reducing stigmatisation and restoring a sense of humanity towards the 'fallen offender'. The Maharashtra State Probation and Aftercare Association,[11] in its annual report of 1962–63,

---

[10] The annual report of the Bombay Aftercare Association stated that in the year 1952–53, the voluntary and probation officers of the association supervised 834 cases, of which 153 were supervised by voluntary probation officers.

[11] The Maharashtra State Probation and Aftercare Association was responsible for organising probation and aftercare in the state under the Bombay Children Act, Bombay Borstal School Act and the Bombay Probation of Offenders Act. The association looked at the supervision of aid to released prisoners. In Maharashtra, Chief Officer's Office was in Matunga, Chembur and Borivali. The probation work included all the activities outlined under the Bombay Probation of Offender's Act, 1938, and help was extended in finding employment opportunities, educational facilities and reconciliation with families. The aftercare included letter of introduction and recommendations to the released prisoners, help finding employment, accommodation and money grants for vocational training and studies, monetary assistance for petty trade, railway fare, reinstatement in service, loans, vehicle license, legal assistance, clothes and medical attention, and establishing contacts with relatives and families. Also, various Bombay Association offices were fieldwork settings for students from social work. The annual report of the year 1959–60 stated that there were 4–6 students from TISS, who as a part of their fieldwork assisted the association in case work and day-to-day work of the association. The responsibility was shouldered by voluntary probation officers in areas where probation officers were not available. In the Presidential address of the

stated that it was desirable to employ more voluntary probation officers in the probation services. It was thought that doing so would bring together concerned individuals from the public and correctional institutions and would ensure efficiency in the handling of cases as the voluntary probation officer would not have a large case load and would also help to reduce stigmatisation of those in correctional institutions. The report acknowledged the role the public could play in the rehabilitation of those in correctional institutions.

The Post-Independence Period

There was an expansion in correctional facilities in India after Independence. Leaders involved in the freedom struggle had been imprisoned by the British government time and again and had first-hand experience of the prevailing prison conditions. They were, therefore, well aware of the need for reforms in the CJS, especially in its correctional institutions. As explained earlier, the correctional institutions[12] were largely for children and young adults. The correctional facilities from the post-Independence period till the early 1980s witnessed increasing public–private partnership, government and policy support

---

Nineteenth Annual General Meeting of the Maharashtra State Association after its revised constitution in the year 1942 and the fifth meeting after the states reorganisation, it was stated that the Annual Report 1958–59 would be useful for the social workers in the field as a reference and also encourage and support them in their work.

[12] The institutions/correctional facilities that existed within the CJS in India did not address all the vulnerable and marginalised groups in India. Some groups that the correctional facilities in the CJS looked at included children—orphans/delinquents/neglected/destitute; women—deserted/widows; beggars; prisoners; physically handicapped—lame, cripple, blind, deaf and mute. Many groups were left out and those included the Nomadic and Denotified Tribes; families and children of prisoners/undertrials; victims; single women; sexual minorities; migrants, etc. This is not an exhaustive enumeration of all the vulnerable and marginalised groups in India. There was silence around many vulnerable groups at the policy and programme levels, in research and academic circles, and civil society at large.

and funding, emergence–recognition–establishment of social work within the CJS and a concern for the offender's rehabilitation and well-being. These developments were the outcome of the contributions made by the United Nations correctional expert and the then renowned American criminologist, Dr Walter Reckless, who was invited to India in 1951 by the first democratically elected government of India, to study the prison conditions and administration, as well as to suggest policy reforms (Chowdhury, 2002, p. 283). Consequently, the first six-month training programme for prison and correctional officers was organised by the TISS in 1952, with the assistance of the Ministry of Home Affairs, Government of India, and the active involvement of Dr Reckless and Dr Edward Galway, a United Nations adviser on social defence (Panakal, 1967, p. 90).

Continuing this trend, the first Five-Year Plan (1951–56) of the Government of India stressed the need for criminal justice reforms. It stated that prisons should be utilised for the rehabilitation of prisoners and should operate on modern principles of penology. It emphasised the importance of probation and after-care, treatment of offenders, reconditioning of prisons and Borstal schools and their vocational units as well as giving impetus, support and funding to aftercare and prisoners' aid societies (Government of India, 1951–56). The waves of change and the fresh perspective towards correctional institutions continued in the Five-Year Plans during the period 1950–79, which led to the establishment of correctional institutions across the country as well as policy commitments accompanied by budgetary allocations.[13] This period witnessed the establishment of university

---

[13] Outlay Table on Social Welfare Programmes in the Five-Year Plans:

First plan (1951–56)	16 (in million)
Second plan (1956–61)	134 (in million)
Third plan (1961–66)	194 (in million)
3 annual plans (1966–69)	120.8 (in million)
Fourth plan (1969–74)	413.8 (in million)

The fourth Five-Year Plan had a total outlay of ₹413.8 million, out of which research, training and administration had an allocation of ₹10.5 million; educational work for prohibition of ₹1 million and ₹2 million for Central Bureau of Correctional Services.

departments of social work with a correctional focus, development of social agencies and departments, training of personnel for social work, undertaking social research, introducing social legislation and a community-based approach in social welfare and correctional administration. For example, the implementation of the second Five-Year Plan saw the establishment of many institutions including 17 certified schools, 5 Borstal schools and 40 remand homes. In the third Five-Year Plan (1961–66), under the Programme for Social Defence, Social and Moral Hygiene and Aftercare Services, 327 institutions were established and 128 probation and welfare officers were appointed. The third plan clearly acknowledged the need and role of probation officers and stated that in the second Five-Year Plan, their number grew from 100 to 304. It also expressed the need for hiring more of such personnel for the third plan (Government of India, 1961–66). The Central Bureau of Correctional Services was set up in 1961 and later renamed as the National Institute of Social Defence (NISD) in 1975, to coordinate, standardise and develop social defence programmes in the country (Madan, 2009).

The focus of working with offenders became more rehabilitation-oriented, rather than the previous emphasis of safeguarding society from them. The roles and governing philosophy of the staff and voluntary workers shifted to ensuring the well-being of the offenders and transforming them into productive members of society on their release from their correctional institutions. The value and skills that the visionary and compassionate voluntary and paid staff of the correctional institutions brought also built a strong platform for the recognition of social work within the CJS. Sethna (1952), while highlighting the changing expectations from prison staff, states that

> It is of highest importance that prison officers must be able and sympathetic persons capable of understanding the psychology of the criminals under care. By persuasion, sympathetic treatment, corrective methods, through moral guidance, religious teaching, music, art, ... the criminal (even a hardened one) may be brought to repentance and correction. (p. 305)

The essence of working with prisoners shifted towards enhancing the well-being of the individual prisoner as well as of the society. There was an increasing realisation for the need to build capacities, train, exchange ideas, share best practices and social work intervention in the field of corrections across the country. There were many concerned individuals driven by compassion and commitment, who had worked as volunteers and prison visitors, and had long been an integral support system for the CJS. The correctional staff and voluntary workers often performed complementary functions towards the objective of rehabilitation, and their work resonated with the ethos of the correctional social worker's role. The third Five-Year Plan acknowledged the contribution of the voluntary workers and accepted the need to further build their capacities through orientation and training programmes. Importantly, the plan laid emphasis on the role of the community in ensuring the welfare, and meeting the needs, of its marginalised sections. It stated that communities grew and were strengthened by involving voluntary workers from the community, especially women, into the field of 'creative social service' (Government of India, 1961–66).

In order to strengthen the rehabilitation efforts being made, the Government of India set up an Advisory Committee on Aftercare Programmes in 1954, to provide an overview and 'factual information on the state of the institutional services in the field of social work'. The Committee did not limit its ambit to offender populations, but envisaged aftercare services as an essential element towards the social reintegration of custodial populations and the physically disabled. The preface of the Advisory Committee on Aftercare Programmes,[14] reads:

> The scope of aftercare services, however, need not necessarily be limited to individuals discharged from custodial and correctional institutions ... it can well extend to a variety of other groups who would also experience difficulties in returning to normal life after having spent years in institutions like Orphanages, Destitute Homes, Homes for Women and the Physically Handicapped. (1954, p. i)

---

[14] The Advisory Committee on Aftercare Programmes was set up to provide an overview and 'factual information on the state of the institutional services in the field of social work'. The Advisory Committee reached out to 217 correctional institutions across the country, out of which 114 institutions responded to the questionnaire circulated by the Committee.

In its report, the Advisory Committee laid down the framework for aftercare services in the country, including the required structure, human resources, training and the type of programmes and services. It highlighted the need to strengthen the organisational structure by recommending the establishment of an Aftercare Project Committee and an aftercare office at the district level, with a trained social worker appointed as the aftercare officer to carry out aftercare functions. As the work of aftercare grew, the Committee acknowledged the need for more technical staff in each district and recommended that they could be employed through the Central Social Welfare Board. However, it was left to the state governments to implement the recommendations of the report, which led to an uneven level of development and progress at the ground level, in the absence of a central ministry for corrections and rehabilitation.

The Growth of Training Institutions in Criminal Justice Social Work

The establishment of the Sir Dorabji Tata Graduate School of Social Work in 1936, later renamed the TISS, was a landmark event in relation to the growth and development of social work education in the country. It created a space for galvanising the earlier informal relationship and mutual support that social workers and criminal justice functionaries sought in each other. The first training programme for government officers working in the field of corrections was organised by TISS in 1952 and the first two-year master's degree in social work with a specialisation in criminology and correctional administration (CCA) was started by the Department of Criminology and Correctional Administration at TISS in 1954, in response to the need for trained personnel in criminal justice social work. The programme offered a new perspective that coupled the prevention of crime and treatment of offenders, with an understanding of the nature and causes of crime as well as its impact from social and psychological points of view. Students undergoing the programme gained the knowledge of criminal and correctional laws, the CJS and intervention in the system through social work methods, with a strong component of doing field work in correctional institutions as part of their curriculum (Panakal, 1967).

Subsequently, other schools and university departments started teaching programmes at the graduate and postgraduate levels in criminology, correctional administration and social work, such as the Madras School of Social Work (1952), University of Saugar (1959), Karnatak University, Dharwad (1970), Madras University (1983), Manonmaniam Sundaranar University, Tirunelveli (2003), and the National Institute of Criminology and Forensic Sciences, Delhi (2004). The teaching in these universities and centres was organised through independent departments of criminology, joint departments of criminology and forensic sciences, diploma courses, criminology as a taught paper and distance education courses (Bajpai, n.d.).

In order to promote the training of criminal justice and correctional staff, conducting of inter-disciplinary research and the facilitating of an exchange of ideas through seminars and workshops, the government set up the NISD in 1975, as mentioned in an earlier section. It was given the mandate to act as an advisor to the Ministry of Home Affairs, specifically, and the Government of India, more generally, on policy matters relating to social defence and corrections in the country. Its agenda included the prevention of alcoholism, drug addiction, suicide and gambling; and the setting up of preventive, corrective and rehabilitative services; the welfare of prisoners, prison reforms and probation; as well as juvenile delinquency and beggary (Madan, 2009, pp. 432–33).

Apart from teaching, training was also emerging as a need of criminal justice functionaries. In the beginning, the TISS admitted 'deputed' candidates to the MA programme in social work with specialisation in CCA. These candidates were appointed by the state governments as prison, probation or social welfare officers first and were subsequently admitted to the TISS master's programme to obtain professional training. This practice was continued until the late 1970s and the early 1980s, but was discontinued as the government departments concerned established their own in-house training schools with qualified personnel to train their candidates. Schools for prison officers played an important role in developing constructive attitudes and understanding towards social work and developing social work personnel to work in the CJS. Schools of social work including TISS continue to organise short-term induction and refresher programmes focusing on methods of social work in the CJS (Panakal, 1967).

The first Five-Year Plan emphasised the need for training in social work. This plan clearly stated that it was imperative to understand the nature and extent of social problems, history and philosophy of social work, structure of society, methods and techniques of social work (Government of India, 1951–56) for India, so as to be able to move beyond the shackles of exploitative colonisation and address the pressing issues at hand. This understanding was imperative to build an effective leadership and the necessary philosophical foundations and values essential to run the various social welfare agencies and departments. The plan stated that the aim of social work was to focus on the gradual rehabilitation of the weak, handicapped and anti-social elements in society (Government of India, 1951–56). It recognised that India needed trained social workers in large numbers in rural areas. It also emphasised that the role of social work needed to shift from a curative to the rehabilitative approach.[15] It stated that social work institutions across the country should shoulder the responsibility of providing in-service training to government employees as well as the training of voluntary workers to work in the community.

The second Five-Year Plan under Welfare Programmes suggested that the probation system should be started in those states where it had not yet been established. It emphasised that prison

---

[15] The curative model of social work focuses on the individual's inability to adapt to the system/environment. The impaired relation with the system is understood as the individual's inability to adapt rather than the nature and functioning of the system. The efforts for restoration are focused on the individual. The rehabilitative model of social work extends beyond the individual and attempts at addressing the environment as well as the individual. The strain/repair/restoration encompasses building skills, psychological support, providing resources and shifts/changes in the system.

welfare officers should be appointed for the purpose of contacting prisoners during their stay in jails and for keeping in touch with them and their families after release. Very importantly, it elicited the need for developing social legislation, welfare of children and women, youth, crime prevention and correctional administration.

The third Five-Year Plan stressed the need for training, education, research in areas including social defence and aftercare. This led to the setting up of a Central Bureau of Correctional Services in 1961, with an outlay of ₹280 million. The policy commitments until the sixth Five-Year Plan were aimed at providing training to government employees, the reform of the CJS by strengthening social work, conducting social science research, establishing correctional institutions and building collaborations with social work institutes.

As far as the JJS was concerned, the Children's Act, 1960, was enacted 'to provide for the care, protection, maintenance, welfare, training, education and rehabilitation of neglected or delinquent children and for the trial of delinquent children in the Union territories' (Government of India, 1960). This Act addressed the needs of both neglected children as well as children in conflict with law. This Act attempted to bring homogeneity of response to address problems of these categories of children across the country. Towards this aim, the Act created the structure of the juvenile court headed by a magistrate to look into the needs of both categories of children with the assistance of probation officers who were trained social workers. By now, the presence of social workers and counsellors was well established in children's institutions as well as agencies looking into the aftercare of these children. The first National Policy for Children was adopted by the Government of India in 1974, which gave an impetus to the child welfare sector in terms of programmes and budgetary allocations. The Juvenile Justice Act was passed in 1986; this categorised children into neglected children and children in conflict with the law. Social workers were an integral part of the JJS, and the 1986 Act recognised the importance of social workers in the system (Adenwalla, 2006). The Act further stated that the juvenile courts have to be 'assisted by a panel of two honorary social workers possessing such qualifications as may be prescribed, of whom at least one shall be a woman, and such panel shall be appointed by the State Government' (Government of India, 1986). India ratified the United Nations Convention on the Rights of the Child, 1989, in 1992, in tune with the growing child rights movement internationally and within the country. This led to the passing of the Juvenile Justice Act of 2000, which was a paradigm shift in terms of treatment, care and rehabilitation of children (Government of India, 2000). The new legislation, further amended in 2006, has expanded the scope for social work intervention in the JJS and created legal space for civil society participation in the rehabilitation process (Government of India, 2006).

Exchange of Knowledge and Skills to Strengthen Criminal Justice Social Work

The growth of training institutions in criminal justice social work and the development of trained personnel in this field led to the evolution of platforms for academic and professional exchanges to share knowledge and build intra- and inter-departmental synergies. The first conference of the Inspector-Generals of Prisons was held at TISS from 15 to 17 March 1952. Dr Walter Reckless, Dr J.M. Kumarappa, the then Director of TISS, and Inspector-Generals of Prisons from 21 states participated in the conference. The conference reaffirmed the importance of the probation system with its universalisation across the country; importantly, the need for institutionalised welfare officers in all prisons and the setting up of a Central Bureau of Correctional Services in India to oversee the standardisation and supervision of prison systems (Administration Report of the Probation Department, Madras State, 1952). The Second Probation Conference was organised from 28 to 31 May 1952, in Bombay. The conference concluded that there was a need for a Central Probation Act, or at least a Model Probation Act, sponsored by the Government of India. The First All India Conference of Probation Officers was held from 13 to 20 December 1952 in Madras. The Sixth International Conference on Social Work was held at the same time in Madras. These conferences[16] proved to be a useful platform for the exchange of knowledge, ideas and skills, as well as sharing best practices in social work intervention in the field of corrections across the country for criminal justice functionaries, government employees and social workers.

---

[16] The Second Probation Conference was organised from 28 to 31 May 1952 in Bombay. It was attended by the Chief Probation Superintendent, Madras, Chief Probation Officers of Bombay and Uttar Pradesh, Chief Inspector of Certified Schools of Bombay, Dr Edward Galway, Dr Walter C. Reckless and 47 jail officers across the country. The conference concluded that there is a need for a Central Probation Act or at least a Model Probation Act sponsored by the Government of India. The Chief Probation Superintendent, upon request by the participants, drafted a Model Probation Act and forwarded it to Dr Reckless who submitted the same to the Government of India. The Sixth Session of the Indian Conference of Social Work was held in December 1953 at Hyderabad. One section of the conference was on the theme of social defence and discussed prevention and treatment of crime and children in conflict with law. The Chief Probation Superintendent Shri V. K. Krishna Menon participated in the Indian Conference of Social Work in Travancore–Cochin as a delegate of Madras Government from 22 to 26 October 1955 and presented a paper titled 'Probation and Aftercare'. As a result of request by conference organisers and consent from Madras Government, Shri V. K. Krishna Menon introduced a programme on Probation and Aftercare in the Travancore–Cochin state. Later, he along with the Inspector General of Prisons (Probation) attended the Eighth Annual Session of the Indian Conference of Social Work held at Bangalore from 27 to 31 December 1955. In the same year, Mr Menon was appointed by the Government of India as a National Correspondent to the United Nations in the field of prevention of crime and treatment of offenders. Two probation officers from Madras were selected by the Central Social Welfare Board for training on 'Aftercare' at the Delhi School of Social Work for a period of one year. Three probation officers from Madras participated in the Decennial Anniversary Session of the Indian Conference of Social Work. The Chief Probation Superintendent, Superintendents of Jails and District Probation Officers attended the All India Conference of Correctional Officers at Trivandrum from 26 to 29 December 1957 (Excerpts from the Administration Report of the Probation Department, Madras State, 1952–57).

The Beginning of the Downfall

The 1980s saw a clear shift in the development paradigm in India. The honeymoon period of the people with the political class was well and truly over, and governments were being pressurised to deliver on the promise of development made to them in 1947. As a result, the focus of governance shifted from welfare to development through poverty alleviation. The State had lost faith in institutional treatment towards the social reintegration of marginalised populations. Investment in the welfare sector reduced considerably, and the fields of criminology and corrections began to shrink. Consequently, there were very few job opportunities being created for trained social workers in the criminal justice and correctional systems (Raghavan, 2013, p. 266).

The thrust towards poverty alleviation and the departure from the institutional welfare approach can be seen in the sixth Five-Year Plan (1980–85) document which emphasised that the social welfare sector had only a supplemental role to meet the needs of the most deprived, and the general sectors should ensure that the real benefits reach the poor. The National Rural Employment Programme and the beneficiary-oriented Integrated Rural Development Programme became the face of social welfare. It was perceived that these schemes would substantially contribute to the welfare of people, besides focusing on agriculture, animal husbandry, irrigation and other economic activities. There was a shift from the earlier understanding of social welfare and greater reliance on planning and execution of schemes and programmes. The new approach stressed that preventive and developmental services be given preference over institutional care. It was believed that the latter was very costly. The document stated that, 'institutional services would be strengthened only selectively by encouraging voluntary agencies to the extent possible' (Government of India, 1980–85).

The seventh Five-Year Plan (1985–90) stated that, 'up to the close of the fourth plan, most of the programmes were curative or ameliorative in nature. From the fifth plan onwards, the emphasis has been on the promotion of preventive and developmental services'. The plan document focused on schemes like the Integrated

Child Development Scheme (ICDS), the Mid-Day Meal Programme, Special Nutrition Programme, Women Welfare Schemes and other schemes of the Central Social Welfare Board. Many marginalised communities got left behind, and the long-term focus cantered on combating malnutrition and under-nourishment by the expansion of employment opportunities and stabilisation of income, especially among vulnerable population groups. Institutions providing social work education were drafted by the government to train official and non-official staff of ICDS.[17] The institutional and correctional focus had faded, and the eighth (1992–97)[18] and ninth plans (1997–2002)[19] concentrated on training and non-institutional treatment of offenders. The 10th (2002–07) and

---

[17] During the Seventh Five-Year Plan, two new schemes were planned to be introduced in the field of CJS. These included: (a) 'Prevention and Control of Juvenile Maladjustment' scheme with a component of community-based services. This centrally sponsored scheme would be started on a pilot basis in few urban areas and would include components such as counselling and guidance, family life education and organised recreation; (b) 'Welfare of Prisoners' scheme was created with the aim to strengthen the correctional component of prison programme through the provision of educational and vocational training, aftercare services and training of personnel. The NISD aimed to focus on the areas of research and evaluation, training of functionaries and consultancy for official departments and non-official implementing agencies.

[18] The plan document stated that efforts would be aimed at reducing the problems of social deviance and juvenile crime through preventive, correctional and rehabilitative services. There would be more emphasis on the promotion of non-institutional community-based services. Necessary infrastructure for implementation of the Juvenile Justice Act 1986 would also be set up in all states to provide care, protection, development and rehabilitation of children in conflict with law and in need of care and protection. The document also stated that existing facilities and standards of services in the institutions will be improved, and diversified vocational training programmes will be developed and linked with the existing vocational training institutions.

[19] Under the ninth Five-Year Plan, the social welfare component of the plan discussed the issues of CJS under the heading 'social deviants'. The document stated that non-institutional treatment of offenders is universally recognised as the most scientific and economical alternative to imprisonment, and the Probation of Offenders Act, 1958 should focus on the same. Under the scheme of Prevention and Control of Juvenile Social

11th Five-Year Plans (2007–12) were completely silent on the CJS and had taken the road of distributing the various marginalised groups into different labour groups as well as under the Scheduled Castes, Scheduled Tribes, Other Backward Classes, Religious Minorities, Nomadic, Semi-nomadic and Denotified Tribes and other vulnerable group categories.

From the 1970s onwards, institutions were established to build capacity, teach, and develop research within the CJS. There was impetus for growth in research and training in criminal justice, whereas the same period also witnessed the collapse of the institutional base of corrections in the country, coupled with withdrawal at the policy and budgetary levels. It was an irony that the shrinking of the welfare state was accompanied by the growth of institutions to promote education, research and training in criminal justice and correctional social work. Some of these institutions included the Central Bureau of Correctional Services in 1961 (later renamed as NISD in 1975), the Bureau of Police Research and Development in 1970, the National Institute of Criminology and Forensic Sciences in 1972, the Academy of Prisons and Correctional Administration in 1978, the National Crime Research Bureau in 1986 and the Institute of Correctional

---

Maladjustment, about 280 Observation Homes, 251 Juvenile Homes, 36 Special Homes and 46 Aftercare Homes were supported and 271 Welfare Boards and 189 Juvenile Courts were functioning in the country. The NISD, functioning under the Ministry of Welfare, continued to serve as the central advisory body in the field of prevention of crime, treatment of offenders in the areas of juvenile justice administration, welfare of prisoners, probation and allied measures. The NISD organised training courses for various categories of personnel including government officials, social workers, counsellors, project managers, programme officers, prison welfare officers, enforcement machinery, etc. in collaboration with state governments, universities and voluntary organisations in different parts of the country. During the eighth Five-Year Plan, the NISD organised 70 one-week regional training courses, 25 two-week training courses and 4 training courses of four days duration benefitting about 3,400 personnel and workers engaged in the area of drug abuse prevention. The Institute is an advisory body in the field of 'Prevention of Crime and Treatment of Offenders' and provides a research base for the identification and formulation of schemes suitable to different regions of the country.

Administration in 1989. The first Five-Year Plan (1951–56) not only advocated the need for social work in the country, but also stressed that social work institutions should shoulder the responsibility of providing in-service training to government employees as well as training to volunteers to work in the community (Government of India, 1951–56). With the shift to a 'development' focus since the late 1970s and early 1980s, the nature of training provided by these institutions changed. The in-service training for criminal justice personnel was largely technical in nature and focused on administration and custody, often reducing social science-based criminal justice education, correctional, welfare and social work interventions in the CJS to the minimum (Khan & Unnithan, 2008).

With the introduction of economic reforms and neoliberal policies over the last two decades, the socio-political and economic scenario has undergone an unrecognisable change. The focus is on economic growth through privatisation of public utilities, disinvestment in the public sector, outsourcing of services and promotion of contractual employment. The focus of the State is on infrastructure development and creating conditions for the private sector to flourish, especially through foreign direct investment in sectors that were earlier under a protectionist regime in favour of the 'national interest'. The poor and the marginalised have ended up on the margins in the political decision-making process and are 'taken care of' through what has come to be popularly known as 'inclusive development'. This paradigm de facto accepts that there is a price to be paid for ushering in economic growth and that the price is often paid by the poor and the dispossessed.

Neoliberalism has led to unprecedented economic and social inequalities and a widening gap between the rich and the poor. In such a scenario, as Wacquant (2008) points out, a large proportion of the poor join the ranks of the urban outcastes who are kept in control by the neoliberal state through a dual policy of work fare and prison fare. The neoliberal era is also witness to increasing crime rates and a rising number of brutal offences, triggered by the harshness of poverty, relative deprivation, increasing marginalisation and the withering away of the welfare state. Through a process of demonisation of the criminal (whose faces are mostly from the poor), the focus has shifted, as highlighted by *risk society* proponents, from justice and equality to *managing risks* and *developing security systems* to counter those risks. Garland (1996) says that the 'culture of high-crime societies' leads to two contradictory criminologies—*criminology of the self* and *criminology of the other.* The former views the offender as a rational consumer of a society where crime is a normal feature of modern life, whereas the latter views crime as the behaviour of the *alien other* and represents criminals as dangerous members of distinct racial or social groups, bearing little resemblance to *us* (Carrabine, Iganski, Lee, Plummer, & South, 2004, pp. 103–07).

This imagery of the modern-day criminal, created through a discourse played out in the mainstream media, has led to a loss of empathy in the minds of the general public, towards the offender. The script has shifted towards the protection of the victim, who could be one from amongst us, from the earlier paradigm of rehabilitating the offender, whose deviant behaviour was believed to be an outcome of psycho-social factors. There is increasing pressure today from the media and civil society on the State to come up with laws and policies to protect the rights of crime victims rather than offenders. This trend has led to a dilution of the existing architecture of rehabilitation for custodial populations, especially those housing adult populations, who are seen as part of the *undeserving poor*. This is evidenced in the crumbling infrastructure and the large number of vacant posts (not being filled up), which employ social workers as welfare and probation officers, lack of new positions requiring social work knowledge or roles and reducing budgets for correctional institutions and departments.

The Challenge before Criminal Justice Social Work

Despite the rather depressing picture presented in the earlier section, it is heartening to note that the challenge before the social work profession vis-à-vis the CJS has been accepted by civil society organisations, which continue to believe in the potential of professional input to protect the rights of citizens at the inter-face of the system and to facilitate the social re-entry of custodial populations (Vadiraj & Gopal, 2011). One important player in this process, with which this author has been associated for the last 25 years, is the School of Social Work at the TISS, which has been demonstrating the role that social workers can play in the CJS, through its field action projects (FAPs).[20]

These projects have worked for the rights and rehabilitation of vulnerable sections coming into contact with the CJS—whether as victims, offenders or as 'ordinary citizens', and their families—and have created a platform for advocating law and policy change towards creating a citizen-friendly CJS. For exam-ple, the special cells for women have been working in Maharashtra for the rights of women victims of violence by placing social workers in the police system to provide socio-legal guidance and support to women who approach the police with complaints of violence. The model has been adopted by the Government of Maharashtra and is in the process of locating special cells attached to police stations at the district and taluka levels. The work of the project has contributed to significant changes at the law and policy levels, including the passing of the Protection of Women from Domestic Violence Act, 2005 (Dave, Raghavan, & Solanki, 2012). Prayas has been working in prisons, police sta-tions, courts and women's and children's institutions over the last 24 years (in Maharashtra and Gujarat) to promote the legal

---

[20] FAPs are experimental and demonstration projects which have played a 'major role in piloting or pioneering new services' through social work inter-vention by its faculty, students and project staff 'with the objective of demon-strating to the public, the need for such services'. 'Field action projects are thus an integral part of validation or revision of such a practice–theory con-tinuum. These projects fulfil several objectives of professional education, and have evolved over the years due to various internal and external factors. They have emerged as a form of demonstration of new interventions and possibili-ties in order to test their efficacy, which then could be emulated by others; as a response to new needs, to changing social realities, or from other social movements or campaigns; to enable faculty to develop academically and keep in touch with field practice; and to provide students opportunities for learn-ing new interventions and formulation of creative strategy for greater rele-vance in practice' (TISS, 2001, unpublished).

rights and rehabilitation of vulnerable sections processed by the CJS. It has reached out to women prisoners, male youth in prison or in juvenile homes, children of prisoners, released prisoners, women rescued from commercial sexual exploitation and their families. Apart from its field-based intervention, it has been working towards the creation of a rehabilitation policy for custodial populations (Dave, Raghavan, & Solanki, 2012; Raghavan, 2013). For example, Prayas has worked for over two decades to highlight the plight of neglected and invisible groups such as children of prisoners through research and advocacy which has led to their inclusion in child welfare policy and programmes. This has resulted in their inclusion in the National Plan of Action for Children in 2002, under the category of 'children in difficult circumstances'. Prayas submitted a report on the situation of children of prisoners before the Supreme Court (R.D. Upadhayay vs. State of Andhra Pradesh and others) as a result of which, in 2008, the court laid down guidelines for the care, protection and education of children living with their mothers in prison. The work of the project has also highlighted the lack of coordination between different wings of the CJS and welfare system, leading to the poor implementation of existing laws and programmes which were originally meant to reach out to vulnerable and marginalised sections coming into contact with the CJS. Prayas has been instrumental in facilitating the creation of inter-departmental coordination mechanisms in Maharashtra, such as the State Inter-Departmental Committee on Prisoners, district inter-departmental subcommittees and the State Advisory Committee on Immoral Trafficking. Such mechanisms have created a platform for government departments and civil society organisations to engage with each other over issues relating to custodial justice and the rehabilitation of custodial populations to come up with practical solutions to complex problems.[21] Koshish has been working since 2006 in beggars' homes and with the homeless and the destitute in Maharashtra, Delhi and Bihar. It has also been working towards the repeal of the anti-poor beggary prevention laws in the country through research and advocacy (Tarique & Raghavan, 2011). The

---

[21] For details on Prayas work and its impact on law and policy, please visit http://www.tiss.edu/TopMenuBar/field-action/projects/prayas.

Resource Cell on Juvenile Justice has been working since 2008 towards the effective implementation of the Juvenile Justice Act 2003, especially in relation to the rehabilitation of Juveniles in Conflict with Law (JCL). TANDA (Towards Advocacy, Networking and Developmental Action) has been working since 2011 for the rights and entitlements of nomadic and de-notified tribes in Maharashtra, who were criminalised by the British through the Criminal Tribes Act, 1871. These projects have provided a range of services such as individual and family counselling, legal aid and guidance, vocational training, awareness sessions, emergency financial or medical assistance, temporary shelter, job placement, access to citizenship documents and welfare schemes, and the formation of women's self-help groups and local community institutions.[22]

Although such initiatives are significant, they are not likely to change the overall scenario in the field of criminal justice social work in India, unless the State reverses its policy of withdrawal from the responsibility of working towards the welfare and rehabilitation of custodial populations. The current trend of privileging the rights of victims over, and often at the cost of, rights of offenders is a worldwide one. Newer crimes such as terrorism, cybercrime, human trafficking and transnational organised crime operate today at the global level, while age-old crimes such as crimes against women and children have assumed ugly faces like never before. The world has never seemed a more dangerous place to live in. The *human rights regime* is under threat of being subsumed by the *security and safety first regime*. There is sufficient literature to show that the criminal justice social work which emerged to facilitate the social re-entry of institutional populations has been turned on its head to protect the rights of victims and ordinary citizens in the neoliberal West (Burke & Collet, 2010; Cullen & Gendreau, 2001; Harker & Worrall, 2011; Herzog-Evans, 2011; Rosenthal, 2004; Teague, 2011). Earlier efforts of rehabilitating offenders are now seen 'as permissive,

---

[22] For more details about these projects, please visit http://www.tiss.edu/ TopMenuBar/field-action/projects. It is important to note that many of these projects are shouldering the State's responsibilities outlined in the Indian Constitution under the Chapter on the Directive Principles of State Policy.

uncaring about crime victims, and committed to a rehabilitative ideal that ignores the reality of the violent, predatory criminal' (Petersilia, 1997, p. 150). In India, criminal justice social work got off to a head start in the postcolonial period, especially in the period between the 1950s and the 1970s. However, with the gradual withdrawal of the welfare state, criminal justice and correctional social work has been reduced to mere tokenism. This has led to the shrinking of jobs in the welfare sector and has consequently shifted the focus of the social work profession from one of working in or with the CJS to one of engaging and confronting the system. The situation has come to pass whereby the onus of keeping alive the rehabilitative objective of the CJS is now left to civil society organisations and an activist judiciary. There is a need to bring about a paradigm shift in the discourse around the aetiology of crime, the socio-economic profile of those involved in crimes and the rehabilitation potential of offender populations, through research and practice knowledge. For this to happen, social scientists, criminologists, criminal justice functionaries and social work practitioners in criminal justice need to engage in what Loader and Sparks (2010) have termed as public criminology. Extinction threatens before criminal justice social work can be converted into an opportunity for re-imagining futures, through a calculated and concerted effort by all stakeholders concerned.

References

Adenwalla, M. (2006). *Child protection and juvenile justice system: For juvenile in conflict with law.* New Delhi: Childline India Foundation.

Bajpai, G. S. (n.d.). *Criminology: An appraisal of present status and future directions.* Retrieved from https://forensic.to/webhome/drgsbajpai/criminology%20appraisal.pdf

Brownell, P., & Roberts, A. (2002). A century of social work in criminal justice and correctional settings. *Journal of Offender Rehabilitation, 35*(2), 1–17. doi: 10.1300/J076v35n02_01

Burke, L., & Collett, S. (2010). People are not things: What new Labour has done to probation. *Probation Journal, 57*(3), 232–49. doi: 10.1177/0264550510373957

Carrabine, E., Iganski, P., Lee, M., Plummer, K., & South, N. (2004). *Criminology: A sociological introduction.* London, New York: Routledge.

Children's Aid Society. (1938). *Annual report.* Bombay: Children's Aid Society.

Chowdhury, N. R. (2002). *Indian prison laws and correction of prisoners.* New Delhi: Deep and Deep Publications Pvt. Ltd.

Cullen, F. T., & Gendreau, P. (2001). From nothing works to what works: Changing professional ideology in the 21st century. *The Prison Journal, 81*(3), 313–38.

Dave, A., Raghavan, V., & Solanki, D. (2012). Centrality of field action in social work education: A case for socio-legal education. *Social Change, 42*(4), 451–66.

Garland, D. (1996). The limits of the sovereign state. *British Journal of Criminology, 36*(4), 445–71.

Government of India. (1951–56). *First Five-Year Plan.* New Delhi: Planning Commission of India. Retrieved from http://planningcommission.nic. in/plans/planrel/fiveyr/1st/1planch36.html

————. (1954). *Advisory Committee on Aftercare Programmes.* Bombay: Usha Printers.

————. (1960). *The Children's Act, 1960.* New Delhi: Ministry of Women and Child Development. Retrieved from http://wcd.nic.in/children-act1960.htm

————. (1961–66). *Third Five-Year Plan.* New Delhi: Planning Commission of India. Retrieved from http://planningcommission.nic.in/plans/plan-rel/fiveyr/3rd/3planch35.html

————. (1980–85). *Sixth Five-Year Plan.* New Delhi: Planning Commission of India. Retrieved from http://planningcommission.nic.in/plans/plan-rel/fiveyr/6th/6planch28.html

————. (1985–90). *Seventh Five-Year Plan.* New Delhi: Planning Commission of India. Retrieved from http://planningcommission.nic.in/plans/plan-rel/fiveyr/7th/vol2/7v2ch13.html

————. (1986). *The Juvenile Justice Act, 1986.* Retrieved from http://www.vakilno1.com/bareacts/juvenilejusticeact/juvenilejusticeact.html#INTRODUCTION

————. (2000). *The Juvenile Justice (Care and Protection of Children) Act, 2000.* Retrieved from http://wcd.nic.in/childprot/jjact2000.pdf

Government of Madras State. (1954). *Administration report of the probation department, Madras State, 1952.* Madras: The Government Press.

Khan, M. Z., & Unnithan, N. P. (2008). Criminological and criminal justice education in India: A comparative note. *Journal of Criminal Justice Education, 19*(1), 97–109. doi: 10.1080/10511250801892987

Harker, H., & Worrall, A. (2011). From 'community corrections' to 'probation and parole' in Western Australia. *Probation Journal, 58*(4), 364–71. doi: 10.1177/0264550511421517

Herzog-Evans, M. (2011). Probation in France: Some things old, some things new, some things borrowed, and often blue. *Probation Journal, 58*(4), 345–54. doi: 10.1177/0264550511420795

Loader, I., & Sparks, R. (2010). *Public criminology?* London: Routledge.

Madan, G. R. (2009). *Indian social problems* (Vol. 1, 7th ed.). Mumbai: Allied Publishers Pvt. Ltd.

Nieto, M. (1996). *The changing role of probation in California's criminal justice system*. Sacramento, CA: California Research Bureau.

Panakal, J. J. (1967). Training for correctional workers. *Indian Journal of Social Work, 28*(1), 91–94.

Patterson, G. T. (2012). *Social work practice in the criminal justice system*. New York, NY: Routledge.

Petersilia, J. (1997). Probation in the United States. *Crime and Justice, 22*, 149–200.

Raghavan, V. (2013). Social work intervention in criminal justice: Field-theory linkage. In S. Singh (Ed.), *Social work and social development: Perspectives from India and the United States*. Chicago: Lyceum Publications Inc.

Roberts, A., & Springer, D. (2007). *Social work in juvenile and criminal justice settings*. Springfield, IL: Charles C. Thomas.

Rosenthal, M. G. (2004). *The punitive (un)welfare state: U.S. penal policy in comparative perspective*. Retrieved from http://www.adelphi.edu/peoplematter/pdfs/Rosenthal.pdf

Sethna, M. J. (1952). *Society and the criminal*. Bombay: Leader's Press Ltd.

Stohr, M. K., & Walsh, A. (2008). *Corrections: The essentials*. Los Angeles, CA: SAGE Publications.

Streets, Heather. (2001). The Rebellion of 1857: Origins, consequences and themes. *Teaching South Asia, 1*(1), 85–104.

Tarique, M., & Raghavan, V. (2011). India's war on its poor. *50.50 inclusive democracy*. Retrieved from http://www.opendemocracy.net/5050/mohammed-tarique-vijay-raghavan/indias-war-on-its-poor

Teague, M. (2011). Probation in America: Armed, private and unaffordable? *Probation Journal, 58*(4), 317–32. doi: 10.1177/0264550511421518

The Association for Moral and Social Hygiene in India. (1939). *The probation services in India and England*. New Delhi: Liddell's Printing Works.

TISS. (2001). Report for the National Assessment and Accreditation Council on field action projects, unpublished.

Vadiraj, S., & Gopal, A. (2011). *Social work in India's criminal justice institutions: Need, experiences and challenges*. Mumbai, India: Sir Dorabji Tata Trust and the Allied Trusts.

Wacquant, L. (2008). *Urban outcasts: A comparative sociology of advanced marginality*. Malden: Polity Press.

Wilson, M. (2010). *Criminal justice social work in the United States: Adapting to new challenges*. Washington, DC: NASW Center for Workforce Studies.

2

Explaining Criminal Behaviour

K. Jaishankar and Amit Gopal Thakre

Introduction

Crimes and criminal behaviour have always aroused varied reactions from society. The reactions to criminal behaviour were responded to with retribution which progressively transformed into rehabilitation because of scholarly and forensic contributions in deciphering criminal behaviours. The criminal justice system (CJS) architecture (such as correctional facilities, juvenile homes, mediation centres and so on) acts as a platform for practitioners and social workers to study criminal behaviour with an aim to understand how these settings impact the effective rehabilitation, reformation and reintegration of offenders back into society. Garland (1997) stated that the understanding of criminal behaviour in CJS settings has direct implications on intervention and deterrence policies because criminological theories (in pursuit of studying criminal behaviours) eventually become transformed through 'government rationalities' into actual practice.

Hesselink and Herbig (2009) illustrated how better understanding of criminal behaviour will improve law enforcement capabilities to take more effective interventional steps and also to construct more efficient correctional facilities. This answers the question of 'how important is it to study criminal behaviour?', but what exactly is 'criminal behaviour' and how can it be used to operationally mould the justice system to be focussed on reforming offenders? Criminal behaviour is 'any antisocial act that places the actor at risk of becoming the focus of attention of the criminal and juvenile professionals' (Andrews & Bonta, 2003). It is evident from this definition that criminal behaviour is an antisocial act (usually involving some breach of the criminal code) which can be studied empirically to measure/predict future crimes, and hence can make such conduct amenable to intervention, deterrence and ultimately reformation.

Understanding 'why crime happens' is actually a bedrock for formulating governmental strategies to regulate criminal behaviour (Sherman & Hawkins, 1981). A better understanding of criminal behaviour will eventually reflect on policies formulated to interpret, intervene and reform criminal behaviour. For example, it makes sense when policies driven by developmental criminological theories attempt to reduce crimes committed by delinquent youth. Criminological theories have focussed on a range of different criminogenic factors through time, right from the classical school explaining criminal behaviour through concepts like 'free will and rationality' (mid to late eighteenth century), thereafter transitioning to the 'atavistic born criminal' (late nineteenth century) and finally to the contemporary era where theories like bio-social and psycho-social explanations of criminal behaviour paved the way for the rehabilitation and reintegration of offenders. While we certainly need to know the importance of understanding criminal behaviour and its implications on the overall social order of a community, it is equally important for us to know exactly where the root causes of deviance lie. This will be discussed in greater detail in the next part of the chapter. This chapter is divided into two parts. The first part will give a historical overview of criminological theories that explain criminal behaviour and the second part will discuss the theories most used by social workers, that is, bio-social and psycho-social theories.

Part I

Pre- and Early-modern Reasoning of Criminal Behaviour

The foremost reasoning in explaining criminal behaviour came from spiritualism (Tannenbaum, 1938), where the cause of crime was explained as an 'act of the devil' or as a result of being 'possessed by evil'. Society subsequently witnessed absurd punishments coming out of judgements from religious leaders based on their subjective interpretation of the 'will of God' (Vold & Bernard, 1986). The prevalence of spiritualism, where crimes are explained by phenomena unknown to humans (metaphysical) coexisted with another group of theorists, termed 'naturalists', who explained that criminal behaviour was either driven by reason or passion (Vold, 1958). During the sixteenth and seventeenth centuries, scholars started searching for a deeper understanding of criminal behaviour that shifted the emphasis from the metaphysical to the natural. This paved the way for the Enlightenment-based Classical School of Criminology which argued that criminal behaviour was rationally justified on the basis of being either pleasure-seeking or pain-avoiding conduct (late eighteenth century). The proponents of this school rejected the spiritual justification for crime and saw the offender as being totally responsible for his/her acts because they chose to behave in that deviant manner (free will). Cessare Beccaria's and Jeremy Bentham's classical theory, using utilitarianism as its philosophical basis, laid the foundations for the reformation of the medieval CJS (Monachesi, 1973) which attempted to abolish the judges' barbaric and discretionary powers to punish offenders (often arbitrarily and extremely severely) during that period (Paolucci, 1963). Some of the important points of Beccaria's work that transformed the public's outlook on criminal behaviour and the treatment of offenders were as follows: equal treatment of all before the law, the need for a well-defined code of law, justification for punishment (purely for deterrence, and not for vengeance or retribution), fair and swift justice, reformation of offenders and an emphasis on crime prevention.

Nevertheless, the late modern period drove scholars to search for more scientific and empirically based causal explanations, leading to the rise of the Positivist School of Criminology in the nineteenth century.

The Late Modern Era and Its Scientific Study of the Criminal's Body, Mind and Society

Philosophical contributions to explaining criminal behaviour were not totally acceptable in late modern nineteenth century, so steps were initiated to understand criminal behaviour by scientifically examining the offender. Cesare Lombroso (the father of modern criminology), in the late nineteenth century, was influenced by Darwin's work and performed anatomical comparative studies of prisoners and published a book *Criminal Man* with findings that explained that an individual's constitutional/biological make-up is a determining factor in relation to whether a person is or not a criminal (Wolfgang, 1973). During this period, many academics and criminal justice practitioners explained criminal behaviour on the basis of certain physical parameters, for example, the works of Kretschmer (physique), Mohr and Gundlach (physique), Hooton (physique and racial factors) and Sheldon (somatotypology) (as cited in Vold, 1958). Testing Lombroso's theory, Charles Goring (1913, p. 370) noted that '[t]he physical and mental constitution of both criminal and law-abiding persons, of the same age, stature, class, and intelligence, are identical. There is no such thing as an anthropological criminal type'. Further, the findings of Lombroso were refuted by his own apprentice, Enrico Ferri, who was convinced that criminality stemmed more from psychological and sociological factors rather than biological ones (1905/1917). Raffaele Garofalo, another student of Lombroso, in his work 'Criminology' argued that the cause of criminal behaviour lies not so much in the biology of an individual, but in his/her social circumstances (economic and political factors) which influence crimes in society at a macrolevel (Vold, 1958).

Social Structure Causing Criminal Behaviour

The period from the 1900s to the 1960s saw an upsurge of youth committing crime which called for academic attention to explain such disturbing social dynamics in the period between the economic Great Depression (1929) and the aftermath of World War II (from 1945 onwards). The criminological explanations of criminal behaviour during this era were very much driven by the dynamics of rapid change in our social structures. The scholars of this generation explained these apparent crime waves using control theory (e.g., childhood developmental processes and external social constraints on behaviour). This period also saw a notable shift in criminological academic dominance from Europe to the United States.

Some of the risk factors identified by control theorists include poor parental supervision, dysfunctional family environments, coercive child–parent relationships and deviant peer associations, many of which were later integrated into governmental policy so as to prevent further social breakdown. Many research studies concluded that these risk factors occurring during childhood correlated strongly with future criminal behaviour (Bernard & Snipes, 1996). This, of course, highlights the importance of studying these risk factors more closely so as to develop effective interventions to prevent youth deviance.

The aforementioned framework (i.e., childhood risk factors) is one of many chains of understanding criminal behaviour, for example, psychological, biological, environmental, hormonal, genetics, economic and so on. Understanding criminal behaviour thus, in many instances, requires a multidisciplinary approach. Criminal justice social workers can leverage on the works of criminologists to establish an empirical base for the purposes of evaluation, determining severity of deviancy as well as the causes and ways of preventing criminal behaviour (Herbig & Hesselink, 2012). The integrity and reliability of studying criminal behaviour is very well demonstrated in Hesselink-Louw's (2004) study which emphasised that researching criminal behaviour involves an in-depth analysis of precursors, arousal factors, causes and intention, as well as psychological and externally influential elements. The methodologies employed to reach such critical findings of the offender's behaviour are empirical/evidence based and accredited techniques that help to reliably and accurately uncover the case histories of the offender's behavioural traits under consideration. Such data will increase the likelihood of creating interventions that will reduce criminal behaviour (Bonta, 2002; Duguid, 2000; Hesselink-Louw, 2004; Myer, 2001). In furtherance of this, Hesselink-Louw (2004) illustrated ways to enhance offender rehabilitation through 'microlevel in-depth' assessments (individual case-specific psychological diagnosis) to be conducted by a conglomeration of experts from various fields (e.g., social workers, health care officials, religious figures, educationists, psychologists, psychiatrists and so on).

Control theories are also deeply interested in external social structural factors that can influence behaviour as well. In the United States, Shaw and McKay (1942) showed the significance of how a highly transitional neighbourhood is an important factor in increasing the likelihood of youth deviance in the area. Other external factors, for example, the disjuncture between cultural goals of material success and the socially acceptable ways of achieving those cultural goals, can give rise to youth crime amongst certain socio-economically marginalised youth— Merton's anomie/strain theory shows how, due to the disparity of socially acceptable opportunities available to lower class youths, intense frustration can be caused, thereby increasing the likelihood of them adapting and adopting deviant alternatives to achieving material success (Merton, 1938). Cloward and Ohlin's (1960) study on delinquent juvenile gangs is an extension of Merton's anomie/strain theory, as well as Cohen's (1955) deviant subcultural theory (which argued that responses to social strain did not occur at an individual level, as Merton asserted, but at a group one, thereby creating criminal or deviant subcultures), and Sutherland's (1940) differential association theory which argued that the learning of deviant attitudes, techniques, values, motives and so on occurred in intimate personal relationships. These studies were devoted to explaining the significance of social structures in the occurrence of crimes and are still considered to be fundamental studies which act as the foundations of contemporary theories explaining criminal behaviour even today.

How Power 'Causes' Criminal Behaviour

In the mid-1960s, critical criminology materialised with the emergence of academic critique into conservatism, the status quo, capitalism and its consequences. In the early part of the twentieth century, Marxist scholars, using a conflict paradigm, were already blaming capitalism (and its highly influential capitalists) as being the root cause for lawlessness (Bonger, 1969[1916]). Labelling theory (Becker, 1963) would later accentuate the role of the powerful within society to 'create' deviants through its argument that the causes of criminal behaviour lie not in pathological individuals or communities, but in a society where the powerful are able to successfully label a person a 'criminal' by having him/her convicted and thereafter placed in correctional institutions, thereby stigmatising them and creating a perceptual image of a 'social misfit' (note its roots in phenomenology and symbolic interactionism: Tannenbaum, 1938). While agreeing with its basic premise, Marxist scholars would nevertheless criticise labelling theory for not identifying who these powerful actors were, that is, the capitalists. Another prominent group of criminologists focussed on 'gender' as part of their understanding of female criminality. The criminogenic factors that came to light under 'feminism' were the patriarchy (male dominance), masculinities and a disparity in socioeconomic status between the genders (Adler, 1975).

A Shift in Explaining Criminal Behaviour from 'Society' Back to the 'Individual'

During the 1980s, however, many researchers suggested that harsher sanctions were the most appropriate response to criminal behaviour, thus evidencing a swing of the pendulum from a critical criminological dominance in the 1960s to a resurgence of conservatism and right realism in the 1980s. The explanation for crimes by scholars of this ilk concentrated on the situational factors that affected the opportunity for a person to commit a crime, giving birth to rational choice perspective and routine activity theory (Bottoms, 1994). Situational crime-prevention measures (Cohen & Felson, 1979) use both these theories to minimise criminal opportunities by, for example, increasing the effort to commit a crime (target hardening), reducing the rewards of committing a crime or increasing the likelihood of being arrested (installing CCTV or anti-burglar alarms). This is because according to Clark and Cornish (2001), a criminal is not biologically or psychologically pathological. Criminals are mostly free willed and rational individuals, making decisions to commit a crime using a cost–benefit analysis approach. Consequently, preventing or deterring crime (though not through traditional classical means of punishment) could be achieved by modifying the situational factors that potential offenders find themselves confronted with when deciding whether to commit a crime or not (Akers & Sellers, 2004).

Thus, criminological theories are dynamic and eclectic, borrowing from a range of disciplines. Nevertheless, there is still a concern that such theoretical frameworks may still be inadequate to explain all forms of criminal behaviour because of their particular roots in time, space and culture. Will a subcultural theory of youth deviance conceived in Europe during the 1950s or America during the 1920s be applicable to explain criminal youth gangs in contemporary India? In this regard, a criminological theory designed to explain criminal behaviour in cyberspace (space transition theory of cybercrimes) that was introduced by the lead author of this chapter (Jaishankar, 2008) demonstrates the dynamic nature of criminological theories and explores some of these challenges therein.

In the next part of this paper, theories which are bio-social or psycho-social in nature will be discussed, as they are mostly used by social workers in the course of their criminal justice practice.

Part II

Social workers employed by organisations dealing with offenders are deeply familiar with a range of criminological theories that aid them in better understanding human criminal behaviour. Many of these paradigms tend to be bio-social and psycho-social in nature.

Bio-social and Psycho-social Perspectives of Criminal Behaviour and Their Implications for Social Workers

As previously highlighted, the interdisciplinary nature of criminology strongly encourages the merging of complementary biological, psychological and social/environmental theories so as to improve our ability to explain criminal behaviour (Ball, 1978). Cullen (2009) stated that bio-social perspectives, in particular, would play a crucial role in the twenty-first century criminal justice policies. It should be noted though that such merged theories do not at all subscribe to a reductionist base that is biologically deterministic (Walsh, 2012, p. 130). They are, rather, dynamic paradigms that suggest that human behaviour is a product of our inherent biological or psychological makeups interacting with the surrounding environment, be it material or cultural (Walsh, 2012, p. 130). Thus, the question is not whether 'nature' or 'nurture' creates delinquents, but rather to what extent does 'nature via nurture' produce or increase the likelihood of deviancy (Walsh, 2012, p. 130).

Bio-social Perspectives

So, for example, behavioural genetics is an exciting approach that takes into account how a person's genes (which are inherited) interact with the environment to develop human traits like 'low empathy, low IQ and impulsiveness' (Walsh, 2012, p. 130). It should be noted, however, that the genes themselves do not 'cause' people to commit crime; there is no 'criminal gene' per se but the expression of particular genes in a person nevertheless 'facilitate tendencies or dispositions to respond to environments in one way rather than in another' (Walsh, 2012, p. 130) and that may well include offending conduct. Such an approach has been supported by concordance (twins) as well as adoption studies that attempt, where possible, to separate the influence genes vis-à-vis upbringing. But if there is no actual genetic theory of criminal behaviour, what then is its significance? According to Walsh, 'behavior genetic studies help us to better understand traditional criminological theories' (2012, p. 132), that is, some of the theories cited earlier in this chapter. By way illustration, Walsh highlights the problem of low impulsivity (a common trait among juvenile delinquents). Gottfredson and Hirschi's (1990) general theory of crime explains that low self-control among young offenders is primarily attributable to defective parenting. However, Walsh points out that

> there are now well over 100 studies that have shown rather strong links between low self-control and low levels of the neurotransmitter serotonin.... In other words, while we all have to be taught to control our impulses, some of us are naturally easier to teach than others. Levels of serotonin are governed both by genes and by the environment. That is, genes govern the base levels of serotonin a person has, but what is going on in the environment results in serotonin levels increasing and decreasing. (2012, p. 132)

Other scholars have posited that abnormal brain functions can be fundamental causes of criminal behaviour in certain social situations. In this regard, Raine (1993) illustrated that dysfunctions in the frontal and temporal lobes of the brain may cause aggressiveness and improper sexual behavioural response, respectively. Further, in tandem with severe levels of stress experienced within a social setting (i.e., the environmental stimulus), Fishbein (2003) noted how the body excessively releases cortisol which eventually shrinks the hypothalamic–pituitary–adrenal axis, thereby leading to depression, an insensitive autonomic nervous system, and behavioural complications, which could include offending conduct.

Another interesting bio-social theory that may develop greater significance as India becomes more industrialised is the relationship between increasing levels of environmental toxins and social disorder (Lynch, Schwendinger, & Schwendinger, 2006). Studies have found that increasing pollution and toxin concentration in the environment plays a significant role in inducing attention disorders, IQ deficits and primary risk factors which could then result in antisocial behaviours (Colburn, Dumanoski, & Myers, 1997; Rodericks, 1992). In particular, Lynch et al. (2006) studied how sporadic growth of industries in the midst of residential communities, and the waste products released from them in close proximity to people living nearby, caused central nervous system impairment, aggressiveness, frustration, hyperactivity, ADHD (attention-deficit/hyperactivity disorder), antisocial behaviour and crime. The researchers further argued that the over-representation of residents from low-income communities, minority groups and slum areas in the official crime statistics could be due to the fact that many of them are located in the vicinity of chemical accidents or hazardous waste sites.

Psycho-social Perspectives

Walsh and Ellis explained that '[p]sychological theories of criminal behavior were in vogue before sociology got into the picture and were more interested in individual differences in the propensity to commit crimes than in environmental conditions assumed to facilitate it' (2007, p. 170).

That said, Walsh and Ellis made it clear that 'these explanations do not compete with sociological explanation; rather, they strengthen and complete them' (2007, p. 170). Such theories would traditionally argue that there were strong correlational links between criminal or antisocial behaviour, and low IQ (resulting in erroneous decisions to commit crime or being unable to get a proper job for subsistence living, and hence needing to commit crime to survive and so on), as well as abnormal personality/temperament (e.g., having an overly dominant id or superego, lacking in empathy, highly impulsive, sensation-seeking and so on) (Walsh & Ellis, 2007, p. 170). Other, more modern psychosocial paradigms would include, however, arousal theory, net advantage theory and lifestyle theory.

Arousal theory posits that human beings experience varying degrees of arousal to their central nervous systems when exposed to the same environmental stimulation, that is, some may be optimally aroused, over-aroused or under-aroused (Walsh & Ellis, 2007, p. 182). Those who were over- or under-aroused, however, will feel some psychological discomfort (either being overly stressed or bored, respectively). Those suffering from the former are called 'augmenters', while those experiencing the latter are called 'reducers'. Walsh and Ellis observed that

> augmenters prefer more constancy than variety in their world and seek to tone down environmental stimuli that most people find to be 'just right'. Such people quickly learn to avoid engaging in behavior that raises the intensity of stimuli to levels they find unpleasant and are rarely found in criminal populations. (2007, p. 182)

Reducers, however, were

> easily bored with 'just right' levels of stimulation and continually seek to boost stimuli to what are for them more comfortable levels. They also require a high level of punishing stimuli before learning to avoid the behavior that provokes it. According to arousal theory, the latter are the individuals who are unusually prone to criminal behaviour. (2007, p. 182)

Without going into too much detail here, net advantage theory is essentially a paradigm that is

> based on conditioning principles and adds individual differences to account for the outcome of conditioning. People are differentially responsive to rewards and punishment, and they differ in what they find to be rewarding or punishing. People who are impulsive, have learning difficulties, and have not developed an adequate conscience focus on immediate rewards from crime without concern for the hurt they cause others while dis-counting punishment for themselves. (Walsh & Ellis, 2007, p. 194)

Glen Walters's lifestyle theory is a practice-oriented framework that attempts to modify criminal thinking patterns rather than uncover how they are initially formed. In Walter's approach, such criminal lifestyles (or criminal behavioural patterns) character-ised by 'irresponsibility, impulsiveness, self-indulgence, negative interpersonal relationships, and the chronic willingness to violate society's rules' (Walsh & Ellis, 2007, pp. 184–85) are developed as a 'result of faulty thinking patterns, which arise from the conse-quences (reward and punishment) of choices in early life, which are themselves influenced by biological and early environmen-tal conditions' (Walsh & Ellis, 2007, p. 185). These daily choices or decisions are conditioned by an interaction of our individual traits (low IQ, impulsivity and so on) and the environmental circumstances (attachment to significant others and so on) in which we are burdened with (Walsh & Ellis, 2007, p. 184). Some of these choices, unfortunately, may lead to the creation of criminal cognitions or 'thinking errors', and would include, for example,

> cutoff (the ability to discount the suffering of their victims), entitlement (the world owes them a living), power orientation (viewing the world in terms of weakness and strength), cognitive indolence (orientation to the present; concrete in thinking), and discontinuity (the inability to integrate thinking patterns). (Walsh & Ellis, 2007, p. 185)

These thinking errors in turn lead to four interrelated behavioural patterns that, according to Walters, 'almost guarantee criminality', that is, rule breaking, interpersonal intrusiveness, self-indulgence and irresponsibility (Walsh & Ellis, 2007, p. 185).

Implications for Social Workers

Criminological theories, and, in particular, those that are biosocial or psycho-social in nature, can greatly assist criminal justice social workers in implementation of clinical rehabilitative measures. Progressive interventions can be used to impart social skills, impulse regulation, as well as engender introspective behaviour, construct goal-oriented cognitive schemas and to develop an acute awareness of the consequences of criminal behaviour. The policies coming out of biological perspectives of criminology may regulate criminal behaviour significantly if antisocial populations are clearly associated with biological disorders interacting with sociological factors (Fishbein, 2001). These policies should be followed up by studies showing impact on macroscale regulation of criminal behaviour. Fishbein (2001) further stressed the point that intervention policies will bring about desirable changes in criminal behaviour through counselling, cognitive rehabilitation programmes and behaviour-modification strategies.

The roles that social worker can play in the CJS are varied given that they have the ethos, skills and expertise to assist victims, offenders (as well as their families) and the community-at-large blighted by environmental factors that increase the likelihood of criminal behaviour (Raghavan & Singh, 2013). Looking at the current crisis of the Indian CJS, overcrowding by those awaiting trial in prisons (undertrials, i.e., those who have not been proved guilty by the court yet) raises the risk of them acquiring or intensifying antisocial traits from those who are indeed guilty of crimes. Furthermore, intervention is necessary to protect the inmate from social stigma and the blunt force of isolation. The 'kith and kin' of persons in correctional institutions should be insulated from physical and emotional deprivation, through assistance of social workers. Psycho-social theories emphasise the role of an addiction-prone lifestyle, 'self-concept' and biological interactions with the environment which could be utilised to frame intervention strategies by social workers that are more effective in its rehabilitative aims.

Conclusion

The effectiveness of any CJS can be measured by the provision, implementation and outcomes of its intervention strategies. That said, the development of knowledge in understanding criminal behaviour in order to prevent it from occurring is nothing less than a roller coaster ride of theories moving from rational free will, biology, psychology to social disorganisation and many more. Nevertheless, there are a number of theoretical frameworks that have shown themselves to be effective in rehabilitating, reforming and reintegrating offenders into the community. In tandem with those theories, though there is still a need humanise the CJS machinery through the employment of social workers to provide not only technical assistance, but also to offer their clients, that is, offenders hope for a better and decent life by reinstating a positive 'self-concept' *sans* antisocial traits (Winnicott, 1962). Social workers equipped with a strong understanding of the causes of criminal behaviour and the literature on 'what works' could use their judicious discretion on occasion to adapt the CJS norms to better address the needs and interests of the offender with their client-focussed interpersonal relational skills.

References

Adler, F. (1975). *Sisters in crime: The rise of the new female criminal.* New York: McGraw-Hill.

Akers, R. L., & Sellers, C. S. (2004). *Criminological theories: Introduction, evaluation, and application* (4th ed.). Los Angeles, CA: Roxbury.

Andrews, D. A., & Bonta, J. (2003). *The psychology of criminal conduct.* Cincinnati, OH: Anderson Publishing Co.

Ball, R. A. (1978). The dialectical method: Its application to social theory. *Social Forces, 57*(3), 785–798.

Becker, H. S. (1963). *Outsiders: Studies in the sociology of deviance.* New York: Free Press.

Bernard, T. J., & Snipes, J. B. (1996). Theoretical integration in criminology. *Crime and Justice: A Review of Research, 20*, 301–48.

Bonger, W. (1969). *Criminality and economic conditions.* Bloomington, IN: Indiana University Press (Original work published in 1916).

Bonta, J. L. (2002). Offender risk assessment: Guidelines for selection and use. *Criminal Justice and Behavior, 29*(4), 355–79.

Bottoms, A. E. (1994). Environmental criminology. In M. Maguire, R. Morgan & R. Reiner (Eds.), *The Oxford handbook of criminology* (pp. 585–656). New York: Oxford University Press.

Clark, R. V., & Cornish, D. B. (2001). Rational choice. In R. Paternoster & R. Bachman (Eds.), *Explaining criminals and crime: Essays in contemporary criminological theory* (pp. 23–42). Los Angeles, CA: Roxbury.

Cloward, R. A., & Ohlin, L. E. (1960). *Delinquency and opportunity: A theory of delinquent gangs.* New York: Free Press.

Cohen, A. K. (1955). *Delinquent boys: The culture of the gang.* Glencoe, IL: The Free Press.

Cohen, L. E., & Felson, M. (1979). Social change and crime rate trends: A routine activities approach. *American Sociological Review, 44*, 588–608.

Colburn, T., Dumanoski, D., & Myers, J. P. (1997). *Our stolen state.* New York: Plume.

Cullen, F. T. (2009). Preface. In A. Walsh & K. M. Beaver (Eds.), *Biosocial criminology: New directions in theory and research* (pp. xv–xvii). New York: Routledge.

48   K. Jaishankar and Amit Gopal Thakre

Duguid, S. (2000). *Can prisons work? The prisoner as object and subject in modern corrections.* Canada: University of Toronto Press.

Ferri, E. (1905/1917). *Criminal sociology* (translation from the French edition of 1905). Boston, MA: Little, Brown, and Co.

Fishbein, D. H. (2001). *Biobehavioral perspective in criminology.* Belmont, CA: Wadsworth.

————. (2003). Neurophysiological and emotional regulatory processes in antisocial behaviour. In A. Walsh & L. Ellis (Eds), *Biosocial criminology: Challenging environmentalism's supremacy* (pp. 185–208). Hauppauge, NY: Nova Science Publishers.

Garland, D. (1997). Governmentality and the problem of crime: Foucault, criminology, sociology. *Theoretical Criminology, 1*(2), 173–214.

Goring, C. (1913). *The English convict: A statistical study.* London: HMSO.

Gottfredson, M., & Hirschi, T. (1990). *A general theory of crime.* Stanford, CA: Stanford University Press.

Herbig, F. J. W., & Hesselink, A. M. E. (2012). Seeing the person, not just the number-need-based rehabilitation of offenders in South African Prisons. *South African Crime Quarterly, 41,* 29–37.

Hesselink, A. E., & Herbig, F. J. W. (2009). Scientific basis of criminology. *Journal of Psychology in Africa, 19*(2), 275–79.

Hesselink-Louw, A. E. (2004). *Criminological assessment of prison inmates: A constructive mechanism towards offender rehabilitation.* Unpublished DLitt et Phil. Department of Criminology, Pretoria: University of South Africa.

Jaishankar, K. (2008). Space transition theory of cyber crimes. In F. Schmallager, & M. Pittaro (Eds), *Crimes of the internet* (pp. 283–301). Upper Saddle River, NJ: Prentice-Hall.

Lynch, M. J., Schwendinger, H., & Schwendinger, J. (2006). The state of empirical research in radical criminology. In F. T. Cullen, J. P. Wright, & K. R. Blevins (Eds), *Taking stock: The status of criminological theory* (Advances in criminological theory, Vol. 15, pp. 191–215). New Brunswick, NJ: Transaction.

Merton, R. K. (1938). Social structure and anomie. *American Sociological Review, 3*(5), 672–82.

Monachesi, E. (1973). Cesare Beccaria. In H. Mannheim (Ed.), *Prisoners in criminology* (2nd ed., pp. 36–50). Montclair, NJ: Patterson Smith.

Myer, R. A. (2001). *Assessment for crisis intervention: A triage assessment model.* Canada: Brooks/Cole and Thomson Learning.

Paolucci, H. (1963). Preface. In C. Beccaria, *On crime and punishment* (H. Paolucci, Trans.). Indianapolis, IN: Bobbs-Merrill (original work published in 1764).

Raghavan, V., & Singh, S. (2013). *Social work and social development: Perspectives from India and United States.* Chicago, IL: Lyceum Publications.

Raine, A. (1993). *The psychopathology of crime.* San Diego, CA: Academic Press.

Rodericks, J. V. (1992). *Calculated risks: The toxicity and public health risks of chemicals in our environment.* Cambridge, UK: Cambridge University Press.

Shaw, C. R., & McKay, H. D. (1942). *Juvenile delinquency and urban areas.* Chicago, IL: University of Chicago Press.

Sherman, M., & Hawkins, G. (1981). *Imprisonment in America: Choosing the future.* Chicago, IL: University of Chicago Press.

Sutherland, E. H. (1940). White collar criminality. *American Sociological Review, 5*(1), 1–12.

Tannenbaum, F. (1938). *Crime and the community.* New York: Columbia University Press.

Vold, G. B. (1958). *Theoretical criminology.* England: Oxford University Press.

———. (1986). *Theoretical criminology.* New York: Oxford University Press.

Vold, G. B., & Bernard, T. J. (1986). *Theoretical criminology* (3rd ed.). New York: Oxford University Press.

Walsh, A. (2012). *Criminology: The essentials.* Thousand Oaks, CA: SAGE Publications.

Walsh, A., & Ellis, L. (2007). *Criminology: An interdisciplinary approach.* Thousand Oaks, CA: SAGE Publications.

Winnicott, C. (1962). Casework and agency function. *Case Conference, 8*(7), 178–84.

Wolfgang, M. E. (1973). Cesare Lombroso. In H. Mannheim (Ed.), *Pioneers in criminology* (2nd ed., pp. 232–91). Montclair, NJ: Patterson Smith.

3

The Prevalence of Mental Illness within the Indian Criminal Justice System

Mark David Chong, Jamie Fellows, Sonny Jose, Abraham P. Francis and Kelly-Ann Williams

Introduction

In recent years, the provision of social work services has become an increasingly indispensable element within the criminal justice system (Treger & Allen, 2007), most notably in countries such as the United States, Canada and Scotland (Champagne & Felizardo, n.d.; Scottish Government, 2010; Treger & Allen, 2007). Variously labelled as criminal justice, correctional or forensic social workers (Wilson, 2010), these practitioners now represent one of the foremost providers of bio-psychosocial services to offender populations and victims of crime in these countries. Whether in collaboration with other criminal justice professionals—the police, prison wardens, probation/parole officers—or with colleagues who specialise in diverse fields such as housing, employment, child welfare, mental health, clinical or education, social work intervention and support is now regarded as fundamental in frontline services as well as administrative functions. These specialist skills may be utilised in a number of ways, for example, in adult prisons, youth detention centres, probation and parole agencies, the courts, community-based non-profit or non-governmental organisations (NGOs), faith-based agencies as well as primary health and behavioural clinics that serve low socio-economic status clients, many of whom themselves are ex-convicts (Wilson, 2010, p. 1).

Social work in India has followed a similar, but not necessarily an identical path. It is generally viewed as benevolent work conducted by individuals or groups driven by humanitarian and/or religious values, as a supplementary or voluntary service. In the 1930s, a more professional and systematic approach was adopted, with initial activities targeting children and adults in lower-class areas of Mumbai (Sir Dorabji Tata Trust and the Allied Trusts [SDTT], 2011). Thereafter, in the 1930s and 1940s, specialist social work schools and courses were developed owing to a greater demand for professional social workers. Among some of the first subjects studied at these schools were juvenile delinquency and criminology. Specialist training for correctional work was initiated in 1952 to benefit social workers, social welfare officers and probation officers (SDTT, 2011). The Tata Institute of Social Sciences (TISS) in Mumbai was at the forefront of this extremely promising movement (Raghavan, 2013, p. 265).

As a result of the efforts of TISS, other prominent institutions and various philanthropists, there are now a range of organisations providing social support and assistance to offenders institutionalised in prisons, borstals, women's institutions, observation homes and so on, as well as to victims of crime, across India. In this regard, the Commonwealth Human Rights Initiative (CHRI) examined the activities of 52 non-government social work-based initiatives in India and discovered a plethora of services including: moral/spiritual guidance and counselling; the provision of appropriate shelter, health and educational services to children of prisoners; rehabilitation services; legal aid and other legal assistance; as well as education- and health-related facilities (CHRI, 2008).

And yet, despite the existence of such services from as early as the 1930s, it is nevertheless arguable that criminal justice social work in India is still not as developed as it is in the United States, Scotland or Canada. Agllias (2004) suggested that some social workers may fear a loss of 'professional identity' if they were to be too closely associated with the correctional justice system. Such ethical tensions arise as a result of complicity with diagnostic models that are essentially coercive (i.e., criminal justice) in nature (Agllias, 2004, p. 332).

However, we would argue, like Agllias, that these tensions should in fact be seen as opportunities instead of impediments to undertaking such tasks because the criminal justice field offers social workers a wide platform to advocate on behalf of some of the most vulnerable and marginalised populations in society (Agllias, 2004). As Bland noted, '[p]eople with a mental illness and their families represent the most disadvantaged and vulnerable end of the mental health spectrum' (2005, p. 119). Lamentably, offenders and victims of crime with psychological disorders represent an even more destitute class along this continuum, and hence, are in greater need of assistance and advocacy.

This chapter will therefore attempt to demystify some of these concerns by making more explicit: (a) the types and characteristics of some of the more common mental and behavioural disorders which an offender and a victim of crime might experience; (b) the legitimacy of intervention on the part of the social worker; (c) the positive aspects of such intervention; (d) the specific non-psychiatric mental health services that social workers may provide to either of these two groups, and finally (e) some of the challenges (and possible solutions) faced by social workers in their day-to-day criminal justice duties.

Mental Illnesses Commonly Suffered by Offenders and Victims of Crime

'Mental health' is a broad term used to describe a state of emotional and social well-being, whereby a person is able to: (a) recognise his/her individual skills and potential; (b) cope effectively with everyday life stressors; (c) work productively; and (d) make a positive contribution to his/her community (World Health Organization [WHO], 2007). It also relates to an ability to interact with others and have healthy relationships with them (Bland, 2005). Mental health is thus an integral component of one's overall health (WHO, 2007). Sadly, offenders and victims of crime are at an increased risk of mental health concerns and they therefore represent an especially vulnerable client population.

In the case of offenders who have been confined in 'total institutions', such as secure psychiatric institutions or prisons, their time there is stringently observed, restricted and regulated (Foucault, 1991, pp. 231–56). This can be a terrifying experience for some, and consequently such an environment can put a heavy strain on a person's mental health (Baillargeon, Binswanger, Penn, Williams, & Murray, 2009; Fazel & Danesh, 2002).

As for victims of crime (particularly those subjected to violence or the threat thereof), exposure to such frightening circumstances may negatively affect a victim's quality of life and hence develop social and mental health problems (Maniglio, 2009). In addition to the trauma suffered as a result of being initially victimised, studies have also shown that such victims are actually at a risk of being revictimised 'in the period immediately after [the primary] victimisation' (Farrell & Pease, 1993, p. 8. According to Farrell and Pease, '[i]n general, if you want to discover where a crime will happen, look where it happened last' (1993, p. 7). To compound matters further, criminal justice systems are notoriously dismissive or ambivalent towards the daily struggles of such victims. Thus, in addition to the increased likelihood of being revictimised, it is not uncommon for victims of crime to also undergo a form of 'secondary victimisation'. Secondary victimisation is a process whereby victims feel that they have been disempowered by the way the criminal justice system operates as well as by its agents (Bhat & Wodda, 2013, p. 289). For example, disempowerment may result from a victim's experience in dealing with a perceived callous or insensitive court, prosecution and defence lawyer (Bhat & Wodda, 2013, p. 289). Sharma (2005) observed that secondary victimisation increases the immediate effects of the crime by exacerbating the victim's emotional and psychological distress.

Sadly, psychological disorders can significantly undermine an individual's ability to maintain a healthy self-identity, relationships with others as well as to fully engage in life's opportunities (Bland, 2005). As Murali and Rao observed,

> severe mental disorder tends to run a chronic course and has a devastating impact on the person's functioning. It affects activities of daily living, such as self-care and personal hygiene, social relationships in terms of communication skills and occupational functioning, such as the ability to acquire a job and retain it. (2004, p. 152)

A number of recent meta-analyses have concluded that 5–10 per cent of the Indian population suffer from a mental disorder that requires treatment. This prevalence appears to be higher in: (a) urban areas; (b) females; (c) the 35–44-year age group and (d) in the lower socioeconomic strata (Ganguli, 2000; Gururaj & Gourie, 1999; Reddy & Chandrashekar, 1998).

Several international and Indian research studies (see Goyal, Singh, Gargi, Goyal, & Garg, 2011; Kilpatrick & Acierno, 2003; Kumar & Daria, 2013) have revealed that the most commonly reported mental illnesses were as follows:

1. Affective (related to mood)
   a. Depressive episode
      • depression; loss of interest or pleasure; significant changes in weight; lower levels of energy; restlessness; feelings of worthlessness or guilt; inability to concentrate; and disrupted sleep patterns
      • suicidal thoughts may be present
      • lasts for at least two weeks
   b. Bipolar affective disorder
      • alternating episodes of depression and mania/hypomania
   c. Dysthymic disorder
      • persistently depressed mood with milder and fewer symptoms which continue over a longer period than those of a depressive episode; lethargy; low esteem; sleep disorders; and reduced levels of concentration
      • exists for a minimum of two years
2. Anxiety related
   a. Panic disorder

- non-specific or random, recurrent and severe panic attacks (including sweating, shaking, chest pain, nausea, dizziness and fear of dying)

b. Generalised anxiety disorder
   - non-specific, excessive and uncontrollable anxiety and worry (usually about minor, daily events); restlessness; fatigue; irritability; loss of concentration; muscular tension; and sleep disturbances

c. Post-traumatic stress disorder (PTSD)
   - enduring, continued and re-experienced response following an exposure to a life-threatening event that caused immense fear, helplessness or horror (e.g., violent crime, car accident or natural disaster); flashbacks; numb responsiveness; hyper-vigilance; and avoidance of associated stimuli
   - event may have been experienced or witnessed

d. Obsessive-compulsive disorder (OCD)
   - obsessions (recurrent, intrusive and/or unacceptable thoughts or impulses, such as 'I have germs on my hands from touching the toilet') and/or compulsions (repetitive acts or rituals, e.g., hand washing) that are recognised as being excessive or unreasonable

e. Social phobia
   - persistent and unreasonable fear of performance situations to an unfamiliar audience or to scrutiny by others; fear of subsequent embarrassment; characterised by panic attacks

f. Agoraphobia
   - fear and panic attacks as a result of being in a public situation or place where escape is difficult (characteristics include avoidance behaviour)

3. Substance use related

a. Harmful use of drugs (these include prescribed, non-prescribed and illicit substances such as sedatives, stimulants, marijuana, opioids) and/or alcohol

b. Drug and alcohol addiction
   - substance addiction causing a severe level of impairment of life and daily activities; use impacts work,

school or home; use in hazardous situations; recurrent legal consequences; and substance acquires more importance to the sufferer than other activities/behaviours that previously had greater priority
- may include tolerance (requiring increased quantities of a substance to achieve desired effect, or a diminished effect of the same quantity of the substance) and/or withdrawal issues
4. Adjustment related
   a. Adjustment disorder
      - an inability to adjust to or cope with an event or situation; does not continue for more than six months after the event's conclusion; depressed mood; nervousness; lethargy; lower levels of concentration; and disrupted sleep patterns

Studies have also shown that the prevalence of the above psychological conditions in convicted criminals is extremely high. Fazel and Seewald (2012) reported, in their worldwide systematic review, that one in seven inmates has either depression or a psychotic illness. A 3.5 per cent prevalence rate was reported for prisoners with a psychotic illness, and 11.4 per cent was found for major depression. Cloyes, Wong, Latimer and Abarca (2010) suggested that almost 23 per cent of offenders met the criteria for a serious psychological diagnosis. The National Commission on Correctional Health (2002, p. 22, fn. 16) noted how a study had 'found that about 16 percent of prison and jail inmates, or an estimated 283,800 inmates, reported either a mental or emotional condition or an overnight stay in a mental hospital or program in 1998'. Australian data suggest that, of those who had been incarcerated, between 19 and 28 per cent had at some point experienced an anxiety, affective or substance use disorder, whereas for those who had not been incarcerated, it ranged from 4.7 to 14.1 per cent (Australian Bureau of Statistics [ABS], 2008). These data are consistent with findings in Canada, Ireland and the United Kingdom (Brinded, Simpson, Laidlaw, Fairley, & Malcolm, 2001; Duffy, Linehan, & Kennedy, 2006; Howard & Christophersen, 2003; Mullen, Holmquist, & Ogloff, 2003; Ogloff, 1996; Ogloff, Davis, Rivers, & Ross, 2006).

Rates of psychosis and depression in prisoners have been reported as appreciably higher in low- and middle-income countries such as India and Malaysia (psychosis: 5.5% and depression: 22.5%), than in high-income countries such as the United States and Australia (3.5% and 10%) (Fazel & Seewald, 2012). Goyal et al. (2011), in a study of Indian inmates (excluding maximum security and psychiatric unit prisoners), reported psychiatric illness prevalence at 23.8 per cent, which encompassed affective disorders (21%), adjustment disorders (1%), anxiety disorders (1.2%), schizophrenia (0.4%) and substance-induced psychosis (0.2%). They also found that 11.2 per cent of prisoners were dependent on various substances. These findings were supported by Kumar and Daria (2013). The latter reported an overall psychiatric disorder prevalence of 33 per cent; however, this study was conducted only within one prison and with fewer participants involved. While there appears to be variation in the prevalence data between these studies (due to differences, e.g., in the definition of mental illness, the varying mental disorders investigated and the statistical analyses used), the notion that psychological disorders are widespread among offenders remains constant.[1] That said, please note, however, the surprisingly low prevalence of mental illness reported by the National Crime Records Bureau of just over 1 per cent (2015, p. i).[2]

Currently there is far less data for victims of crime; however, a similar correlation between being criminally victimised (particularly in cases of violent physical or sexual assault) and mental illness has been suggested. Maniglio (2009) presented rates of victimisation among individuals with a severe mental

---

[1] Despite the apparent connection between mental illness and criminal behaviour suggested by these statistics, one should not assume a causal relationship (Forsythe & Gaffney, 2012). Comorbidity might be a reason for offending behaviour for some offenders (Day & Howells, 2008).Forsythe and Gaffney (2012) further asserted that the highest proportions of mental disorders were found in males arrested for property offences. For females, the rates of psychological disorders was generally higher across all offence categories, however those with the highest proportion were ones charged with drug offences.

[2] This low incidence would most certainly be a matter deserving of greater scrutiny and research in the future.

illness of between 4.3 and 35 per cent, and 2.3–140.4 times higher than in the general population. It was stated that victimisation was frequently associated with substance-use disorders and more severe symptomology. As shown by Jennings, Gover and Piquero (2011), a variety of conditions appear to be more prevalent among victims of violent sexual offences. These include disorders such as PTSD, agoraphobia, depression, OCD and a range of phobias. According to Cohen and Miller (1998), approximately one-fourth of those who are victims of crime have a mental illness.

As highlighted earlier, many offenders and victims of crime have already experienced social marginalisation, and stigmatisation, for reasons other than their mental condition. Thus, the presence of mental illness, such as schizophrenia, depression or PTSD, will only make a criminal justice social worker's attempt to maintain an even keel of their clients' emotional, mental and social well-being all the more difficult.

While helping crime victims is not at all controversial, the same cannot be said for assisting offenders, especially those who have used violence in order to get what they want. And yet, the expectation that criminals receive treatment from the criminal justice system is also not unreasonable, at least from a legal point of view. As Justice V. R. Krishna Iyer explained, '[c]onvicts are not by mere reason of the conviction denuded of all the fundamental rights which they otherwise possess'.[3] In addition to the municipal legislation that reflects this ideal (such as the Indian Constitution or the Mental Health Act 1987), there are other overarching international laws and principles that mandate the adoption of such practices (Chong & Fellows, 2014). In this context, Chong and Fellows (2014, p. 185) listed the following provisions that relate specifically to the rights that offenders have in relation to mental health services:

1. Article 12 of the 1966 United Nations International Covenant on Economic, Social and Cultural Rights (UN-ICESCR) stipulates:

---

[3] Sunil Batra v. Delhi Administration (I), AIR 1978 SC 1675 (India).

The States Parties to the present Covenant recognize the right of everyone to the enjoyment of the highest attainable standard of physical and mental health.

2. Principle 9 of the 1990 United Nations Basic Principles for the Treatment of Prisoners makes it clear that:

    Prisoners shall have access to the health services available in the country without discrimination on the grounds of their legal situation.

3. The WHO's 2003 Moscow Declaration on Prison Health as a part of Public Health noted:

    > Member governments are recommended to develop close working links between the Ministry of Health and the ministry responsible for the penitentiary system so as to ensure high standards of treatment for detainees, protection for personnel, joint training of professionals in modern standards of disease control, high levels of professionalism amongst penitentiary medical personnel, continuity of treatment between the penitentiary and outside society, and unification of statistics.

While Article 12 of the UN-ICESCR applies equally to victims of crime, Chong and Fellows (2014, pp. 185–86) further noted that psychologically impaired victims of crime could additionally point to the following international instrument in order to establish an expectation of assistance from its government:

The 1985 United Nations Declaration of Basic Principles of Justice for Victims of Crime and Abuse of Power:

> Principle 14: Victims should receive the necessary material, medical, psychological and social assistance through governmental, voluntary, community-based and indigenous means.

> Principle 15: Victims should be informed of the availability of health and social services and other relevant assistance and be readily afforded access to them.

> Principle 16: Police, justice, health, social service and other personnel concerned should receive training to sensitize them to the needs of victims, and guidelines to ensure proper and prompt aid.

> Principle 17: In providing services and assistance to victims, attention should be given to those who have special needs because of the nature of the harm inflicted or because of factors such as those mentioned in paragraph 3 above (i.e., race, colour, sex, age, language, religion, nationality, political or other opinion, cultural beliefs or practices, property, birth or family status, ethnic or social origin, and disability).

It is clearly axiomatic that these international laws and principles are needed to ensure that there is no ambiguity in relation to such issues. This is especially pertinent because people suffering from psychological disorders are already more susceptible to a number of problems that may further exacerbate their mental health. This could take the form of, for example, being: (a) socially stigmatised, marginalised and discriminated against; (b) subjected to violence and abuse; (c) unable to exercise all of their civil and political rights; (d) excluded from opportunities to generate income, seek employment or acquire education; and (e) unable to access health and other essential services (Funk, Drew, Freeman, & Faydi, 2010). Finally, there is also an increased vulnerability to premature death and disability (Funk et al., 2010).

Given the above afflictions, the Indian National Human Rights Commission strongly recommended that specific guidelines should be adhered to when addressing mental illness in prisons (as cited in Sivagnanam, 2012). These would include, for example: (a) all central and district jails should employ a qualified psychiatrist, assisted by a psychologist and a social worker,[4] to provide early detection, treatment, counselling and legal assistance to mentally ill inmates; (b) prisons should collaborate with local psychiatric institutions and NGOs, and (c) that sub-jails should transport such offenders to psychiatric facilities.

---

[4] Note however, that this plan to employ more mental health care professionals looks highly improbable given the fact that there is already a dearth of psychiatrists available to handle the therapeutic needs of the regular population. Given this problem, the Mental Health Authority has attempted to integrate psychiatry into Primary Health Care Centres. That said, it will be some time before the prison population is brought under the purview of these Primary Health Care Centres. It should be further noted that in India, psychiatry is a less preferred choice of specialisation among the doctors.

Moreover, there should be an onus on the part of the government to prevent mental illness within prisons by methods such as: (a) having open environments with gardens and lawns; (b) providing daily programmes; (c) employing humane, well-trained staff; (d) limiting the use of force to control behaviour; (e) providing information to all prisoners regarding regulations governing their treatment, and (f) providing appropriate grievance and complaint mechanisms (as cited in Sivagnanam, 2012, p. 9).

Justification for Social Work Intervention

Whilst some criminal offenders may have had a psychological disorder before being incarcerated, it has been contended that the severe and draconian conditions of imprisonment can potentially aggravate an existing mental illness or, in fact, trigger or produce a new psychopathology in a previously healthy individual (Baillargeon et al., 2009; Fazel & Danesh, 2002; WHO, 1999). Even prisons in wealthy, developed countries, such as Australia and the United States, have far from ideal conditions. Issues such as overcrowding and limited access to rehabilitation programmes have been raised (Cook, 2012; Jerga, 2010).

Prisons, and therefore offenders, in developing countries face even more deleterious conditions. In India, the criminal justice system has remained largely unchanged since independence from colonial rule and this lack of progress is most notably evidenced in the plight of poor and underprivileged inmates. The majority of inmates are illiterate, or semi-literate, and are yet to be convicted of any crime; they are the 'undertrials' awaiting legal proceedings or lack the ability to get bail (Goyal et al., 2011; SDTT, 2011). Undertrials can spend long periods in judicial custody, sometimes longer than the actual sentence for their alleged crime. This occurs because they are unable to provide appropriate sureties, have been denied bail due to the nature of their crime or because of lengthy trial delays (SDTT, 2011).

Indian prisons are by any standards overcrowded (National Crime Records Bureau, 2015, p. i). While the National Human

Rights Commission guidelines recommend a number of strategies to ensure the mental health of prisoners (such as, humane staff, gardens, sports and meditation programmes and the availability of psychological or psychiatric counselling), there is a still a gap between these aspirations and the reality of the prison environment (CHRI, 2009). The same report from the CHRI (2009) highlighted some of the major concerns afflicting the Indian prison system, including overcrowding, lengthy trial delays, torture and ill-treatment, neglect of health and hygiene, and inadequate food and clothing. In 2012, the prison occupancy rate was at 112.2 per cent, while in 2013, the overcrowding was even higher at 118.4 per cent (National Crime Records Bureau, 2015, p. i). Prisoners of the Arthur Road Jail in Mumbai have complained that toilets are not cleaned for days, and that living in such close, overcrowded proximity is leading to the spread of skin conditions (Raja, 2013). The largest prison in South Asia, Tihar Jail, is also running at almost twice its capacity; and apart from the obvious overcrowding, allegations of corruption, bribery, sexual abuse and high suicide rates likewise proliferate (Polgreen, 2011; Raza, 2013). While official statistics remain very conservative, it nevertheless estimates that slightly over 1 per cent of the total inmates housed in various jails in the country are mentally ill (National Crime Records Bureau, 2015, p. i).

While there are legal protections for those confined in Indian criminal justice institutions, there are unfortunately insufficient or inadequate systems of compliance to ensure that these provisions are fully observed. Criminal justice social workers can thus play a critical role in this context, especially for more vulnerable inmates, such as women separated from their families, lower socio-economic offenders and those with a mental illness (SDTT, 2011).

Not only are these poor conditions negatively affecting both physical and mental health, the WHO has contended that a contributing factor to severe mental harm is caused by incarceration and deprivation of a person's freedom (1999, p. 4). Consequently, it was proposed that by supporting therapeutic mental health practices and programmes in prisons, a range of additional benefits could accrue for all relevant stakeholders (WHO, 1999).

The benefits would be manifold; and would include potentially insulating the offender from certain effects of incarceration such as psychological harm or to reduce the effects of pre-existing psychological/emotional conditions (WHO, 1999). Additionally, an overflow effect may be anticipated, with advantages also extending to an offender's family members (via improved intra-familial relationships), the prison system, as well as to the wider community (by increasing social inclusion and community safety) (WHO, 1999).

While individuals with a mental illness are at an increased risk of being criminally victimised due to their vulnerable state (Maniglio, 2009), a large proportion of mental health concerns for victims of crime are actually focussed on the direct consequences of being offended against. Disorders such as PTSD, severe depression and/or substance abuse can develop or worsen when an individual is victimised by an offender (what is often referred to as 'primary victimisation'; Kilpatrick & Acierno, 2003; Jennings et al., 2011). To make matters worse, involvement in the ensuing criminal justice proceedings amplify the victim's emotional suffering. In this regard, Herman (1992) discussed the notion of secondary victimisation (a concept that was highlighted in an earlier section of this chapter). Herman argued that if there was ever a system that could be designed to bring on a PTSD, it would very much take on the characteristics of a court of law (1992, as cited in Herman, 2003, p. 159). This is partly due to the legal presumption of innocence that stipulates an accused person is innocent until proven otherwise (Douglas & Harbidge, 2008). The criminal process and trial thus cannot be seen to be used as an instrument of revenge, notwithstanding whatever suffering the victim has had to endure as a result of the offence. As a consequence of the presumption that the criminal justice system affords to the alleged offender (i.e., innocent until proven guilty), it is not surprising that a victim would feel systemically disempowered and emasculated. For instance, criminal procedural rules are generally promulgated not on the basis of the victims' needs but rather to ensure that 'justice' is done, and seen to be done, to the offender. Feelings of frustration on the part of the victim might also arise because of the range of due process rights (i.e., legal protections) provided to the offender. The defence will also be allowed to aggressively challenge the victim's credibility and the veracity of his/her allegations in an open court. Furthermore, by being examined and cross-examined in court, the victim will have to publically re-live each terrible moment of their victimisation. Finally, the victim is bound by strict procedural rules that militate against free expression and catharsis during the trial (Herman, 2003, pp. 159–60).

Offenders Suffering from Psychological Disorders

Whilst a significant part of an offender's mental health and psychological treatment is managed by psychiatrists, psychologists and forensic and/or mental health nurses, there is still scope for the services of a social worker. There are many opportunities for him/her to play an integral role in assisting clients to maintain their mental health or manage their mental illness. More specifically, social work intervention within the criminal justice system has the potential to reinforce an incarcerated offender's emotional resilience by helping to increase or improve their

- physical and emotional health;
- coping strategies to reduce criminal behaviour;
- confidence and social interactions;
- effective time management;
- capacity to devise a credible future;
- social inclusion; and
- prospects of rehabilitation (WHO, 1999, p. 9).

However, achieving these aims will not be easy. In particular, it should be noted that comorbidity of psychological disorders has been associated with increased levels of reoffending or recidivism (Smith & Trimboli, 2010), thereby making rehabilitation all the more difficult. That said, Young (2002, pp. 69–70) has detailed a broad range of more specific, non-psychiatric mental health services that social workers can offer to incarcerated offenders with a mental disorder. Whilst not an exhaustive list, it encompasses a variety of specialised tasks, including:

1. Intervening at the time of crisis
   This relates to urgent intervention by the social worker during times of personal crisis that the offender may be experiencing, for example, where an offender exhibits signs of self-harm (Young, 2002). The social worker's role in this case is to emotionally stabilise the inmate by employing mental health first aid until the situation is de-escalated or until psychiatric or medical intervention is applied.

2. Personal Counselling
   A social worker can conduct personalised one-on-one counselling sessions for the purpose of developing social resilience and life skills (Young, 2002).

3. Group Work
   These sessions provide psycho-educational support and direction to a number of offenders simultaneously. Such thematic intervention might include anger management, substance abuse desistance, emotional regulation, self-esteem building, maintenance of personal care, breaking cycles of domestic violence and recreational activities (Young, 2002).

4. Ongoing Assessment
   Inmates generally undergo initial intake health screening and psychological assessment at the outset of their incarceration. However, further ongoing mental health evaluation augments this, and directs future mental health management. This task can be conducted by a social worker (Young, 2002).

5. Monitoring Sessions
   During these follow-up sessions, the inmate does not receive any counselling but the social worker is able to check the progress of the client and provide any further information to him/her (Young, 2002).

6. Psychiatric Referrals
   If necessary, the social worker should refer the inmate to the psychiatrist—especially if medication would appear necessary (Young, 2002).

7. The Use of other Service Providers
   Inmates can be referred to other health professionals aside from a psychiatrist. These might include a referral to a nurse, another social worker or other 'in-house' professionals (Young, 2002, p. 69).

8. Evaluation for Prison Housing Change
   Social workers are able to make recommendations regarding the housing arrangements of their inmate clients. The offender's mental health (including mood, affect and suicidal ideation) will influence a recommendation for the inmate to be consigned to the general population, kept under close supervision, or be deprived of objects that may enable self-harm/suicide (Young, 2002).

9. Working with other Mental Health Services
   Social workers can work with a range of allied mental health professionals, such as mental health nurses and psychologists. Social workers are also able to work alongside prison wardens or other prison staff as required (Young, 2002).

10. Discharge Planning
    Social workers are involved in the planning of a client's eventual release from incarceration. Assistance can be offered in mental health and support services such as accommodation, employment, family reunification, training and government/welfare entitlements (Young, 2002).

11. Self-referrals
    Inmates may seek the services of a social worker for a variety of reasons. These may involve medical, legal, psychological or interpersonal issues (Young, 2002).

12. Requests for Evaluations from the Court
    Judges and other criminal justice personnel may request the inmate to undergo an assessment by a social worker to be used to supplement other psychiatric data (Young, 2002).

13. Contact with the Legal System
    The role of a social worker may also involve facilitation of correspondence between criminal justice agencies (e.g., probation department) and an offender with a mental illness (Young, 2002).

14. External Psychiatric Services
    Other psychiatric providers can be contacted to obtain information pertaining to the client's current medical prescriptions (Young, 2002).
15. Contact with the Inmate's Support System
    Social workers can be integral in facilitating or assisting the inmate client with regards to support networks and family. For example, this might include assisting with tasks that involve communicating with members of the client's family, landlord or caseworker (Young, 2002).

In addition to these clinical and case management roles, Agllias pointed out that social work is a 'political activity' and is committed to policy reform at various levels in order to address social justice issues (2004, p. 338). Criminal justice social workers, due to their understanding of the criminal justice system, are in a good position to advocate for favourable policy and administrative changes (SDTT, 2011). Therefore, a social worker, while committed to clinical practice and case management, must also be informed about the process of policy development. This should include an ability to

- critically assess and challenge government policies that impact upon or infringe the human rights of an offender with a mental disorder;
- introduce new policies that help increase a mentally ill inmate's access to support services and social networks;
- serve as a functionary for inmates to express their opinions to the appropriate authorities and policy makers; and
- facilitate the implementation of policy (as adapted from Agllias, 2004, pp. 338–39).

Victims of Crime Suffering from Psychological Disorders

Criminal victimisation can result in feelings of powerlessness, confusion, guilt, shame, self-blame and grief (Young, 1993). Due to the nature of victimisation, PTSD is a common diagnosis

(Kilpatrick & Acierno, 2003). These authors pointed out that women who are victims of rape and other physical assaults will most likely acquire PTSD (Kilpatrick & Acierno, 2003, p. 130). Likewise, men who are subjected to sexual assaults were equally susceptible to PTSD. However, if the attacks were of a non-sexual nature, men appeared to withstand the onset of PTSD better than women (Kilpatrick & Acierno, 2003). However, PTSD is not the only psychological disorder found in victims of crime. Many studies have indicated that comorbidity is also an issue where conditions such as anxiety, depression, phobias and substance abuse are also commonly reported in combination with PTSD (Kilpatrick & Acierno, 2003; Kessler, Sonnega, Bromet, Hughes, & Nelson, 1995). Depression, the misuse of substances and the onset of other emotional issues are, according to Kilpatrick and Acierno (2003, p. 129), a result of the combination of a traumatic offence and the associated PTSD.

Whilst mental disorders can result as a consequence of being criminally victimised, it is also important to remember that some victims may have been mentally ill prior to the offence. Severely mentally ill individuals are vulnerable to victimisation due to the nature of their impairment (e.g., poor judgement, social skills and planning) as well as the related social consequences (such as, unemployment and social isolation) (Maniglio, 2009). Moreover, there is a definite risk that pre-existing poor mental health may deteriorate due to being offended against.

If criminal charges are pursued, involvement in the ensuing criminal justice proceedings can cause additional trauma to the victim, especially if it was a violent offence (Herman, 2003; Wemmers, 2013). 'Secondary victimisation' can disempower a crime victim and exacerbate distress in a number of ways: (a) by the involvement of unsympathetic authorities (e.g., police or legal professionals); (b) victim blaming; (c) examination and cross-examination of the victim; as well as (d) the obvious fear and uncertainty of the entire investigation and trial experience (Herman, 2003; Schoeman, 2012; Wemmers, 2013). Those who have been subjected to violent crime may have the trauma of such events compounded by the operation of the criminal justice system itself (Herman, 2003, p. 159).

Despite the potential for further distress, Herman (2003) argued that victims of crime should nevertheless pursue their assailants through the courts. She contended that by engaging in the criminal justice system, the victim may derive a better sense of well-being achieved by the deterrent and empowerment aspects of the criminal justice system, as well as receive: (a) acknowledgement of their suffering; (b) financial compensation through 'victims of crime' legislation; and possibly even (c) an apology from the offender. Ideally, a just result in this regard would likewise validate the victim's trust in the community (Herman, 2003, pp. 160–61).

In order to counteract the adverse psychological and emotional effects of both the initial criminal act (primary victimisation) and the subsequent secondary victimisation outlined earlier, a criminal justice social worker could be employed to mitigate these problems by supporting the victim to

- feel safe;
- articulate and express their emotions through positive outlets;
- better cope with the criminal justice proceedings;
- resume normal activities and routines;
- increase awareness of their legal entitlements; and
- recover their general health and well-being (University of Missouri-Columbia & NASW, 2006, pp. 1–2).[5]

The involvement of a social worker to assist a victim of crime is thus critical to ameliorate not only the deleterious consequences of the initial criminal act, but also the more insidious effects of secondary victimisation. In response to the potential risks associated with the latter, a very useful model that encapsulates the

---

[5] However, it should be noted that some individuals may not wish to report a crime or to proceed with legal measures. Others may be unable to do so due to having insufficient evidence against the offender. Furthermore, a victim's potentially unstable mental state may be adversely affecting their decision-making in these circumstances. As such, victims like these will most likely require even more substantial support and assistance from social workers (Schoeman, 2012).

roles of the social worker in relation to victims of crime was developed by the National Organization for Victim Assistance in the United States. This model consists of 8-stages and operationalises the tasks of a social worker in relation to victims of crime who may be psychologically traumatised (as cited in University of Missouri-Columbia & NASW, 2006, p. 4). An outline of this framework is set out below:

> *Stage 1: Crisis intervention.* The first stage requires the social worker to provide therapeutic crisis intervention and trauma assessment, as and when deemed necessary. This may occur at a variety of locations, including the crime scene, police station or in a hospital (University of Missouri-Columbia & NASW, 2006, p. 4).
>
> *Stage 2: Victim stabilisation.* At this stage, a range of tasks are performed to further stabilise the victim and, if necessary, to provide any additional crisis assistance. The social worker will then help the victim navigate through the often complex procedures of the criminal justice system. Alternative accommodation, transport, police protection, etc., can also be arranged at this time (University of Missouri-Columbia & NASW, 2006, p. 4).
>
> *Stage 3: Resource mobilisation.* The objective at this stage is to mobilise other resources that may benefit the victim. Here, while social workers will be providing ongoing counselling and information sessions to their clients, they will also be making referrals, if necessary, to any relevant professionals such as psychologists or other medical practitioners. The task of resource mobilisation will likewise require the social worker to actively liaise with a variety of stakeholders involved in the well-being of the victim, such as the police, the courts, government agencies, insurers, employers, financial services and so on (University of Missouri-Columbia & NASW, 2006, p. 4).
>
> *Stage 4: After the arrest of the offender.* Further crisis intervention, counselling and other support may be required during and after the alleged offender's arrest. Support for the victim might include assistance with the media, and guidance on how to navigate around problematic issues

associated with the criminal justice system (University of Missouri-Columbia & NASW, 2006, p. 5).

Stage 5: Pre-court appearances. The objective at this stage is to assist the victim and possibly the victim's friends/family with matters involving the courts and court processes (University of Missouri-Columbia & NASW, 2006, p. 5).

Stage 6: Court appearances. Appearing in an open court and facing the alleged attacker can be particularly distressing and intimidating experiences. Therefore, the victim will benefit from the provision of emotional support from the social worker, as well as protection from the accused and any overly aggressive reporters. Matters including transport, childcare and financial concerns can also be managed at this stage by the social worker. Furthermore, the social worker can also provide answers to any queries pertaining to the impending trial from the victim, and their support network at this juncture (University of Missouri-Columbia & NASW, 2006, p. 5).

Stage 7: Pre-sentencing. If the trial ends in a conviction, the court might permit the victim to read aloud a victim impact statement, the purpose of which is to assist the court in punishing the offender. As one can imagine, this is yet another extremely daunting (but often cathartic) process for the victim, and hence having a social worker by his/her side may make this experience more manageable and less frightening (University of Missouri-Columbia & NASW, 2006, p. 5).

Stage 8: Post disposition of the case. In this final stage, the social worker provides ongoing counselling to the victim regarding the victimisation itself, or the outcome of the trial. The social worker might also assist the victim to testify at subsequent court hearings (University of Missouri-Columbia & NASW, 2006, p. 5).

As the above framework illustrates, there is an important need for social workers to act as intermediaries between victims of crime and the formal criminal justice system (Schoeman, 2012). Consequently, criminal justice social workers must have a comprehensive understanding of the relevant legal procedures, as well as victims' rights (Chong & Fellows, 2014, pp. 197–98). Moreover, without an understanding of the secondary victimisation process, a social worker might actually add to, instead of alleviate, a victim's trauma (Schoeman, 2012).

Challenges Faced by Criminal Justice Social Workers

As stated in the introduction to this chapter, social workers practising within the criminal justice system are regularly confronted by numerous challenges. From an ideological perspective, there is the fundamental question as to who is owed the social worker's primary obligation; is it the client (who is a criminal) or the community (who has been victimised by that criminal) (Treger & Allen, 2007)? This is by no means an academic or pedantic question. Criminal justice social workers often struggle with balancing the conflicting roles of having to be both a 'good cop' and 'bad cop' to their criminal clients. That is, offering empathetic social support, providing rehabilitation services, and protecting the offender's rights, on the one hand; and surveillance, applying sanctions and implementing breach actions for offender non-compliance when required, on the other (Moore, 2005). To complicate these circumstances even further, offenders with mental disorders may, for example, breach their parole or supervision orders, not so much out of defiance to authority but rather due to the sometimes overwhelming impulses of their mental illness.

Resolving this conflict of interest is not an easy task, and Treger and Allen (2007) lamented that criminal justice social workers have to carefully walk a tightrope between discharging their duty to uphold the rights of the offender, while at the same time ensuring that the offender complies with any legal requirements imposed upon them by the justice system. It is therefore not surprising that some social workers may feel conflicted in terms of their career aspirations vis-à-vis their ethical values if they are required to implement policies that they believe operate to 'dehumanize clients' (Treger & Allen, 2007, p. 46). This is especially so in light of Treger and Allen's position that any competing demands should be resolved in favour of the community's safety over that of the offenders' rights (2007, p. 46). That said, there is no suggestion on the part of these authors that criminal justice social workers should be unethical or unreasonably submissive to their government employer. Far from it, in fact, Treger and Allen suggested that social workers should work to reform the system from within, and they should actively participate in public policy development so as to 'create a balance between the justice system and the offender' (2007, p. 46).

While involvement in policy development is ideal, this does not, however, address the more immediate practical and routine challenges that social workers can expect to face when balancing the demands of the criminal justice system and the needs of a mentally ill, and hence highly vulnerable, offender. Moore (2005) stated that a key feature of social work practice within criminal justice institutions involves adhering to both legal obligations and being held accountable for their actions. This would require the social worker to comply with a range of reporting requirements involving law enforcement authorities. However, in fulfilling these legal obligations the social worker might come into conflict with their professional obligations regarding client confidentiality (2005, p. 219).

In some cases, prisoner clients are considered involuntary, in that they are forced to accept social work support or intervention as a result of a court order or mandated legislation (Trotter, 2006). The presence of a mental illness further complicates the therapeutic relationship and the ethical obligations of criminal justice social workers. Bland (2005) suggested that these ethical dilemmas concerning mentally ill clients be managed on a case-by-case basis, via three checks:

1. Protecting the civil rights of the client must take precedence when deciding to take any action. As such, the social worker must raise the client's and their family's, awareness of the applicable laws to be fully informed of their available options;
2. In order to decide on a course of action, critical analysis and deep reflection will be required. Social workers should not concede to organisational expectations if these are in conflict with their carefully considered decisions. This can require significant moral courage; and

3. Finally, the social worker must be well informed and/ or willing to acquire all relevant information, by way of research and consultations with other practitioners, including the client's physician, psychiatrist, psychologist and other social workers.

In addition to these, a fourth consideration should be included: the social worker must be acutely aware of all the relevant legal duties, obligations and reporting requirements that have been imposed on him/her in the circumstances (Chong & Fellows, 2014, pp. 199–200). Only then can the social worker make a properly informed choice. Legal advice, however, should be sought in situations where a social worker is considering a course of action that is, unfortunately, in breach of such laws (Chong & Fellows, 2014, pp. 199–200).

Social workers practicing in the criminal justice field, with mentally ill clients, must also consider that they will inevitably encounter volatile, unreasonable and unpredictable behaviours, especially in the case of violent offenders. One example that illustrates the volatility associated with social workers working within the criminal justice system occurred at Ashworth Hospital in Merseyside, England. Despite Merseyside being a high security psychiatric institution, social workers were harshly criticised by the Department of Health for not taking adequate steps to protect a young person who was visiting the facility. Part of the reason for not taking the necessary precautions might stem from a lack of understanding of the dangers inherent in criminal justice social work (Fallon, Bluglass, Edwards, & Daniels, 1999, p. 24). As such, social workers must ensure that they will never compromise their own physical safety or the safety of others. In order to achieve this, social workers must be aware of, and strictly adhere to, security procedures and protocols. Ongoing training in relation to such matters is a key feature in complying with these obligations.

There are also challenges specifically relevant to social workers in developing countries, and these tend to be of a policy and institutional nature. In India, when an individual person charged or convicted with a crime is diagnosed with a mental illness, he/ she is transferred to a government mental health facility, where they are maintained in a forensic ward. This is, of course, an extremely restrictive environment. The Mental Health Centre's administration will not normally be privy to the details of the criminal case that the patient is involved in, and hence will treat these patients on the basis that the courts will ultimately call for them to be brought before the judges in due course. However, this is usually also the job for the prisons to monitor. Sadly, many prisons are ill equipped to handle such cases, and may even consider the transferring of such prisoners to secure mental health facilities as fortuitous for them and thereafter conveniently 'forget' about them altogether. With no formalised coordination between the Prison Administration, the Court system and the Mental Health Authority, these mentally ill prisoners could potentially end up being incarcerated for decades!

Despite specific acknowledgement by the Supreme Court of India of the importance of social workers in the social rehabilitation of prisoners,[6] there is at present no national policy framework recognising the need for social workers in the criminal justice system.

Prayas, a large NGO that offers social work services to prison inmates in India, actively lobbied for such a framework in the mid-1990s. Unfortunately, the Maharashtra State Home Department took no action to implement their recommendation (SDTT, 2011). It appears that more lobbying and political pressure from other social work organisations working within the criminal justice system are required to bring this laudable aim to fruition. Such efforts would likewise be aided if more research into such matters were undertaken by local social work academics and practitioners (preferably in collaboration with one another), thereby building a strong evidence base which can then be used to support wide-ranging criminal justice reforms in the future.

Conclusion

This chapter has attempted to highlight the critical need for the involvement of social workers in the criminal justice system, particularly where there exist vulnerable clients such as criminal offenders and victims of crime who suffer from psychological or

---

[6] Sunil Batra v. Delhi Administration (II), AIR 1980 SC 1579 (India).

psychiatric disorders. It is arguable that the incidence of mental illness in victims of crime and offenders is high when compared to the general population, and the detrimental effects on their well-being and social functioning are significant. To address such psychological disorders within offender and victim groups (in particular, the consequent effects these illnesses have on their social lives), social work intervention and support are essential for their successful rehabilitation and/or reintegration into the community. Fortunately, there are comprehensive and robust models of intervention that social workers can employ in order to achieve these objectives. Lamentably, however, encouraging social workers to become more involved in matters pertaining to criminal justice is difficult. Criminal justice social work is fraught with difficulties, especially when many of their clients will be mandated ones. Being saddled with mental illness only makes the job much harder, and social workers often find balancing the needs of their offender clients, with that of community safety, a challenging task to accomplish. Yet, social workers, with their professional ethos, temperament and training, are ideally positioned to make a significant positive impact in the lives of mentally ill offenders and victims of crime who normally feature very heavily in the lower socio-economic levels of Indian society. As mentioned earlier, even the Supreme Court of India publicly acknowledged how important social workers were in the social rehabilitation of prisoners. Consequently, it is hoped that this chapter will continue to encourage social work students and early career practitioners to seriously consider taking up the cudgel so as to improve the lives of some of the most marginalised individuals in their community.[7]

---

[7] Although perhaps outside of the scope of this chapter, it is important to point out the possibility that some members of the judiciary and the prison administration may not truly appreciate the correlational/causal nexus between mental illness and criminal behaviour. If this is indeed the case, then there will be a need to educate key criminal justice officials about, first, the complex interaction between mental illness and crime; second, the need to be able to have proper diagnostic tools to properly identify inmates who are mentally ill, and finally, the necessity of having in place viable treatment avenues for such prisoners. In this regard, criminal justice social workers may be able to act as advocates and educators to bring this to fruition.

References

Agllias, K. (2004). Women in corrections: A call to social work. *Australian Social Work, 57*(4), 331–42.

Australian Bureau of Statistics (ABS). (2008). *National survey of mental health and wellbeing: Summary of results, 2007.* Canberra: ABS.

Baillargeon, J., Binswanger, I. A., Penn, J. V., Williams, B. A., & Murray, O. J. (2009). Psychiatric disorders and repeat incarcerations: The revolving prison door. *American Journal of Psychiatry, 166*(1), 103–09. doi: 10.1176/appi.ajp.2008.08030416

Bhat, M., & Wodda, A. (2013). Examining legal responses to sexual violence: A review of courts systems in India. In N. P. Unnithan (Ed.), *Crime and justice in India* (pp. 269–99). New Delhi: SAGE Publications.

Bland, R. (2005). Social work practice in mental health. In M. Alston & J. McKinnon (Eds), *Social work: Fields of practice* (2nd ed., pp. 119–30). South Melbourne: Oxford University Press.

Brinded, P. M., Simpson, A. I., Laidlaw, T. M, Fairley, N., & Malcolm, F. (2001). Prevalence of psychiatric disorders in New Zealand prisons: A national study. *Australian and New Zealand Journal of Psychiatry, 35*(2), 166–73.

Champagne, D., & Felizardo, V. (n.d.). Social work practice in corrections. *Canadian Association of Social Workers.* Retrieved from http://www.casw-acts.ca/en/social-work-practice-corrections

Chong M. D., & Fellows, J. D. (2014). Crime and mental health: Implications for social work practice. In A. Francis (Ed.), *Social work in mental health: Contexts and theories for practice* (pp. 182–204). New Delhi: SAGE Publications.

Cloyes, K. B., Wong, B., Latimer, S., & Abarca, J. (2010). Time to prison return for offenders with serious mental illness released from prison: A survival analysis. *Criminal Justice and Behavior, 37*(2), 175–87.

Cohen, M. A., & Miller, T. R. (1998). Cost of mental health care for victims of crime. *Journal of Interpersonal Violence, 13*(1), 93–110.

Commonwealth Human Rights Initiative (CHRI). (2008). *Community participation in prisons: A civil society perspective.* New Delhi: CHRI. Retrieved from http://www.humanrightsinitiative.org/publications/prisons/community_participation_in_prisons.pdf

————. (2009). *Rights behind bars: Landmark judicial pronouncements and National Human Rights Commission guidelines.* New Delhi: CHRI. Retrieved from http://www.humanrightsinitiative.org/publications/prisons/rights_behind_bars.pdf

Cook, H. (2012, January 18). Prisoners arm themselves, climb roof. *Sydney Morning Herald.* Retrieved from http://www.smh.com.au

Day, A., & Howells, K. (2008). Problems in responding to co-occurring mental health and drug-related problems: A criminal justice perspective. In S.

Allsop (Ed.), *Drug use and mental health: Effective responses to co-occurring drug and mental health problems* (pp. 68–79). Melbourne: IP Communications.

Douglas, H., & Harbidge, S. D. (2008). *Criminal process in Queensland.* Pyrmont: Lawbook Co.

Duffy, D., Linehan, S., & Kennedy, H. (2006). Psychiatric morbidity in the male sentenced Irish prisons population. *Irish Journal of Psychological Medicine, 23*(2), 54–62.

Edney, R., & Bagaric, M. (2007). *Australian sentencing: Principles and practices.* Port Melbourne: Cambridge University Press.

Fallon, P., Bluglass, R., Edwards, B., & Daniels, G. (1999). *Executive summary: Report of the committee of inquiry into the personality disorder unit, Ashworth Special Hospital.* London: Stationery Office.

Farrell, G., & Pease, K. (1993). Once bitten, twice bitten: Repeat victimisation and its implications for crime prevention. *Police research group, crime prevention unit* (Paper 46). London: Home Office Police Department.

Fazel, S., & Danesh, J. (2002). Serious mental disorder in 23,000 prisoners: A systematic review of 62 surveys. *Lancet, 359*(9306), 545–50.

Fazel, S., & Seewald, K. (2012). Severe mental illness is 33,588 prisoners worldwide: A systematic review and meta-regression analysis. *British Journal of Psychiatry, 200*(5), 364–73.

Forsythe, L., & Gaffney, A. (2012). *Mental disorder prevalence at the gateway to the criminal justice system.* Canberra: Australian Institute of Criminology.

Foucault, M. (1991). *Discipline and punish: The birth of the prison.* New York: Vintage Books.

Funk, M., Drew, N., Freeman, M., & Faydi, E. (2010). *Mental health and development: Targeting people with mental health conditions as a vulnerable group.* Geneva: WHO Press.

Ganguli, H. C. (2000). Epidemiological findings on prevalence of mental disorders in India. *Indian Journal of Psychiatry, 42*(1), 14–20.

Goyal, S. K., Singh, P., Gardi, P. D., Goyal, S., & Gard, A. (2011). Psychiatric morbidity in prisoners. *Indian Journal of Psychiatry, 53*(3), 253–57. doi: 10.4103/0019-5545.86819

Gururaj, G., & Gourie, D. M. (1999). Epidemiology of psychiatric and neurological disorders: Indian scenario. *NIMHANS Journal, 17*(4), 291–94.

Herman, J. L. (1992). *Trauma and recovery.* New York: Basic Books.

———. (2003). The mental health of crime victims: Impact of legal intervention. *Journal of Traumatic Stress, 16*(2), 159–66.

Howard, D., & Christophersen, O. (2003). *Statistics of mentally disordered offenders 2002* (Cat. No. 1403). London: Offending and Criminal Justice Group, Research Development and Statistics Directorate, Home Office.

Jennings, W. G., Gover, A. R., & Piquero, A. R. (2011). Integrating the American criminal justice and mental health service systems to focus on victimization. *International Journal of Offender Therapy and Comparative Criminology, 55*(8), 1272–90.

Jerga, J. (2010, August 10). Overcrowded prison is degrading. *Sydney Morning Herald.* Retrieved from http://news.smh.com.au

Kessler, R. C., Sonnega, A., Bromet, E., Hughes, M., & Nelson, C. B. (1995). Posttraumatic stress disorder in the national comorbidity survey. *Archives of General Psychiatry, 52*(12), 1048–60.

Kilpatrick, D. G., & Acierno, R. (2003). Mental health needs of crime victims: Epidemiology and outcomes. *Journal of Traumatic Stress, 16*(2), 119–32.

Kumar, V., & Daria, U. (2013). Psychiatric morbidity in prisoners. *Indian Journal of Psychiatry, 55*(4), 366–70.

Maniglio, R. (2009). Severe mental illness and criminal victimization: A systematic review. *Acta Psychiatrica Scandinavica, 119*(3), 180–91.

Moore, E. (2005). Criminal justice: Extending the social work focus. In M. Alston & J. McKinnon (Eds), *Social work: Fields of practice* (2nd ed., pp. 207–21). South Melbourne: Oxford University Press.

Mullen, P. E., Holmquist, C. L., & Ogloff, J. R. P. (2003). *National forensic mental health scoping study.* Canberra: Department of Health and Ageing.

Murali, T., & Rao, K. (2004). Psychiatric rehabilitation in India: Issues and challenges. In S. P. Agarwal, D. S. Goel, R. L. Inchhpujani, R. N. Salhan & S. Shrivastava (Eds), *Mental health: An Indian perspective, 1946–2003* (pp. 152–62). New Delhi: Directorate General of Health Services, Ministry of Health and Family Welfare and Reed Elsevier India Private Limited.

National Commission on Correctional Health Care. (2002). *The health status of soon-to-be-released inmates: A report to Congress,* Volume 1. Chicago, IL: National Commission on Correctional Health Care.

National Crime Records Bureau. (2015). *Prison statistics in India.* New Delhi: Ministry of Home Affairs, Government of India.

Ogloff, J. R. P. (1996). *The Surrey pretrial mental health program: Community component evaluation.* Coquitlam: British Columbia Forensic Psychiatric Services Commission.

Ogloff, J. R. P., Davis, M. R., Rivers, G., & Ross, S. (2006). *The identification of mental disorders in the criminal justice system.* Canberra: Criminology Research Council.

Polgreen, L. (2011, July 18). Rehabilitation comes to a prison and to its inmates. *New York Times.* Retrieved from http://www.nytimes.com

Raghavan, V. (2013). Social work intervention in criminal justice: Field-theory linkage. In S. Singh (Ed.), *Social work and social development: Perspectives from India and the United States* (pp. 265–89). Chicago, IL: Lyceum Books, Inc.

Raja, A. (2013, March 17). Rotting behind bars: As claims of daily violence, sexual assault and hell-hole conditions dog Tihar Jail, mail today takes a look at life in India's toughest prisons. *Daily Mail.* Retrieved from http://www.dailymail.co.uk

Raza, D. (2013, March 15). No security, medicine or protection: The horrors of living in Tihar jail. *Firstpost India*. Retrieved from http://www.firstpost.com

Reddy, M. V., & Chandrashekar, C. R. (1998). Prevalence of mental and behavioural disorders in India: A meta-analysis. *Indian Journal of Psychiatry, 40*(2), 149–57.

Schoeman, M. (2012). Working with victims of crime. In L. Holtzhausen (Ed.), *Criminal justice social work: A South African practice framework* (pp. 76–98). Cape Town: Juta.

Scottish Government. (2010). *National outcomes and standards for social work services in the criminal justice system*. Edinburgh, Scotland: Scottish Government.

Sir Dorabji Tata Trust and the Allied Trusts (SDTT). (2011). *Social work in India's criminal justice institutions: Need, experiences, and challenges*. Mumbai: SDTT. Retrieved from http://www.dorabjitatatrust.org/pdf/SocialWorkinIndiasCJIs.pdf

Sivagnanam, T. S. (2012, February 24). *Rights of prisoners and convicts under the criminal justice administration*. Paper presented at National Judicial Academy Regional Judicial Conference, Chennai. Retrieved from http://www.hcmadras.tn.nic.in/jacademy/article/Role%20of%20Prisoner%20and%20Conv%20TSSJ.pdf

Sharma, P. (2005). Mental health aspects of victims of crime with special reference to children. *Journal of Indian Association for Child and Adolescent Mental Health, 1*(4). Retrieved from http://files.eric.ed.gov/fulltext/EJ847490.pdf

Smith, N., & Trimboli, L. (2010). Co-morbid substance and non-substance mental health disorders and re-offending among NSW prisoners. Sydney: NSW Bureau of Crime Statistics and Research.

Treger, H., & Allen, G. F. (2007). Social work in the justice system: An overview. In A. R. Roberts & D. W. Springer (Eds), *Social work in juvenile and criminal justice settings* (3rd ed., pp. 44–52). Springfield, IL: Charles C Thomas.

Trotter, C. (2006). *Working with involuntary clients: A guide to practice* (2nd ed.). Crow's Nest: Allen & Unwin.

University of Missouri-Columbia, & National Association of Social Workers. (2006). *Introductory workshop participant manual*. Washington, DC: U.S. Department of Justice.

Wemmers, J. (2013). Victims' experiences in the criminal justice system and their recovery from crime. *International Review of Victimology, 19*, 221–33.

Wilson, M. (2010). *Criminal justice social work in the United States: Adapting to new challenges*. Washington, DC: NASW Centre for Workforce Studies.

World Health Organization (WHO). (1999, November). Mental health promotion in prisons. Report presented at the WHO Meeting, The Hague,

Netherlands. Retrieved from http://apps.who.int/iris/bitstream/10665/108156/1/E64328.pdf

————. (2007). *What is mental health?* Retrieved from http://www.who.int/features/qa/62/en/

Young, D. S. (2002). Non-psychiatric services provided in a mental health unit in a county jail. *Journal of Offender Rehabilitation, 35*(2), 63–82.

Young, M. (1993). *Victim assistance: Frontiers and fundamentals.* Washington, DC: National Organisation for Victim Assistance.

SECTION II

Criminal Justice Social Work Practice

4

Police Social Work: Active Engagement with Law Enforcement

Ruchi Sinha

Introduction

The police are the primary institution responsible for the maintenance of public order and the rule of law. India is a union of 28 states and 7 union territories, and governed by the tenets of the Constitution of India. Article 246 of the Constitution of India, which delineates the legislative powers of the states and the Centre (i.e., the federal government), places the police, public order, courts, prisons, reformatories, borstal and other allied institutions in the State List (List II). While policing is primarily a state subject, specific provisions in the Constitution gives the Centre certain powers in matters related to police.

It has been strenuously argued that the police in India generally lack legitimate authority and public trust. To address the shortcomings within the police system, the Government has constituted many commissions, which besides adequately highlighting issues ailing the police system also acknowledge that there is a need to strengthen the role of civil society in policing. Most reports suggest that by involving citizens in evaluating the quality of service at police stations and other police offices, and by providing incentives for citizens' initiatives, the police as an institution can be made more accountable to citizens. Some of the later reports have deliberated on the scope of devising formal mechanisms at different levels that involve citizens/citizen's groups in various aspects of public order management. Thus, while the commissions have visualised short-term issue-based partnerships with civil society, they have failed to explore police social work (PSW) as an option.

PSW recognises that policing encompasses more functions than simply ensuring security for its citizens. The police also have a positive obligation to help create an environment in which people feel that they are, and in actual fact are, free and secure. PSW recognises that the police themselves are entitled to this positive obligation of the state and that the police are entitled to the same rights as anyone else. Despite this broad all-encompassing, yet challenging, role that PSW engages with, it remains strongly contested by both the state and social work education establishments across India (Sinha, 2012a).

Policing in India

In order for PSW practitioners to function effectively, they should be aware of the evolution and organisation of the police as well as the duty span of each police officer. The following sections will demystify policing by first contextualising its evolution with a brief overview of the commissions constituted to look into policing, and then by discussing the complex organisational set-up of the police.

Evolution of Policing in India

Sir Charles Napier, inspired by the Irish Constabulary, developed a separate and self-contained policing organisation in Colonial India. He began with organising policing for Sind province, and his model was then replicated in Bombay in 1853 and in Madras in 1859 (Arnold, 1986). To strengthen policing, the Colonial rulers in British India appointed a Police Commission in 1860. Based on the recommendations of this Commission, the Colonial Government submitted a bill, which became a law as Act V of 1861 or the Police Act, 1861. As per the Act, the police became a subject to be administered by the provinces that were divided into police jurisdictions corresponding with the districts and divisions. The Indian police organisation originally conceived in 1861 was remodelled in 1902, based on the report of the 1902 Indian Police Commission.

It is evident that the British needed a police structure to suppress political dissent and unrest by collecting political intelligence and maintaining public order. Hence, they introduced policing in India not to serve the people of India but principally to maintain the authority of the Crown. It thus evolved as an agency of oppression, of subjugation, primarily used for protecting the interests of the British Empire.

When India gained independence, the country retained the structure of policing, with the expectation that the role of the police force would transform based on the mandate of the Constitution. Policing, however, failed to transform itself from being a coercive force. Its structure, functions and ethos defined by the archaic Acts prevent the transformation of the present structure to align itself with the demands of democratic policing. Thus, the relationship between the police and the public is both antagonistic and based on suspicion (Government of India, 2007).

During the post-Independence period, the police have been the subject of a number of Commissions and Committees (Table 4.1), appointed by various state governments as well as the Government of India to probe into the various problem areas of the police force. Different commissions have time and again expressed concern over the practice of non-recording of crimes by police officers to erroneously project a lower rate of crime in their jurisdictions and hence enhance perceived efficiency. They have highlighted issues related to the ineffectiveness of the police, poor quality of investigation and prosecution, political interference, factionalism in the ruling party and how this plays into the

Table 4.1:
Select List of Police Acts and Commissions

S/No.	Year	Legislation/Report/Commission
1.	1860	The Police Commission
2.	1861	The Police Act V
3.	1888	The Police Act III
4.	1902	The Indian Police Commission
5.	1922	The Police (Incitement To Disaffection) Act XXII
6.	1949	The Police Act LXIV
7.	1952	The State Armed Forces (Extension Of Laws) Act LXIII
8.	1960	UP Police Commission
9.	1960	West Bengal Police Commission
10.	1961	Bihar Police Commission
11.	1966	The Khosla Commission (Delhi Police)
12.	1966	The Administrative Reforms Commission
13.	1966	The Police Forces (Restriction Of Rights) Act XXXIII
14.	1969	Tamil Nadu Police Commission
15.	1971–73	Gore Committee on Police Training
16.	1979–81	National Police Commission (NPC)
		NPC: First Report—February 1979
		NPC: Second Report—August 1979
		NPC: Third Report—January 1980
		NPC: Fourth Report—June 1980
		NPC: Fifth Report—November 1980
		NPC: Sixth Report—March 1981
		NPC: Seventh Report—May 1981
		NPC: Eighth Report—May 1981
17.	1998–99	Ribeiro Committee (RC)
		RC: First report—October 1998
		RC: Second Report—March 1999
18.	2000	Padmanabhaiah Committee
19.	2005–06	Police Act Drafting Committee (PADC)
20.	2007	Second Administrative Reforms Commission (SARC)
	(January)	SARC: Fifth report—Public Order—June 2007

way the police perform some of their tasks, and association of criminals with political parties and their control over the police. Almost all these Commissions have made a number of concrete suggestions to reduce corruption across its ranks. Some Commissions have also made wide-ranging recommendations related to the welfare of police personnel. For this, they have looked into the conditions of service, duties and responsibilities, modernisation of the police force and so on.

These Commissions have repeatedly sought to improve the relationship between the police and the public as well as to loosen the stranglehold of politics over the police. They have emphasised the importance of public cooperation and have concluded that principal support to the police should come from society itself. As a result of all these recommendations at the national level, the Gore Committee on Police Training (1971–73) was set up to review the training of the police at all levels. The National Police Commission (NPC), 1977, is one of the most important police commissions as it has made an exhaustive list of recommendations based on its comprehensive review of the Indian Police. The NPC had a fairly wide and comprehensive term of reference, requiring a fresh examination of the role and performance of the police, both as a law enforcement agency and as an institution to protect the rights of the citizens enshrined in the Constitution.

The NPC produced eight reports between February 1979 and May 1981. The first report came out in February 1979 and was made public by the Janata Government. This Commission had finished the first two reports, when the government changed at the Centre. With Indira Gandhi's return to power in January 1980, the very existence of the NPC came under threat. The remaining seven reports (the 2nd to the 8th) were released to the public after much delay in March 1983. The most important recommendation of the NPC centred on the problem of insulating the police from illegitimate political and bureaucratic interference. They also recommended a draft police bill that incorporated the recommendations of the Commission. The 'power lobby' were disconcerted by these recommendations; at the prospect of losing control over an organisation that, they had been misusing for so long.

Following the NPC, the Ribeiro Committee (RC) (1998) strongly recommended the setting up of Police Performance and Accountability Commissions at the state level, the constitution of a District Complaints Authority and replacement of the Police Act, 1861 with a new Act and so on. In 2000, the Padmanabhaiah Committee on Police Reforms was constituted to study, inter alia, recruitment procedures for the police force, training, duties and responsibilities, police officers' behaviour, police investigations and prosecution.

Because of growing discontent with policing and mounting pressure, in September 2005 the Government of India constituted a Police Act Drafting Committee (PADC) to draft new legislation to replace the Police Act of 1861. This Committee drafted a model police bill, keeping in view the changing role/responsibility of the police and the challenges before it. It has proposed a corresponding need for attitudinal changes within the police and the necessity for a functional mechanism to elicit cooperation and assistance from the community. The Second Administrative Reforms Commission (SARC), and especially its Fifth Report on Public Order, comprehensively encapsulates all the above and suggests that the recommendations be implemented if the government is serious in its intent to substantially improve the police as an institution.

Most commissions recognise that to inspire public confidence, the police require a new doctrine of policing embedded in an inclusive approach to governance and to reflect a process open to public partnership in policing decisions. Most of the shortcomings, according to these commissions, are due to the institution's colonial development as a means of oppression, and its alleged corruption and criminalisation in the postcolonial period. The commissions, however, also acknowledge that the institution of police in India is also structurally disempowered due to the multiple conflicting authorities that challenge and often overwhelm the authority of the police (Jauregui, 2013).

While they strongly advocate that policing be viewed as a service, which needs to be responsive, preventive and proactive, the government has refrained from fundamentally restructuring the police. All that one can see in terms of the intent to transform policing is a fragmented approach towards inculcating soft skills such as communication, counselling, team building and leader-ship as additional training components. Thus the police, regarded as a gatekeeper of the criminal justice system (CJS), remains a neglected institution and has subsequently failed to transform itself into a true public service agency.

Police Organisation

The Ministry of Home Affairs manages the police as an institu-tion. The organisation of the Indian Police reflects India's central-ised federalism, as specific provisions in the Constitution gives the Centre certain powers in police matters and even authorises it to set up certain central police organisations. The Central Police Force is divided into two distinct areas of command, namely the Central Police Organisations (CPO) and the Central Paramilitary Forces (CPF). The CPO work in coordination with Indian Federal Police agencies, state police forces and other Indian law enforce-ment agencies. The CPF are the armed forces of the police, which work closely with the Indian Armed Forces. It should be noted that this chapter contextualises PSW with the civil police organi-sation, as the operations of CPF are more aligned with the mili-tary and hence should be considered under the aegis of Military Social Work.

Figure 4.1 gives a comprehensive overview of police organisa-tion in India at both the Central and state levels. The police, even though they are a concern of a state, has its leadership provided by the Indian Police Service (IPS) which is an All India Service—recruited, trained and managed by the central government.

Table 4.2 outlines the organisation of the police at the state level. The DGP heads the police force in the state. Some states have zones comprising of two or more Ranges, under the charge of an officer of the rank of an IGP. A group of districts form a Range, which is looked after by an officer of the rank of Dy IGP. An officer of the rank of SP heads the district police force. The SP is the entry point for the IPS cadre. Every district is additionally divided into sub-divisions. A sub-division is under the charge of

Table 4.2:
Organisation of Police in India

Operative Unit	Rank and File	Police Cadre
State	Director General of Police (DGP) Additional Director General of Police (Addl. DGP)	IPS
Zones	Inspector General of Police (IGP)	
Ranges	Deputy Inspector General of Police (Dy IGP)	
Districts	Senior Superintendent of Police (SSP) Superintendent of Police (SP)	
Sub-divisions	Assistant/Deputy Superintendent of Police (ASP/Dy SP)	State Police Cadre
Circles	Senior Inspector of Police (SPI)	
Police Stations	Inspector of Police (PI)	
Police Out-posts	Sub Inspector (SI) Assistant Sub-Inspector of Police (ASI) Head Constables (HC) Police Constables	

an officer of the rank of ASP/Dy SP. Every sub-division is then divided into a number of police stations. Between the police station and the sub-division, there are police circles in some states, which are generally headed by a PI.

The police station is the basic unit of police administration. All crimes have to be recorded at the police station and all preventive, investigative and law and order work are performed from there. A police station is divided into a number of beats, which are assigned to constables. The officer in charge of a police station is a PI. In rural areas, the officer in charge is usually a Sub-Inspector of Police. To improve its reach, and to facilitate access to the public, police posts (*police chowki*) have been set up under police stations, particularly where the geographical jurisdiction of the police station is large.

The sheer expanse of this police organisation explicitly reveals the hierarchical nature of the system, run by an array of operating procedures that work in a complex arena with many different (political, state and community) players serving many different interests, and held in check by different systems of accountability. A police social worker must first understand the system before they can function effectively in this role.

Police Functions

It is the state's ultimate responsibility to preserve public order so that people within its jurisdiction can enjoy their rights to the fullest. Police functions are most relevant for a police social worker as they represent an area in which a dialogue with the police can take place. It also sensitises the police social worker to the fact that the police do not operate in a vacuum and that they are bound by legislation and other regulations.

The police are at the forefront in maintaining law and order. Along with this primary role, increasingly, police officers are expected to assume social responsibility of the community under their jurisdiction and thereby provide access to services for individuals, families and communities in crisis. With the advent and promotion of community policing, the role of the police officer is now viewed differently, and is expected to be compatible with community-based social services. As a result of their interface with the community, it has been noticed that the police do have an astute understanding of the community and as a result are in a position to identify cases needing support or crisis intervention.

However, as per Section 23 of the Police Act of 1861, which specifies the general functions of the police officer, the social responsibility roles for the police do not exist. The Act enjoins the police officers to obey and execute all orders and warrants lawfully issued by any competent authority. They are thus responsible for collecting and communicating intelligence affecting the public peace. Further, they have the authority to prevent the commission of offences and public nuisances; detect and bring offenders to justice; and apprehend all persons that they are legally authorised to apprehend and for whose apprehension sufficient grounds exist.

It is apparent that police functions, as per the Act, are minimalistic and restrictive in nature as they are rooted in a pre-Independence context and thus do not account for changes in the socio-political environment in which the organisation is required to function today. The NPC's model police bill has substantially expanded the functions of the police. While retaining promotion and preservation of public order and investigation of crimes, as well as the apprehension of offenders, it enjoins the police to reduce the opportunities for the commission of crimes through preventive patrol and other prescribed measures. It recommends that police aid and cooperate with other relevant agencies for the prevention of crimes, and also aid individuals who are in danger of physical harm—including providing necessary services to afford relief to people in distressing situations. It visualises the police as an organisation, which would create and maintain a feeling of security in the community by providing counselling, resolving conflicts and promoting amity.

The Fifth Report of the SARC envisions changing the character of the police from a 'force' meant to enforce the writ of the state to a 'service' meant to secure the lives and liberty and constitutional freedoms of the citizens of a free and democratic country. This report states that their focus is on creating new structures, based on the best international examples that would usher in an era of accountability, functional autonomy, transparency, responsiveness and professionalism in the Indian police. Yet, the report does not aver to the robust and positive role and practice that Criminal Justice Social Work (CJSW) can play in this area.

Criminal Justice Social Work

Historically, social work in India has its roots in religious philanthropic efforts. During the nineteenth century, social reform movements led by many reformers instigated the movement of charity from religion to an organised process. Following which the freedom movement facilitated the acceptance of principles of social justice, as enshrined in the Constitution of India. Over the years, social work in India has thus evolved by responding to the changing needs of society in the post-Independence era.

Social work education began in 1936 at the Sir Dorabji Tata Graduate School of Social Work. For a decade, no other social work educational centre emerged. The next decade, that is, 1946–55 saw the emergence of about eight prominent social work departments. From 1955 to 1980, there were about 60 social work educational departments. Interestingly, the post-1990s period then saw a proliferation of social work institutions, resulting in over 500 institutions delivering social work education today.

Despite this boom in social work education, the social work syllabus has failed to include much criminal justice content in its curriculum. In India, most departments/schools/centres of social work offer limited courses, namely juvenile justice, human rights, and law and social work, in their curricula. Since 1956, the Tata Institute of Social Sciences is the only social work educational centre in India that offers a full-fledged Master of Social Work (MSW) course in CJSW. Two universities, namely the Maharaja Sayajirao University of Baroda (MSU) and the School of Social Work (SOSW) in Indira Gandhi National Open University (IGNOU), Delhi, offer diploma, or certificate courses in CJSW, and consequently include a few elements of CJSW in their course curriculum as well.

The beginning of corrections (the forerunner of CJSW in India) is attributed to the commitment India had post-Independence to the implementation of welfare and social policy. The post-Independence government followed an interventionist and developmental state paradigm to achieve the stated aims of the 'directive principles' of state policy—social justice, self-reliance, growth, and the removal of poverty (Palriwala & Neetha, 2009). As a result, many pieces of welfare legislation were passed which led to the institutionalisation of some vulnerable groups susceptible to neglect/abuse. This interventionist state-led welfare initiatives demanded a cadre of trained social workers for social welfare departments to work with institutionalised population groups such as destitute women, children, beggars, the mentally challenged, and women in prostitution and prison.

With neoliberal reforms being propagated since the 1980s, however, there was a clear shift towards advocating for a private sector expansion into health, education, welfare and 'other social services'. This development led to a corresponding gradual withdrawal of the state in the provision of such 'public goods', and is reflected in the declining levels of social sector expenditure (Palriwala & Neetha, 2009). This, combined with the limitations of institutional treatment and rehabilitation as a method for social reintegration, meant that corresponding investments in terms of institutional set-up, work force, training and service delivery were curtailed (Sinha, 2012b). The growing indifference of the government was reflected in the lower budgetary provision and the gradual curtailment of expenditure in this area. This, sadly, likewise led to the decline of corrections in India.

While the state was withdrawing from corrections, the advent of structural social work brought about severe criticism of the existing model of corrections as it discounted the role of oppressive social structures, subscribed to an elitist definition of crime, and exclusively centred on 'deviant' individual behaviour (as opposed to a 'criminogenic' society). This critique of the conventional practice of corrections paved the way for CJSW. CJSW aligns itself with the liberal arts tradition, which laid the foundation of the community-oriented movement and relies on partnerships with other resources, not just the CJS to deal with an issue.

Understanding Police Social Work

CJSW across countries has largely focussed on work in prison, juvenile justice, probation, domestic violence, trafficked women, youth crime, child protection and substance-abusing persons.

Sites for engagement thus have been the prison, courts, institutions, short stay homes and other facilities once the individual has been processed by the CJS. PSW within CJSW is not as widely documented as the other practice sites mentioned above. This section discusses how PSW as a practice domain can be strengthened especially since it is located with the gateway agency of the CJS.

The basic premise of PSW, is that the police ought to engage with those they are to serve—the members of the public—as the most effective way to prevent the police from becoming tyrannical and oppressive in their practice. This premise concurs with the United Nations Code of Conduct, which states that, 'every law enforcement agency should be representative of, and responsive and accountable to, the community as a whole'.[1]

The article 'Coordinating Police and Social Work' is one of the earliest articles published in 1952 (Patterson, 2006) to describe social work–police partnerships. Similarly, the British report, 'Social Workers: Their Role and Tasks' in 1982, recognised the possibility of inter-agency work involving the police and social services, and advocated a closer working partnership between social workers and the police. PSW thus was recognised as a legitimate practice arena with the police (largely a non-voluntary) system subject to some amount of regulation based on existing legislation.

The Encyclopaedia of Social Work in 1987 first included a definition of PSW by Treger. This definition described PSW as a new area of social work practice in which social workers provide assessment and crisis intervention in a timely manner to individuals experiencing delinquency, mental health issues, alcohol and substance use and abuse, family and neighbour conflicts, and crime victimisation. Another definition, in the Social Work Dictionary by Barker (1998) defines PSW as

---

[1] General Assembly Resolution 34/169 adopting the UN Code of Conduct, 17 December 1979.

professional social work practice within police precinct houses, courthouses and jail settings to provide a variety of social services to victims of crime, people accused of crimes and their families. Some workers also counsel police officers and members of their families under job related stresses. They sometimes act as advocates and public relations specialists for police departments and help in mediation with various community groups. A major activity is helping resolve domestic troubles for which the police are often called.

These two definitions largely describe the functions of the police social worker and specify that the 'catchment' of work is primarily para-legal in nature.

PSW has been recognised in countries such as the UK, the USA, Australia and Hong Kong. A majority of the PSW collaborative partnerships in these countries are in the fields of elder abuse, child protection, juvenile delinquency, youth problems, domestic violence, drug addiction and so on (Barclay Report, 1982; Cooper, Anaf & Bowden, 2008; Dolon & Hendricks, 1989; Garrett, 2004; Holdaway, 1986; Patterson, 2004; Thomas, 1994). Dolon and Hendricks (1989) found that police and social service providers share a common concern of finding a safe and secure environment for victims of elder abuse and neglect. Similarly, in the field of domestic violence, studies on police and social work collaborations suggest that abused women benefit from collaborative police attention (Dave, 2000; Treger, Thomson & Sloan, 1974). Another area where collaboration between social workers and police exists is in the field of child protection. Garrett (2004), in his study discussing the role of multidisciplinary teams in child protection in England, has highlighted the advantages of police-social work collaborative practice.

Practice Domains of Police Social Work

The only institutionalised PSW engagement in India is in the context of crimes against women and domestic violence. While social workers also have an important role in social legislation such as the Bombay Prevention of Beggary Act 1959; the Juvenile Justice Act 2004; the Immoral Trafficking Prevention Act 1956;

the Criminal Tribes Act, 1924 and so on are largely NGO collaborations. In this context, the police, while being the first point of contact, have limited skills to deal with the issue or the individual under these Acts. Recognising the shortcomings in police capacity with respect to such social legislation, the National Human Rights Commission (2004) has recommended the appointment of trained social workers in police stations.

The complexity of demands made on the police often puts them in a 'catch 22' situation where on the one hand they are expected to be polite and civil to the public, and on the other hand, to be suspicious of strangers. Despite the fact that the police attempt to deal with all complaints, humanistic and rehabilitative aspects in the police station are often neglected. One reason for this neglect is systemic as the focus is on law and order issues. Another reason is that the police often work excessively long hours, are underpaid, carry out dangerous work with little, if any, protection, are ill-prepared (both in terms of training and infrastructure) to perform tasks, have little social status and receive criticism from all sides.

It is apparent that citizens approach police for a variety of social, civic and criminal problems. Treger (1987), Briar (1985) and Howard (1963) have documented that most police officer functions involve addressing social distress and hence are related to social services. This, they feel, is a strong basis for social workers to collaborate with police. Holdaway (1986), too, has observed that police officers frequently act as untrained temporary social workers for people in diverse situations, and yet the officers performing these roles may not rate this as being central to their work, even though their police workload contains a significant 'social service' element. Goldstein (1979) has argued vociferously for the need of integrating law enforcement agencies into the social policy arena. While the similarity of police functions to social service explores the micro–meso levels of engagement, linking policing to social policy brings forth the macro context and spells out the structural dimensions of engagements.

PSW requires working with victims, offenders, marginalised communities and with different branches of the police. Besides the functional issues of ensuring complaints are registered immediately, re-orientation of training of personnel needs to include neglected soft skills such as communication, counselling, team building and leadership; police social workers need to have the skills to collaborate, challenge, and negotiate as well as facilitate work in the police station.

Police social workers collaborate with multiple stakeholders on all relevant social issues such as domestic violence, juvenile justice, child protection, elder abuse, substance abuse and protecting the rights of all people accessing the police station. They challenge stereotypes that the individual police officer or the system may have with respect to a vulnerable group or marginalised community. They negotiate with the government for changes required within the system to transform the police from an authoritarian force to a public service agency. They attempt to engage with the government to transform the policing philosophy. Thus, police social workers will try to encourage the organisation to shift from an autocratic and crisis-policing philosophy to a community and problem-oriented policing philosophy.

Finally, police social workers facilitate sensitisation across all police ranks regarding issues of the police that police officers themselves often neglect. A police social worker strives to help the individual police officer to realise that they are entitled to all the rights provided for in the various national and international instruments.[2] Amnesty, in its report, also accepts that the police cannot be expected to protect human rights when their own rights are not protected (Osse, 2006). Police social workers have dealt with issues of frustration that the police often face due to people in power who 'interfere and manipulate' the system to their benefit (such as delaying trials, filing complaints, appealing to higher court and so on). PSW strives

---

[2] The only exception is with Article 22(2) of the ICCPR which states that States can restrict the rights of those working within the armed forces or the police to freedom of assembly including the right to form and join trade unions (this is the only explicit mention of police in the entire body of international human rights treaties).

to reduce exploitation by people with vested interests and thereby strike a balance in expectations between the citizen and the system.

Police Social Work or Social Work with the Police

The terms 'PSW' and 'Social Work with the Police' are often used interchangeably. Since both terms connote partnerships with the institution of the police, many accept them as having no difference as well. Practitioners, however, feel that there is a nuanced difference between the two.

Social work with the police broadly encompasses the work of non-police, non-state, organisations such as NGOs (local and international), academic institutions and so on, who establish collaborations with police departments as one of their activities. As a result, their work and intervention is dependent on police priorities and perceptions. Their inclusion/participation is thus by invitation, mostly need-based, and hence, temporary. The decision-making powers in this context are with the police and since the engagement is short term, process engagement and outcomes are largely missing.

In PSW, though, there are two models. In the first model, police departments employ social workers, and in the second, the police integrate social workers of a civil society/human service organisation, into the system as an equal partner and hence they are entitled to use the police infrastructure for their work. In both these models, social workers have their autonomy and mandate defined and hence there are well articulated intervention strategies. They begin with an analysis of the police as an institution and conduct a contextual examination. Based on this, police social workers then formulate their main concerns. They thereafter define objectives and develop a strategy to achieve outcomes both as activities and as a process. It is obvious then that the entry, and hence leveraging capacity for police social workers, is different. For police social workers, their entry is systemic, institutionalised with checks and balances, and consequently, permanent in nature. In PSW, the decision-making power is with the social workers. Police social workers can thus undertake both process-oriented work and short-term engagements. Hence, they engage with the community (micro–macro continuum), initiate work aimed towards organisational transformation and thereby increase police accountability.

Challenges Facing Police Social Work

The complexities of social worker–police relationships arise from the differing roles and mandates of human services and criminal justice organisations. Dolon and Hendricks (1989), in their study, reiterated the need to understand the professional responsibilities and differences that exist between police officers and social workers. Garrett (2004) has also pointed towards a 'blurring of the social work identity' by elucidating the tensions in the working relationship between police officers and social workers, which emerge from the perceived overlaps in their roles.

Police officers tend to have a different perspective from that of the police social workers due to different professional values and cultures that govern these professions. Thus, both often use different languages and reach different conclusions about cause and effect while dealing with the same issue. The crucial differences between the two systems arise from the fact that the police are mandated to respond to a specific offence by collecting evidence and witness statements, whilst social workers view the client as a victim of circumstance requiring the long-term commitment of a dedicated social worker to provide stability, empathy and a therapeutic environment (Cooper et al., 2008). Lack of trust between social workers and the police is due to the latter's culture that is based on masculine ideology which determines their perceptions of perpetrators of crime, and regulated by a hierarchical, patriarchal organisational structure similar to that of the armed forces (Niland, 1996).

This culture reflects the police's mandate to act as a coercive arm of the state to maintain community order and safety with the use of force (Reiner, 2000).

Opening up spaces in the system appears to be an ideal way to begin organised work for efficient and timely interventions to assist clients. In practice, the restructuring difficulties and social worker dilemmas of breach of trust, confidentiality and privacy are obstacles to be dealt with (Cooper et al., 2008).

Despite their differing cultures, roles and philosophies, social work and policing have intersections (Sinha, 2008). Interestingly, many police officers consider themselves as social workers as they feel they can ensure the well-being of citizens as per the states' mandate. This increases the possibility of ambiguity and tension as well as the need for cooperation. Social workers aim to assist individuals in crisis by focusing on their welfare and human rights (Cooper et al., 2008), and ensuring prompt support for the victims and the vulnerable. The police, on the other hand, work from a legalistic view that involves maintaining order, community protection and safety, fighting crime through the use of force, if necessary (Fielding, 1984). Social workers and the police have different perceptions of issues of crime and deviance, which needs to be addressed to create workable partnerships based on equal commitment, teamwork, mutual respect and trust (Cooper et al., 2008; Dolon & Hendricks, 1989; Garrett, 2004; Holdaway, 1986; Patterson, 2004; Thomas, 1994).

Another unexplored arena is the system's power to influence the social worker's work. Police social workers also face the danger of co-option if the practitioners do not fully comprehend the functions and the environment of the police. A critical issue that police social workers face in India is that they are functioning on an administrative order (on an experimental basis) which does not offer any legal protection. Thus, actions taken on behalf of the victim or offender in good faith can be challenged in a court of law. It is apparent that social workers find working with police fraught with dilemmas and there is a need to define the practice field to meet its objective of facilitating a shift in the nature of the policing philosophy and redefining it as a public agency.

Conclusion

Police social work validates Treger's premise that there is a need for trained social workers in the police station, where citizens interface with the system (Treger et al., 1974). PSW in India today needs to be developed and strengthened. It should increase its presence to mitigate the effects of criminal justice action on the vulnerable and marginalised by situating the differential impact of socio-economic structures on an individual (Sinha, 2012a). PSW as a partnership facilitates access to the CJS for vulnerable and marginalised groups, both as victims and as offenders. At the same time, PSW acknowledges the concerns and realities of the police as its practitioners are aware of their functions, procedures and regulations. While they operate within the system, they have to be extremely careful of the co-option processes within the system. That said, PSW, nevertheless, presents an opportunity for increased cooperation based on areas of mutual interest between social work and policing in seeking to achieve similar goals. Despite this, PSW in India is struggling for recognition, and, as a result, it remains strongly contested by both the state, which is reluctant to integrate social workers in the CJS, and in practice, due to limited competencies and motivation existing in most schools of social work across India to integrate CJSW in the curriculum.

References

Arnold, D. (1986). *Police power and colonial control, Madras 1859–1947.* New Delhi: Oxford University Press.

Barclay Report. (1982). *The roles and tasks of social workers.* London: George Allen & Unwin.

Barker, R. L. (1998). *The social work dictionary* (4th ed.). Washington, DC: NASW.

Briar, K. H. (1985). Emergency calls to police: Implications for social work intervention. *Social Service Review, 59*(4), 593–603.

Cooper, L. Anaf, J., & Bowden, M. (2008). Can social workers and police be partners when dealing with bikie-gang related domestic violence and sexual assault? *European Journal of Social Work, 11*(3), 295–311.

Dave, A. (2000). An ongoing journey: Learning from a field action project in the police system. *The Indian Journal of Social Work, 61*(2), 295–99.

Dolon, R., & Hendricks, J. E. (1989). An exploratory study comparing attitudes and practices of police officers and social service providers in elder abuse and neglect cases. *Journal of Elder Abuse & Neglect, 1*(1), 75–90.

Fielding, N. (1984). Police socialization and police competence. *The British Journal of Sociology, 35*(4), 568–90. Retrieved from http://www.jstor. org/stable/590435

Garrett, P. M. (2004). Talking child protection: The police and social workers working together. *Journal of Social Work, 4*(1), 77–97.

Goldstein, H. (1979). Improving policing: A problem-oriented approach. *Crime and Delinquency, 25,* 236–58.

Government of India. (2007). Fifth Report—Public Order, Second Administrative Reforms Commission, June 2007. New Delhi: Author.

Holdaway, S. (1986). Police and social work relations: Problems and possibilities. *British Journal of Social Work, 16,* 137–60.

Howard, J. (1963). Policemen as social workers. *New Society, 14,* 9–10.

Jauregui, B. (2013). Beatings, beacons, and big men: Police disempowerment and delegitimation in India. *Law & Social Inquiry, 38*(3), 643–69.

National Human Rights Commission. (2004). *NHRC's plan of action to prevent and end trafficking in women and children in India.* Retrieved from http://www.nhrc.nic.in/

Niland, C. (1996). The impact of police culture on women and their performance in policing. Paper presented at the Australian criminology conference, Australasian Women Police Conference, July, Sydney.

Osse, A. (2006). *Understanding policing: A resource for human rights activists.* The Netherlands: Amnesty International.

Palriwala, R., & Neetha, N. (2009). *The care diamond: State social policy and the market* (India: Research Report No. 3). Geneva: United Nations Research Institute for Social Development.

Patterson, G. (2006). *Police social work available.* Retrieved from http://www.oxfordbibliographies.com/

———. (2004). Police-social work crisis teams: Practice and research implications. *Stress, Trauma, and Crisis, 7*(2), 93–104.

Reiner, R. (2000). *The politics of the police.* Oxford: Oxford University Press.

Sinha, R. (2008). *Socio-legal study of Baba Nagar—Slum in the vicinity of the Deonar dumping ground: Under the jurisdiction of Shivaji Nagar police station* (Unpublished Report). Mumbai: Centre for Criminology and Justice, TISS.

———. (2012a). Social work in police stations: Challenges for front line practice in India. *Practice: Social Work in Action, 24*(2), 91–104.

———. (2012b). Therapeutic work and police social work. In A. Ponnuswamy & Y. Vijila (Eds.), *Professional counselling with social work implications* (pp. 135–40). Coimbatore: Zageer Hussain Publications.

Thomas, T. (1994). *The police and social workers.* London: Arena.

Treger, H. (1987). Police social work. In A. Minahan (Ed.), *The encyclopedia of social work* (18th ed., pp. 263–68). Washington, DC: National Association of Social Workers Press.

Treger, H., Thomson, D., & Sloan, J. G. (1974). A police-social work team model: Some preliminary findings and implications for system change. *Crime & Delinquency, 20*(3), 281–90.

5

Correctional Social Work in India

Ilango Ponnuswami, Sonny Jose and
Praveen Varghese Thomas

Introduction

'Hate the crime and not the criminal.'

—Mahatma Gandhi

Criminology (from the Latin *crīmen*, implying 'accusation'; and Greek -λογία, -loia, implying 'study') is the scientific study of the nature, extent, causes, control and prevention of criminal behaviour in both the individual and in society (Martin, 1997; Pearsall & Trumble, 1995). The criminal justice system (CJS) is one of our most significant democratic institutions to combat and deter crime. An effective CJS is important for two main reasons: first, for maintaining law and order as well as a sense of fairness, which is an essential building block for everything else a society wants to do; and second, because it concerns every problem—race, poverty, homeless, addiction, mental illness and so on—that India would ever want to address. This is one of the key underlying insights that this chapter will attempt to impart to the readers. Society can use the criminal justice process as a springboard for addressing a host of critical social issues (Muncie & Fitzgerald, 1981). The world over, the CJS and institutions have always presented enormous challenges to those professionals engaged in the reformation of persons in conflict with the law. However, this is complicated by public opinion and legislative majorities; many of whom are ignorant or slow to appreciate this priority as they see this as a diversion of funds which, in their opinion, are better spent elsewhere (Beccaria & Davies, 1995).

However, problems that prisons are facing in India seem especially grave. While retributive punishment as a penal philosophy has been replaced with ideas of rehabilitation and welfare elsewhere, the custodial approach of the Indian prison system has continued and been fed into the current system's operational ethos. In this chapter, we have attempted to: (a) acquaint the readers with the present status of the occurrence of crimes in India; (b) present a bird's eye view of the nature and status of India's correctional institutions (with a specific focus on prisons), (c) introduce the humble beginnings of correctional social work and its subsequent demise, (d) examine the systemic problems apparent in correctional administration, (e) explain the problems arising out of the incarceration and imprisonment of individuals and (f) identify the areas of social work intervention that might be either improved (if already existing) or introduced where they are non-existent. After a careful analysis of the existing gaps, a few suggestions have also been made concerning the programmatic content of social work interventions in the different correctional settings, and the necessary changes to be made in the pattern and content of professional social work education and training.

Crime Statistics in India

The Code of Criminal Procedure (CrPC) of India classifies offences into

1. cognizable offences—those for which a police officer can arrest a suspect without a court warrant and
2. non-cognizable offences—those for which a police officer cannot arrest a suspect without a court warrant.

The National Crime Records Bureau's (NCRB, 2012) data seem to indicate that 6.04 million cognizable crimes were perpetrated, with 2.38 million being offences committed under the Indian Penal Code (IPC), while 3.65 million have been reported under the category of Special and Local Laws (SLL). That said, the NCRB claims that this is actually a much healthier picture than 2011 given that 2012 saw a reduction of an overall 3.4 per cent of recorded crimes over the previous year. This is not, however, a great consolation when compared to the statistics of five years ago, in 2007, when it was at 5.63 million. The share of violent crimes under the IPC during 2012 was 11.5 per cent as against 11.0 per cent in 2011. The highest rate of violent crimes was reported in Assam (54.2) followed by Manipur (44.6), Kerala (42.7) and Delhi (34.7) as compared to 22.7 on an all-India average. Uttar Pradesh (33,824) reported the highest incidence of violent crimes accounting for 12.3 per cent of the total number of violent crimes in the country (2,75,165).

As for the rate of 'violence against women', the proportion of IPC crimes committed against women increased during the last five years from 8.9 per cent in 2008 to 9.4 per cent in 2012. Andhra Pradesh has reported 40.5 per cent (3,714) of crimes referred to as an 'insult to the modesty of women'. Similarly, cases under the Immoral Traffic (Prevention) Act increased by 5.2 per cent in 2012. Human trafficking incidence was observed to have increased by 1.1 per cent between 2011 and 2012. Still far more disparaging is the crime against the tender-aged; a 15.3 per cent increase in the incidence of crimes against children was reported in 2012 over 2011. For every one hour, 273 cases of rape were being reported in the country, with 373 persons being arrested under different IPC sections in 2012. In other words, crime rates may have declined by a minor margin, but it shows increase in violence against women and children, with men being the 'perpetrators'. Equally worrying as an indicator of criminalisation is the involvement of children; the numbers of juveniles in conflict with the law under both IPC and SLL have increased by 11.2 per cent and 42.3 per cent, respectively, during the year 2012 over 2011. The percentage of juveniles apprehended under the IPC was 66.6 per cent in the age group of between 16 and 18 years in 2012.

High-tech crimes too, abound. The incidence of cybercrimes (IT Act and IPC offences together) has increased by 57.1 per cent in 2012 as compared to 2011. Cyberfraud accounted for 46.9 per cent, while cyberforgery accounted for 43.1 per cent (259 out of total 601) under the IPC category for cybercrimes.

The Nature and State of Prisons in India

Criminal justice institutions (CJIs), as a key part of the CJS, suffer from a range of problems. The 2012 NCRB figures report 385,135 inmates in India's 1,394 prisons. Clearly with occupancy at 112.2 per cent, overcrowding may be said to be at best, an understatement with regard to the Indian prison system. The NCRB (2012) reports that, with the exception of seven States and three Union Territories, the inmate population was greater than the prisons' capacity; in Uttar Pradesh and Chhattisgarh, the number of inmates was twice the capacity of prisons in those states. However, the NCRB (2012) shows that convicts comprise only 33.2 per cent of the total number of inmates in Indian jails, 66.2 per cent of them are undertrials—those not yet proven guilty of their alleged crimes. In the context of India, many detentions by the police are entirely unnecessary. Many get inducted into the CJS as 'undertrials' without any emotional preparedness. Further, delays in the processing of 'undertrials' create problems of overcrowding, thereby exacerbating the already dire prevailing conditions.

As aforesaid, India's CJS is severely strained. Years spent in a CJI—for reasons deserved or undeserved—not only isolate the person from society, but also impact them in very many ways. As the Honourable High Court of Kerala observed in the case 'A Convict Prisoner in the Central Prison vs. State of Kerala' (Nair, 1993), a 'prisoner' as a person, 'loses his identity', and comes to be known 'by a number'. The prisoner is not only 'dispossessed of everything material and personal, but also of personal relationships'. Loss of freedom, status, possessions, dignity and the autonomy of personal life precipitate psychological problems. Unless from privileged backgrounds or tried for high-profile cases, people confined in CJIs suffer even after their release; the label of being a criminal weighs on them heavily, is long-lasting and is difficult to erase. Friends, colleagues and acquaintances prefer to stay away. Past or potential employers want nothing to do with 'such a person'. In many cases, even families disown the 'criminal'. Devoid of emotional and financial support to lead a productive, satisfying life, there is a significant chance that a one-off offender gets pushed into taking up criminal activities as a career, associating with criminals, or leading a life marked by addiction or destitution (Vadiraj, Gopal, SDTT, & Sahni, 2011). At best, state efforts at rehabilitation are restricted to providing vocational training in income-generation as well as exposure to activities and advancing small business loans to prisoners after their release. Continuous and regular support to released under-trials is not formally recognised or offered by state agencies. Herein lies the relevance of social work, perhaps even still further the possibility of evolving a specialist cadre—a reformative service—to identify varied individual-specific needs, plan aligned interventions from the point of being brought into the CJS until such time as the person is rehabilitated and reintegrated into his/her community through a system of case management.

Those running the system experience two things—first, they experience a degree of 'impotency' in working within the system, let alone changing the system; second, they get frustrated seeing little results from whatever sincere efforts are taken, with the undertrials literally emerging into the larger society as hardened criminals. Such systems and structures demoralise those who have the duty of running the prisons, looking after the prisoners, as well as their reformation. True, prison reform cannot be discussed and handled successfully in isolation of these systemic qualities. But, neither can this be taken as an excuse for not attending to systemic issues that have been simmering for decades. A start has to be made somewhere; criticism of a prison service in which criminal justice, police and welfare policy ills are disclosed is simply not enough.

Induction of Criminal Justice Social Work in India

The induction of social work into the CJS was a development that happened in the early part of the twentieth century. In the 1930s, Dr Clifford Manshardt, a young American missionary, carried out a number of non-religious activities for the benefit of children and adults in Nagpada, a densely populated slum in the heart of Mumbai, through an institution called the 'Neighbourhood House'. Recognising the need for professional social workers, Manshardt decided to hold six-week courses for bright young people with an inclination towards social service. The Sir Dorabji Tata Graduate School of Social Work, established in the Neighbourhood House in 1936, later evolved into the Tata Institute of Social Sciences (TISS) in the 1940s, and eventually moved to Deonar (another suburb in Mumbai) in the 1950s. At its very inception, juvenile delinquency, crime and criminology were among the subjects of study at TISS.

In 1952, an effort to provide specialised training for correctional work was initiated. With the help of the Ministry of Home Affairs, the Government of India, and two experts made available by the United Nations, TISS offered a six-month programme to prison officers deputed by various state governments. A separate Department of Criminology and Correctional Administration (CCA) was created in 1953, endorsing full recognition to the professional training requirements in this field. The department became TISS's Centre for Criminology and Justice in 2006. Until the 1970s, most students of the CCA were candidates deputed from departments of 'prisons' and 'social welfare', as well as 'women and child development' across the country, who on completing the Master of Arts degree in social work with a specialisation in CCA, would go back to their parent departments to work as prison officers, social welfare officers and probation officers.

TISS undertook the first ever scoping study (assisted by the Commonwealth Human Rights Initiative [CHRI]) of all non-governmental organisations (NGOs) involved in criminal justice interventions; the study identified seven distinct areas in which social work efforts could be focused:

1. Moral or spiritual guidance/instruction, such as conducting spiritual discourses, individual preaching and counselling
2. Welfare of children of prisoners with regard to their shelter, health and education
3. Rehabilitation activities for women and youth
4. Health-related activities such as conducting health camps and health check-ups
5. Education of inmates, conducting literacy classes, coaching classes for Open University courses and vocational training
6. Legal guidance, referral services and legal aid
7. Generic support to prisoners such as organising lectures, celebrating festivals and attempting one-off activities

This was TISS's investment in influencing state policy to bring in reforms in CJI projects. TISS's interventions have inspired scores of other social justice initiatives—Prayas (Mumbai), Sudhaar (Bhopal), Varhad (Amravati), Sahyadri (Solapur), Sahyog (Pune), just to name a few.

The Indian Criminal Justice System and its Systemic Problems

The Indian CJS may be understood from two angles—one, from the dimension of being an entity with a legal structure; the second, from the point of view of its functionality.

From the legal structural perspective, the Indian CJS is said to be governed overall by four laws (Jose, 2014):

1. The Constitution of India
2. The Indian Penal Code (IPC)
3. The Code of Criminal Procedure of India (CrPC)
4. The Indian Evidence Act

The legislative power is vested with the Union Parliament and the State legislatures and the law-making functions are divided into the Union List, the State List and the Concurrent List, as mentioned in the Indian Constitution. The Union Parliament alone can make laws in domains mentioned under the Union List, the State legislatures alone can make laws under the State List, whereas both the Parliament and the State Legislatures are empowered to make laws on subjects as per the Concurrent List. The Constitution of India guarantees certain fundamental rights to all its citizens. Under the Constitution, criminal jurisdiction belongs concurrently to the central government and the governments of all the states.

At the national level, two major criminal codes, the IPC 1861 and the CrPC 1973, deal with all substantive crimes and their punishments, and the criminal procedure to be followed by the criminal justice agencies (i.e., the police, prosecution and judiciary) during the process of investigation, prosecution and trial of an offence. These two criminal laws, applicable throughout India, take precedence over any state legislation. All major offences as defined in the IPC apply to resident foreigners and citizens alike. Besides the Indian Penal Code, many special laws have also been enacted to tackle new crimes.

For functional purposes, the Indian CJS has four subsystems (Jose, 2014):

1. Legislature—the Union Parliament and State Legislatures;
2. Law enforcement—Police;
3. Adjudication—Courts and
4. Corrections—adult and juvenile correctional institutions, probation and other non-institutional dispositions

The correctional administration system in India primarily consists of three dimensions (Jose, 2014): (a) law enforcement (including preventive and investigative roles); (b) the judiciary; and (c) the correctional system. Like all democratic societies, India has also created a system of correctional services and a system of correctional administration. There are different kinds of correctional institutions, including the Prisons, Borstal Schools, Schools for Juvenile Delinquents, Remand/Observation Homes, Beggar Homes, Reception Centres, Protective Homes, State Homes and Probation Hostels. The government recognises that the process of reformation and rehabilitation of offenders is an integral part of the total process of social reconstruction, and therefore, the development of prisons and correctional services should find a place in the national development policies. However, the ground realities are quite different. While it is true that the country has moved away, at least in principle, from the erstwhile custodial approach to a reformative paradigm, the conditions in correctional institutions leave much to be desired. The concerns such as 'overcrowded prisons, prolonged detention of undertrial prisoners, unsatisfactory living conditions, lack of treatment programmes and allegations of an indifferent and even inhuman approach of prison staff' expressed by the All India Committee on Jail Reforms, chaired by Justice A. N. Mulla way back in the early eighties, seem to be quite relevant even today. In addition to the problems due to overcrowding, prolonged detention, unsatisfactory living conditions, lack of treatment programmes and inhuman approach of the staff, the correctional institutions in India are beset with a much more serious problem of a near total absence of professionally trained social workers to offer a whole range of treatment programmes for the inmates.

In the third functional dimension of correctional settings, as seen in more advanced countries, the social worker may be engaged as a case manager. Post-conviction, as a practice, the 'convicted' is handed over to the police, who 'bundles up' the person convicted and lodges him in a prison, which is administered and monitored by enforcement-oriented officers. Ideally, there must be some sort of a parallel agency to send and receive the person into the correctional setting. The social worker must prepare, induct and orientate the new entrant to the realities of the correctional setting whether it be the prison or juvenile detention centre. Subsequently, the social worker has to design a plan for programmatic intervention. Eventually, as the treatment progresses (and depending on the assessment regarding the extent of reformation) the social worker may allow the person to go on parole. The social worker may also provide feedback to the inmate's family and also allow the convicted to visit their families while on parole. In the case of probation, the necessary follow up should be undertaken by way of the social worker who is managing the case.

Reviewing the present functioning of the prison system based on the responses by key stakeholders, the authors are left to conclude that there is much to be covered to ensure that certain minimum standards of reformative services are met. There is an acute need to establish a separate Prison Department, which has qualified personnel, who are trained in criminology and social work, and have an inclination to work towards the reformation of the convicted. But unfortunately, at this point in time, there is no specific system or any training programme for the enforcers who form part of the correctional setting. Another dilemma awaits those educated and motivated to enter into prison services. They come into the service with genuine intentions and a clear motivation to serve and reform the inmates. However, unfortunately, they will be 'systematically' demoralised by the existing system, which is structured and administered by seniors who have been weaned on traditions and knowledge based on experience, and are perhaps even too numbed to be sensitive to the prevailing problems plaguing the entire correctional framework. These new entrants will be forced to undertake the 'job', and do nothing further, let alone innovate. This will inevitably create a sense of futility among the initially motivated new entrants. That said, there are very rare instances, as in the noteworthy case of Kiran Bedi IPS (Tihar fame) or Alexander Jacob IPS (the former Inspector General of Prisons, Kerala), whose zeal and dogged persistence won the hearts of the convicted and aided their reformation, and in the process beat the 'tried and tested' system.

The Problems Associated with Incarceration and Institutionalisation in India

India's CJS continues to be strained due to a lack of resources. According to the 2007 figures of the NCRB (2007), there were 376,396 inmates in India's 1,276 prisons. The following are the statistics on the CJIs with the figures of 2007 within the parenthesis. Of the CJIs: 127 (113) are Central Jails, 340 (309) are District Jails, 806 (769) are Sub-jails, 20 (16) are Women Jails,

46 (28) are Open Jails, 21 are Borstal Schools, 31 are Special Jails and 3 are Other Jails. The prisons are generally overcrowded. The NCRB (2007) figures show that except in seven states and three union territories, the inmate population was much beyond these prisons' residential capacity. In 2012, the total number of inmates in jails has been put at 3,85,169 as against a capacity of 3,43,169. Of these, 1.2 per cent of the total number of inmates lodged in various jails during 2012, were mentally ill. The occupancy rates were at 112.2 per cent, which is an improvement when compared to 115 per cent in 2010. In Uttar Pradesh and Chhattisgarh, the number of inmates was twice the capacity of prisons in these states (NCRB, 2009). Except for special categories of prisoners, like high-profile terrorists or political prisoners, life in India's jails is hard. The NCRB 2007 data quoted earlier shows that convicts comprise only 32 per cent of the total number of inmates in Indian jails; 66.6 per cent of them continue to be 'undertrials'—people who have not yet been proven guilty of their 'alleged' crimes. In 2012, this is still static at 66.2 per cent. In 2012, Chhattisgarh reported the highest overcrowding in its prisons (252.6%), followed by Delhi (193.8%). A sad tale is that a total of 344 women convicts with their 382 children and 1,226 'undertrial' women with their 1,397 children were lodged in various prisons in the country at the end of 2012.

As discussed earlier, years spent in a CJI—deservedly or undeservedly—not only isolates the person from society, but impacts him/her in other ways too (NCRB, 2007). As the Kerala High Court observed, a prisoner is a person who not only loses personal possessions but also personal relationships, as well as totally 'losing his identity', and ends up being known by 'a number'. Loss of freedom, status, possessions, dignity and the autonomy of a personal life leads to psychological problems.

Unless they are from privileged backgrounds, people who are confined in CJIs suffer even after their release. They continue to be stigmatised even after leaving the system. The label of 'criminal' is stigmatic in nature. Friends, colleagues and acquaintances in general prefer to stay away to avoid similar discrimination simply because they are deemed to be 'guilty by association'. Family relations become strained, and employment is unduly difficult to secure.

Suddenly, a career in crime becomes the 'only' option for them—that or a life tragically numbed by drug and alcohol addiction. With a few exceptions, the current correctional system does little to truly and effectively address such problems.

Areas of Social Work Intervention

The average prison employee has to deal with complexities ranging from having to manage innocent 'undertrials' to petty offenders, and still further down the spectrum, hardened criminals or organised crime. Ideologically, the 'one solution fits all' approach does not work, nor serve the purpose of rehabilitation. Herein comes the relevance of defining the diverse possibilities of social work intervention in the CJS. As previously highlighted, a study undertaken by the CHRI and Prayas, investigated 52 initiatives in eight States in Southern and Western India, and identified seven areas in which social work initiatives may be thematically focused, ultimately with the purpose of influencing state policy (CHRI, 2011): (a) moral or spiritual guidance/instruction; (b) welfare services; (c) rehabilitation activities for women and youth; (d) conducting health camps and health check-ups; (e) providing educational and vocational training/services; (f) offering legal guidance, referral services and legal aid; (g) providing other generic support to prisoners.

A cursory look of the above cited areas will immediately alert you to the fact that these are all very conventional and politically correct matters and appear to be too clinical and depersonalised. There is an absence of the soul of social work if one were to be prescriptive. The very fact that the CJIs are overcrowded as cited earlier suggests that two-thirds of these prisoners are innocents yet-to-be tried, caught in a panoptic setting where they are gullible to the influence of those hardened criminals who have been in the system for a long time. Second, there is a perennial delay in the working of the CJS that delays justice—justice delayed is justice denied. All these go against the principles of social work.

Social work in the CJS needs to perhaps adopt more individualised treatment methods in case management and even incorporate the Management by Objective approach, wherein the inmates discuss their situation with the social worker and negotiate goals pertaining to reform and behaviour modification, and agree to work together towards achievement of the same over a stipulated period of time. Such participative methodologies are likely to generate more sustainable and favourable outcomes compared to a standardised routine treatment. Besides, it is far more important that the innocent be kept out of the system, as she/he is more likely to be predisposed to a faster, conscious and more involved reform process. Herein lies another area of social work intervention. The service gaps as listed below are clear issues that would benefit from greater social work expertise.

Gaps and Recommendations

There is a dire necessity for demonstrating and advocating for greater social work interventions in the CJS. Some of the potential grey areas for social work intervention may include (Prayas, 2006):

1. prisons, to assist in reformation, rehabilitation and prevention of HIV;
2. promote the use of correctional laws towards rehabilitation of vulnerable groups especially women, youth and children;
3. increase awareness in the government and society about issues related to the rehabilitation of persons affected by crime or prostitution through legal and policy change and
4. generate knowledge in the field of social work, criminology and corrections through the analysis of field experiences.

Programmatic Content

Specific programmes may be designed for stipulated areas— custodial care, education, reformation and rehabilitation. The following programmatic interventions may be recommended based on the subsettings within the correctional setting for social work (Chockalingam & Srinivasan, 2009; Prayas, 2006):

1. *Prisons:* Focus work on the youth—women and males (18–23 years)—so as to prevent re-victimisation, by coaching, providing legal literacy, re-establishing family contact; support to families (especially children), counselling, vocational training activities, as well as networking with NGOs and government departments such as police, women and child development; health (especially with the areas of reproductive and child health, and HIV) and the judiciary towards custodial care, pre-release preparation and post-release rehabilitation issues.

2. *Protective institutions for women:* Counselling and follow up during the period of reformation; rendering psychosocial support to aid recovery from trauma, designing vocational activities suitable to their aptitude; networking with NGOs, networking with government departments such as the police, women and child development, health and the judiciary towards custodial care; pre-release preparation, repatriation and post-release rehabilitation issues.

3. *Contact-cum-rehabilitation unit:* Providing a host of services for women, youth, children and their families; approaching NGOs after their release from prison/custodial institution or upon referral by clients, ex-clients, the police, prison or institutional staff, judiciary, NGOs and community-based organisations or members of the community for the purpose of 'total' rehabilitation; extending services such as counselling, legal guidance, shelter, establishing family associations to augment family support, financial support for emergencies, arranging for medical treatment or hospitalisation, vocational training, educational support; arranging a help desk for information about suitable government schemes, access to citizenship rights, and linking up with the NGO sector towards rehabilitation and mainstreaming.

4. *Research and documentation:* Planning and undertaking research studies as well as documentation of services available, efficacy of services provided and issues in the field, with the purpose of increasing knowledge in the field of

criminology and correctional social work for the purpose of teaching, training and intervention.

5. *Policy and advocacy:* Taking up field issues with authorities and government departments concerned, with the police, prison, legal officers and judiciary, women and child development, home, youth affairs and education, both at the state and central levels; lobbying with national and state level bodies such as the National Human Rights Commission (NHRC), State Human Rights Commission (SHRC), National Commission for Women (NCW) and State Commission for Women (SCW), to create a climate conducive to rehabilitation of vulnerable groups in the CJS; involvement in Public Interest Litigation (PILs) both at the High Court as well as at the Supreme Court levels on issues related to prison conditions, trafficking, children of prisoners, rehabilitation of victims of commercial sexual exploitation and so on.

6. *Press and media:* The media plays a significant role in 'sensationalising' crime and those who commit it. It also does play a major role in shaping public perception regarding the 'criminals' and the 'prisons teeming with criminals.' There needs to be strong code of ethics in place to prevent newspapers and electronic media from compulsively holding 'media' trials and convicting women before they are even tried or convicted by the law of the land. Social workers can work towards advocating for a more measured and reasonable depiction of such news.

Issues and Perspectives

Despite the dire need for engagement with the CJS and the considerable promise that criminology holds, professional social work in India, just as any other parent discipline, has treated this subject with avoidable neglect and apathy. The reasons may be attributed to the following disturbing trends (Bajpai, 2004):

1. Teaching and engagement of criminology at the degree and postgraduate level is very limited in India.

2. Absence of a clear cut beneficiary base due to the obscure linkage between practice and profession.
3. Predominance of parent discipline (i.e., social work), which is treated philosophically and academically superior to criminology.
4. Dearth of basic research in criminology in India that would have generated indigenous theories explaining the major problems of criminality in this country.
5. Criminology is largely perceived as a discipline with restricted avenues and limited vertical mobility in relation to career advancement in India.

The Social Work Curriculum

Even though correctional administration was a part of the social work curriculum in the nascent days of the profession, the important field of correctional social work has almost been completely neglected by social work educators all over the country. However, the blame cannot be squarely put on social work educators since social work education in India has been driven largely by market forces rather than a deeply value-based mission to address the ills of society. Right from the beginning, social workers have found job placements in hospitals, and industrial and community settings. Clearly, there has been a strong demand for social work manpower specially equipped with the skills to work with patients in hospitals, employees in industry and so on at the grass root level. Owing to the non-recognition of social work as an important entity in the correctional system by policy makers and the resulting absence of patronage and job opportunities, the specialisation of correctional social work lost its charm very early in the development of the profession. Nevertheless, with its proud existence for over seven decades in the country, the profession of social work has still made inroads into several areas. However, the involvement of social workers in correctional settings has not been very significant. The situation is rather complex because, on the one hand, social work schools do not offer the specialism of correctional social work in their curriculum for fear of not getting sufficient candidates. On the other hand, since social work schools do not offer a correctional social work specialisation, budding social workers never get a chance to understand the important role social workers can play in reforming and rehabilitating inmates of correctional institutions. This, obviously, creates a vicious cycle. Somehow, this cycle needs to be broken and professional social work education should address the psycho-social needs of the inmates of correctional institutions. Correctional administration does feature in the curriculum framework in a few selected social work schools but it is offered only as one course which does not move beyond just sensitising the social work trainees to these extremely important issues.

Social work practitioners, criminologists and human rights activists are increasingly engaging in diverse issues—human trafficking, sexual harassment, domestic violence, psychotropic substances abuse and their conduit, cyberstalking, elderly abuse, child sexual abuse, domestic violence, financial frauds, hi-tech crimes, homicide, organised crime and terrorism. The host of clients range from 'suspects' to victims to convicts, from the abusers to the abused, and hardened criminals (Chockalingam & Srinivasan, 2008a; 2008b). That puts into question the competence of the key actors—especially social workers, criminologists and human rights workers—of being able to deal with and negotiate the CJS maze.

Broader issues include dealing with marginalised groups, and the increasing use of technology in the detection, investigation and prevention of crime (Hayward, 2004). Thus, professional social work needs to be sensitised to issues as diverse as capital punishment, suicide and euthanasia, forensic investigation techniques and the growing menace of cybercrime and the efficacy of related laws to deal with the same.

In a developing country like India, criminal justice settings typically reflect the inherent conflict between the citizen, the society and the Nation State or some part of it on account of the issues concerning development (Jose, 2014). There are numerous instances of social movements perceptively against central government policy being acted on by the State; there are instances of nuclearisation (Koodumkulam), establishment of projects that damage the environment (Plachimada Coca Cola Plant siphoning drinking water; the Aranmula KGN Green Field Airport Project on ecosystems wastelands) or even the burgeoning conflict between the State and the people of a district (the Tata Singaur Car Plant in West Bengal or the Gadgil Committee Reports followed through by the Kasthurirangan Report on the Biodiversity and Environment Sensitive areas of Idukki and Wayyand Districts in Kerala, India). All of these have resulted in conflict with the State allegedly engaging in 'State terrorism' (Jose, 2014). This conflict gets manifested through the enactment of laws that infringe on the life and liberty of citizens and may involve taking individuals into protective or penal custody. These 'involuntary clients' are forced by those around them, such as parents, neighbours and police, to enter into custody or to get help from social service agencies. There is also the issue of the protection of basic human and legal rights of these citizens while they are in custody. Custodialisation and legal processing (whether as victims or as offenders) inflicts social stigma and discrimination, and requires a social work response based on the dynamics of the situation rather than just on the needs of individuals involved. This demands skills in mediation and consensus building between the functionaries, families and the community (Jose, 2014).

With increasing crime in society both in terms of types and levels, there has been a concerted attempt by the State and criminal justice agencies to focus on prevention as a method of reducing crime. Citizen participation in crime prevention is essential if positive results are to be achieved in this area. Social workers in collaboration with state actors can play a crucial role in involving the community to achieve better results in reducing crime through prevention. This course of action will focus on groups vulnerable to violence and crime, site-specific crimes, and discuss the role that social workers can play in the prevention of such crimes. There would also be a focus on the development of prevention strategies with regard to specific types of crimes and against specific groups which are particularly vulnerable to victimisation. Despite the dire need for social workers to be substantively involved in helping offenders and victims of crime—unfortunately, not many have heeded the call. There are of course a number of very good reasons for this, for example, not wanting to be a part of a coercive system of social control; enforcement functions are contradictory to core social work values of caring and empowerment; clients are primarily mandated rather than voluntary and so on. That said, another significant cause could be the lack of understanding of what criminal justice social work entails, the intellectually stimulating expertise one needs to do such work, and the exciting albeit challenging employment opportunities it offers. This latter problem however can be addressed through education and professional course development.

Conclusion

The role of the CJS and correctional institutions is getting increasing attention in India these days, like other countries, due to the soaring rates of crime and detention of offenders, which has a profound detrimental impact on the society. The CJS in India is the target of severe criticism due to the exponentially increasing cases that are pending; resulting in delayed justice. On the other hand, the correctional institutions in the country are severely criticised for the overcrowding, prolonged detention, unsatisfactory living conditions, lack of treatment programmes and allegations of an indifferent and even inhuman approach of CJS staff. Unlike in other advanced countries, professional social work in India has still not made its presence felt in the correctional environment owing to several reasons. The profession has deviated from its original mission which was embedded in the cherished value of service to humanity to a more mundane function of supplying manpower to suit the market-driven economy's demands. However, it is high time the profession of social work realises its mandate, sets its course right and starts addressing humanitarian concerns in all sectors, including the correctional system.

References

Bajpai, G. S. (2004). *Criminology: An appraisal of present status and future directions.* Retrieved from http://www.forensic.to/webhome/drgs-bajpai/criminology%20appraisal.pdf

Beccaria, C., & Davies, R. (1995). *On crimes and punishments, and other writings*. Cambridge, MA: Cambridge University Press.

Chockalingam, K., & Srinivasan, M. (2008a). Evaluation of the implementation of the victims' assistance fund in Tamil Nadu. *The Indian Journal of Criminology and Criminalistics, XXIX*(1), 8–19.

————. Perception of victim treatment by police and courts: A study among university students in India and Japan. *Temida, 11*(3), 63–78.

Chockalingam, K., & Vijaya, A. (2008). Sexual harassment of women in public transport in Chennai city: A victimological perspective. *The Indian Journal of Criminology and Criminalistics, 30*(3), 167–84.

Commonwealth Human Rights Initiative (CHRI). (2011). *Community participation in prisons: A civil society perspective*. Retrieved from http://www.humanrightsinitiative.org/publications/prisons/community_participation_in_prisons.pdf

Hayward, K. J. (2004). *City limits: Crime, consumer culture and the urban experience*. London: Glasshouse Press.

Jose, S. (2014). Criminal justice system in India: A case for social work intervention. *Adelaide Journal of Social Work, 1*(1), 61–82.

Martin, E. A. (1997). *A Dictionary of Law* (4th ed.). Oxford: Oxford University Press.

Muncie, J., & Fitzgerald, M. (1981). Humanizing the deviant: Affinity and affiliation theories. In M. Fitzgerald, G. McLennan & J. Pawson (Eds.), *Crime and society: Readings in history and theory*. London: Routledge & Kegan Paul/The Open University Press.

Nair, C. S. (1993). A convict prisoner in the Central Prison vs. State of Kerala. *Criminal Law Journal*, 3242. Retrieved from https://indiankanoon.org/doc/25915/

National Crime Records Bureau (NCRB). (2007). *National Crime Report—2007*. New Delhi: Ministry of Home Affairs, Government of India.

————. (2009). *National Crime Report—2009*. New Delhi: Ministry of Home Affairs, Government of India.

————. (2012). *National Crime Report—2012*. New Delhi: Ministry of Home Affairs, Government of India.

Pearsall, J., & Trumble, B. (1995). *The Oxford Encyclopaedic English Dictionary* (2nd ed.). New York: Oxford University Press.

Prayas. (2006). *Report of the district level workshop on 'laws related to rehabilitation of offenders in criminal justice' organised by the district and sessions court, Thane & Prayas*. Tata Institute of Social Sciences, held at 'Manthan', Thane: Prayas.

Vadiraj, S., Gopal, A., Sir Dorabji Tata Trust and the Allied Trusts (SDTT), & Sahni, S. (2011). *Social work in India's criminal justice institutions: Need, experiences and challenges*. Mumbai: SDTT.

6

Reviving Criminal Justice Social Work through Probation in India: Historical Solutions to Contemporary Problems

Roshni Nair and Vijay Raghavan

Introduction

Probation as a community-based alternative to imprisonment has been in existence for a little over two centuries now. Its origins have been traced to the harshness of English penal law in the Middle Ages and subsequent developments in Britain and the United States in the early and mid-nineteenth century. It gradually spread as a movement across the world and came to be established as a scientific method of rehabilitation of offenders by the twentieth century. By the 1950s, probation was being celebrated for its cost-effectiveness and harm-reducing results on the offenders' lives in comparison to imprisonment as a penal philosophy. Probation as a sentencing tool was based on the premise that the individual alone cannot be held responsible for the wrongdoing he/she was convicted for; society has a role in helping the person make amends, through a re-learning process which plays out within the social milieu and citizenship space of the offending individual.

The probation officer (PO) has been a key player in the probation system right from the days of John Augustus (considered to be the 'Father of Probation' during the nineteenth century), and literature abounds on the myriad roles he/she plays from identifying 'eligible' cases, filing social investigation reports, supervision, mentoring, to monitoring and reporting relapses. It has also been well recognised that many of the roles and responsibilities of the PO require social work grounding and skills. In fact, social work and probation share a historical connection. There is evidence to show that the correctional social worker and the PO cross their paths at many points in their developmental journeys (Panakkal & Dighe, 1961).

The movement from an institutional to a community focus form of punishment emerged by the 1970s in the United States (Johnson, 1978, p. 527, cited in Srivastava, 1980, p. 135; Rosenthal & Luger, 1974, p. 19, cited in Srivastava, 1980, p. 135). The US National Advisory Commission on Criminal Justice Standards and Goals (1973, p. 1, cited in Srivastava, 1980, p. 136) highlighted the limitations of correctional institutions, stating that they brought about more negative change and made successful reintegration back into the community less likely. It came to be recognised that correctional agencies alone cannot correct criminal behaviour as crime was rooted in social causes (Carney, 1977, p. 43, cited in Srivastava, 1980, p. 135). This change in ideology generated further discussion concerning rehabilitation and its challenges. The rehabilitation of the offender is seen now as the joint effort of the offender, professional social worker and the community.

Changing Focus of Probation Systems around the World

Despite its glorious past, probation as a system and the social work role of the PO has undergone radical shifts and changes in the last three decades or so. This shift was triggered by the increasing despair amongst experts, policy makers and civil society since the mid-1970s about the apparent failure of correctional strategies to combat the rising crime trends in Western countries, particularly the United States and the United Kingdom. This gave rise to the 'nothing works' ideology and an era of policy reversals with regard to the rapid strides made towards the de-institutionalisation process and community-based correctional treatment methods in the preceding half a century (Cullen & Gendreau, 2001). A cursory glance of the literature highlights the crisis of probation, whereby the system, almost turned on its head, is now aimed at keeping tabs on offenders to prevent crime and protect potential victims, rather than facilitating the social re-entry of offenders. The literature also suggests that with the growth of neoliberal regimes, the focus of criminal justice systems (CJSs) have shifted from penal welfarism (Garland, 2001) to harsher laws, more and longer terms of imprisonment and the rise of the penal state, which Wacquant (2010) so eloquently describes as a political economy of restrictive *workfare* and expansive *prisonfare* in the context of growing social insecurity. The following section will take a closer look at some of the changes that have taken place across the globe in this direction.

The CJS in the United States has come a long way from its earlier focus on community corrections, probation and parole to its current heavy reliance on imprisonment for all categories of offences, harsher sentences and an increasing trend of privatisation of prisons, marked by a reduced focus on social services (Rosenthal, 2004). In the United States, as in England and Wales, the traditional function of probation was to support clients towards their rehabilitation and reintegration into society, a role not dissimilar to social work intervention. With the penal regime ideology changing from rehabilitation to risk management, the thrust of the US probation system is now less on therapy and more on surveillance, control and risk management. The PO's role has changed from being a professional rehabilitation agent to that of a referral negotiator, with reduced direct involvement with individuals (Teague, 2011).

In the United Kingdom, the 'prison works' philosophy of the Conservative government in the 1990s gave way to the 'what works' adage, coined by the Labour Party when it was elected to office in 1997. These developments have eventually led to a managerialist approach and technical policy fixes in the probation system, at the cost of the human element and client–worker dynamic so characteristic of the probationer–probation officer relationship (Burke & Collet, 2010).

France has held on to traditional practices like one-to-one supervision, but POs have very heavy caseloads, with many of them functioning in a part-time capacity. French probation services have long abandoned social work. In 1993, they introduced a new cadre called CPIP, or Insertion and Probation Councillors, mainly comprising of lawyers as POs. They even deleted the term 'social worker' from the probation rules in its Criminal Procedure Code (CrPC). The current staff face stress and pessimism and function as remote supervisors. Elements of managerialism and increased paperwork designed to standardise procedures have further affected the quality of services. POs were earlier in two spaces: in the prison and in the community. Later, these two were merged and attached to the prison administration. Probation was thus influenced by the prison disciplinary system of governance. There was, therefore, a general decline of social work in the French probation system, due to a 'tick box' type of supervision, and increased recruitment of lawyers, due to disinterested and disillusioned staff. The prison system's domination of probation has damaged its efficiency. The future of probation in France is in turmoil, with the political economy not supporting new positions, a lack of evidence-based programmes and a section of academics (especially lawyers and sociologists) campaigning against the use of criminology itself in probation work. It is now up to the policies and ideology of the existing governments that will influence the direction of probation in France (Herzog-Evans, 2011).

Probation was introduced in Belgium in 1964 and was limited to cases of drug and sexual offences. In 1994, it was extended to all offences punishable with a maximum of five years of imprisonment. POs are university graduates in social work, psychology, criminology, sociology or education. In recent years, probation services have been at the receiving end of public ire and political pressure, leading to reforms introduced since 2000 in the form of a business process re-engineering (BPR) programme. The aim of the BPR was to bring greater objectivity, standardisation and managerialism towards the delivery of a consistent service to the public and to offenders (Bauwens, 2009).

In response to the myriad changes taking place in probation systems across Europe, in 2010 the European Probation Curriculum Group (EPCG) was set up to carry out research into probation curricula and to develop a European approach to probation training. It found different practices being followed. For example, in some countries, POs work as trained social workers, whereas in others, they are part of the prison service, albeit with distinct roles. They called for a benchmarking of European probation training and a clarifying of the relationship between probation and prison services. The issue of location of training—within social work or outside of it—was also a bone of contention. Another issue was whether case work based on the social work approach and case management based on a risk assessment approach were compatible with one another. The EPCG identified seven competencies in probation rules:

1. To develop working relationships with voluntary and involuntary clients
2. To communicate with voluntary and involuntary clients
3. To write reports
4. To assess offender behaviour
5. To plan and deliver evidence-based interventions
6. To work with diversity
7. To work in an inter-agency way

The report found that communication and forming working relationships with clients are essential aspects of probation work everywhere. It expressed a concern about how to blend the social work orientation and the risk assessment approach into one coherent educational programme, suggesting that this could be achieved through a modular framework. It called for developing new competencies among POs towards management of working with victims (Durnescu & Stout, 2011).

The Japanese system, like in parts of Europe, is heavily reliant on voluntary POs, and non-governmental organisations (NGOs) managed aftercare hostels and post-release supervision processes. The involvement of NGOs is an attempt to shed the load off the government, overwhelmed by rising costs of providing services to released prisoners. It has been found that voluntary POs are not trained or paid well, giving rise to issues of quality. Japan treats crime as a community phenomenon and so believes in public involvement in the control of criminal behaviour. The Japanese system administers a 'straight [form of] probation' with an attendance requirement but no other conditions or programmes attached to it (Ellis, Lewis, & Sato, 2011).

In Australia, the probation and parole system was replaced with community-based corrections framework that was attached to the prison service in 1987. The social work approach thus gave way to achieve a greater alignment with the role of prison officers. There was a paradigm shift from the needs-based, welfare-rehabilitation model to a justice model, based on offender management. The adoption of the title 'Community Corrections' led to a de-professionalisation of the role of the correctional staff and affected the type and level of training received by new entrants. Some concerns that emerged were of the adoption of international trends unquestioningly (e.g., 'prison works'), without due consideration to their appropriateness in the local context. Legislative efforts are now focussed on reverting to probation and parole, since the latter was found to have greater public acceptance. While Australia has begun its journey to reclaim probation, it still needs to adjust itself to the change in ideology and its related demands and concerns (Harker & Worrall, 2011).

Russia's journey in corrections has been fairly recent. Since 1989, some of the changes adopted include the introduction of rights-based work and improvement of prison conditions (Bowing, 2009; Piacentini, 2007, both cited in Harding & Davies, 2011, p. 355). With the influence of international protocols, and being a member of the European Council, two new experiments were carried out around 2007–09: one, a microlevel training of POs and the other, a macrolevel policy change with regard to strengthening alternative sentences. Psychologists are part of the probation system both in the prisons and in the community (Piacentini & King, 2007, p. 357, cited in Harding & Davies, 2011). Overall, there has been a hesitant and uncertain development of the probation system in Russia. The probation system has faced the same problems as its European counterparts—overworked staff, resource crunch, short staffing of partner agencies, standardised assessments tools and limited accredited intervention programmes. Some of the problems identified were lack of adequate training, insufficient time spent by staff with probationers and the dismissive attitude of the CJS staff of POs (Harding & Davies, 2011).

The Korean probation system is also comparatively young, about 20 years old, and is currently engaged in organisational change and ethical reshaping. The Koreans use community volunteers who assist POs in the process of rehabilitation of probationers, especially with job placement, individual counselling and family support. By using volunteers, the community is directly involved in the supervision of the offender. The focus of the probation system, however, has been changing from the offender's rehabilitation to community protection in recent years, as has been witnessed in the West. This has led to a shift away from human rights, welfare and humanitarianism towards public security emerging as the core priority. This is to be achieved through the use of technology in the management of dangerous offenders. The Korean probation system uses technology more than Western Europe. The future of probation supervision may be less of a traditional face-to-face and individualised supervision approach and more carried out through the use of technological innovations like cyber probation offices and web-based education programmes. Contemporary probation practice in South Korea is somewhat in a state of flux, and future practice seems to prioritise the use of technology as the core tool of effective supervision of offenders. It may also try to align itself with police work in terms of alleviating the fear of crime in society (Gough, 2011).

It emerges from the above discussion that the winds of change accompanying neoliberalism have hardly spared any nation in the move towards a shrinking welfare state and consequent fiscal cuts in penal welfare expenditures (Raghavan, 2013). It is in this context that we need to understand the changes taking place in probation services in India, which were part of the penal welfare architecture.

Probation Services in India

The roots of probation in India can be traced to the penal laws of the country enacted in 1878. Sections 562, 563 and 564 of the CrPC provided for the release on a bond of good behaviour of male offenders below the age of 21 years and women of all ages, as long as they were not convicted of an offence punishable with death or transportation for life. In a case where there was no previous conviction, the court could release the offender on condition of his or her entering into a bond with or without sureties and to appear and receive sentence if he or she does not maintain the terms of release.

The first legislative effort in India in the direction of probation was the enactment of Section 562 in the CrPC in 1898. It was applied to offenders of theft, theft in a building, dishonest appropriation, cheating or any other offence under the Indian Penal Code punishable for not more than two years. This was amended in 1974 as Section 360 of CrPC, to read as follows:

> When any person not under 21 years of age is convicted of an offence punishable with fine only or with imprisonment for a term of 7 years or less, or when any person under 21 years of age or any woman is convicted of an offence not punishable with death or imprisonment for life and no previous conviction is proved against the offender, if it appears to the Court before which he is convicted, regard being had to the age, character or antecedents of the offender, and to the circumstances in which the offence was committed, that it is expedient that the offender should be released on probation of good conduct, the Court may, instead of sentencing him at once to any punishment, direct that he be released on his entering into a bond, with or without sureties, to appear and receive sentence when called upon during such period (not exceeding three years) as the Court may direct and in the meantime to keep the peace and be of good behaviour.

Section 361 of the CrPC made it mandatory for the judge to declare the reasons for not awarding the benefit of probation to the offender. The Probation of Offenders Act was passed in 1958 with jurisdiction throughout the territory of India (except the state of Jammu and Kashmir, which legislates its own laws, as per Article 370 of the Indian Constitution). 1971 was celebrated as the 'Year of Probation' and this period indicates a collective interest in probation philosophy. A national law was in place, various states enacted their state rules and its implementation structure was defined and located either with the government, quasi-government or civil society organisations.

However, since the 1980s, the probation system has witnessed a steady decline in terms of the importance it carries as a judicial mechanism and the infrastructure made available by the state to implement the law. It is interesting to note that this decline has corresponded with the decline in correctional philosophy in the West, as highlighted in the earlier section. By the late 1970s and the early 1980s, social welfare policy in India gradually shifted from the protection of socially excluded populations to a larger focus on poverty alleviation. One of the outcomes of this process was that investments in the welfare sector reduced considerably in terms of institutional mechanisms, human resources, training and service delivery (Raghavan, 2013).

The authors have a first-hand experience of witnessing the decline in probation services in the state of Maharashtra in India, where they have been engaging with the probation services wing of the administration since the early 1990s through the placement of students for their field work, as part of the curriculum of the Master's programme in Social Work at the Tata Institute of Social Sciences (TISS). One of the authors has been actively associated with Prayas ('effort' in the Hindi language), a field action project[1] of the Centre for Criminology and Justice, School of Social Work, TISS, which has been working with the CJS since 1990 through social work intervention to promote legal rights and rehabilitation of vulnerable populations being processed by the justice system.[2] The experiences of the authors led to the idea of doing a study on the implementation status of the Probation of

---

[1] Field action projects are experimental and demonstration projects which have played a 'major role in piloting or pioneering new services' through social work intervention by its faculty, students and project staff 'with the objective of demonstrating to the public, the need for such services' (TISS, 2001, p. 5, cited in Dave, Raghavan, & Solanki, 2012.). To know more about field action projects of TISS, visit http://www.tiss.edu/TopMenuBar/field-action/projects.

[2] For more details about the work of Prayas, visit http://www.tiss.edu/TopMenuBar/field-action/projects/prayas.

Offenders Act, 1958, in the state of Maharashtra from the view-point of the key actor in the implementation of the Act, that is, the PO. The study was based on qualitative methodology, using in-depth interviews with POs, prison officers and the district level judiciary across the state, and supplemented by interviews with key informants. The findings from the study confirmed some of the hunches that the authors had and also gained some new and interesting insights on what ails the probation services in the state (Nair, Mukundan, & Raghavan, 2008). The following section is largely based on the findings from this study.

It needs to be mentioned that it may be hasty to conclude that this study is representative of the situation of probation and correctional social work in India, given the diversity of a country as vast and as complex as India. However, Maharashtra is a state of great contrasts; parts of the state have far better than national averages when compared with the best performing states in the country, while other parts fall well below the national average when compared with the worst performing states, in terms of economic growth and human development indicators. Mumbai is its capital and is often referred to as the commercial capital of the country. It is seen as a city of dreams, of surviving against the odds, with many a-rags-to-riches stories to be told. Conversely, more than 60 per cent of the population lives in extremely congested and unsanitary conditions, with poor access to water, health and education facilities. Mumbai has also been the centre of under-world activities with a flourishing illegal economy, directed and regulated by criminal gangs and mafia dons (Raghavan, 2012, pp. 356–58).

Probation Services in Maharashtra

History of Probation in Maharashtra

Very little documentation about the history of probation in Maharashtra is available. The TISS study (Nair et al., 2008) made an attempt to construct the history of probation services in Maharashtra based on interviews with retired POs and senior officials who were a part of the probation system over the past four decades. The following section is constructed from these interviews.

The first probation law in the state was passed during the colonial period known as the Bombay Probation Act, 1938, applicable to the Bombay Presidency, and its rules were framed in 1940. The Act was meant for the rehabilitation of young adult offenders, especially in the age group of 16–21 years. The Act was administered under the supervision of the Director, Department of Social Welfare, who was also designated as the Director, Correctional Services and Chief Inspector under the Act. A Chief Probation Officer was appointed to oversee the implementation of the Act and he/she was assisted by POs and clerical staff appointed at the district level.

After India gained independence, the Bombay Probation Act, 1938, was repealed and replaced with the Probation of Offenders Act, 1958 (PO Act), with jurisdiction throughout the territory of India, except for the state of Jammu and Kashmir (as explained in the earlier section). In 1960, Maharashtra was carved out from Bombay state. Thereafter, the Maharashtra Probation Rules were formulated in 1966. The onus of the implementation of the law was placed with the Department of Social Welfare.

As per the 1966 State Rules, probation work is under the control of a District Probation Officer (DPO) at the district level. Initially, District Probation Offices were established, and DPOs were appointed in a few districts in Maharashtra. By 1970, the probation system was established in nearly all 28 districts of the state. But the implementation of the Act required coordination with the prison department which came under the Home Department. The then Inspector General (IG) of Prisons highlighted these difficulties to the government, leading to a decision transferring the implementation of the PO Act from the Department of Social Welfare to the Prison Department, under the Office of the IG Prisons, with additional role as the Director of Correctional Services.

The literature suggests that during this period, the POs would regularly visit prisons in the state, contact inmates and take up cases *suo moto* for follow-up and rehabilitation. They would visit courts and request judges to refer cases under the PO Act for pre-sentence inquiries. Apart from this, the POs would arrange for shelter, vocational training, self-employment and explore employment opportunities for probationers and released prisoners. Through such efforts, the POs had carved out a role for themselves within the CJS, with a focus on corrections.

The Home Department, under which the IG Prisons' Office existed, restructured the composition of the PO wing to appoint a Probation Superintendent at the state level, Probation Inspectors at the divisional level and DPOs at the district level with POs working under them. A liaison officer was appointed in each of the eight Central Prisons, from among the POs, to look into the psycho-social and rehabilitative needs of convicted prisoners. The job profile of these officers was to 'liaise' between the prisoner and his/her family and carry out their requests such as looking into property disputes in their native place, the institutionalisation of their children in the absence of local guardians, arranging for emergency assistance to the family, etc.

Though the implementation of the PO Act was under the IG Prisons (as the Director of Correctional Services), the powers of recruitment, transfer and promotions were reserved with the Department of Social Welfare. The probation staff was part of the cadre belonging to the Department of Social Welfare and was 'deputed' to the IG Prisons' Office to work as POs. In 1976, based on a complaint forwarded to the government by the Director of Correctional Services, a representative of the IG Prisons' Office was involved in the recruitment process of the probation staff, and the transfer of POs was likewise brought under the control of the IG Prisons. Similarly, reimbursement of expenses and leave were handed over to the IG Prisons' Office. However, the authority for promotions remained with the Department of Social Welfare.

There was, however, an exception to the rule. Bombay, though a part of Maharashtra and the capital city, was not under the control of the Director of Correctional Services. It was under the control of the Maharashtra Probation and Aftercare Association, an NGO. This NGO had also made a request to the government for handling the work of probation in four to five adjoining districts of Bombay.

Changing Focus of Probation

As a result of continued demands made on the government relating to structural issues, the Correctional Wing was finally separated from the Prison Department in 1994 and brought under the Department of Women and Child Development (DWCD), which had been carved out from the erstwhile Department of Social Welfare. Over time, the post of the DPO and POs was brought under the supervision of the District Women & Child Development Officer (DWCDO) and the post of probation inspectors was abolished. In the newly established structure, the DPOs reported to the DWCDO at the district level and to the Probation Superintendent and the Commissioner, DWCD, at the state Headquarters. All POs and staff earlier reporting to the DPO are now directly reported to the DWCDO. The financial powers of the 'Drawing and Disbursal Officer' (DDO) that had been given to the DPO were withdrawn and handed over to the DWCDO. Gradually, the DPO and the POs were engaged in other tasks assigned to them by the DWCDO, such as inspection of children's and women's institutions and the implementation of a plethora of social legislation which came under the purview of the DWCD. The PO Act was ranked very low in the priority of the work assigned to the DWCDO, and the DPO and POs became de facto support staff of the DWCDO. Posts for liaison officers for the Central Prisons in the state have since similarly been discontinued.

It was during the decades of the 1960s and the 1970s that probation was a subject of interest for both practitioners and the academia. Research papers, articles and seminar proceedings around the subject during this period are evidence of this. Subsequently, there has been academic silence for many years, while the few writings emerging on the issue have largely arisen from field-based interventions in their attempts to draw attention to the law and its importance. A study conducted in two of Mumbai's prisons indicated that of the undertrial prisoners interviewed, nearly 90 per cent were eligible for release on probation (Prayas, 2002).

Probation could have naturally grown as the face of corrections in India. Its ideology was based on individual intervention which it shares closely with case work as a method of social work practice. But the diminishing focus on welfare and corrections since the late 1970s and 1980s and the increasing focus on security have led to the gradual neglect and decay of the system.

Issues Emerging from the Study

Some of the findings from the TISS study (2008) highlight the current state of probation and correctional social work. For example, the human resource allocation in terms of the number of POs was found to be standardised across the districts (one DOP and three POs), irrespective of the number of courts and the population in each district, thus creating a differential impact on their workload and, therefore, the quality of their work.

With regard to the profile of the POs, it was found that the number of male POs far exceeded that of the female POs. This has implications for women prisoners' access to POs. It was found that the last direct recruitment of POs was done in 1999, after which channels of promotion were opened up to clerical staff and supervisors of other government programmes, who had neither the necessary social work qualifications nor the relevant experience relating to probation or rehabilitation work. Post-induction training was reduced to a couple of weeks from the earlier 3–6 months of training. The frequency of refresher training has also substantially reduced over time. These changes have seriously compromised the quality of work undertaken by the POs in the state.

With regard to the interface with the judiciary, very few judicial officials were well acquainted with the names of the DPOs and POs in their districts, thus indicating the nature and frequency of their interaction. We also found the absence of a feedback mechanism from the courts regarding the final outcome of the pre-sentence investigation reports submitted by POs, which demotivates them from submitting good quality reports. It was also observed that some magistrates release convicted persons on probation without calling for the report of the PO, due to the pressure on them for early disposal of cases.

As far as the interface with the prison system was concerned, it was found that there were no fixed days of the week or the month for prison visits by the POs, which impacted the visibility of the POs in the system. It also emerged that there were no regular meetings between the POs, prison officials and the judiciary, and the lack of communication among them leads to the creation of mistrust and crisis of confidence about probation services.

We found that a high percentage of posts of the POs were lying vacant, due to expenditure cuts and given that they are used for other work related to the DWCD (as mentioned earlier), the POs came across as highly demoralised and lacking in drive and enthusiasm to deliver results. The fact that POs are ranked very low in the hierarchy of government officers[3] adds to their poor image and impact quotient.

Conclusion

In India, as has emerged from this chapter, the philosophy of community-based corrections is a long way off. Critical criminology, which places the onus of crime commission as much, if not more, on social structure and social exclusion processes has had little impact on penal policy in India. Neoliberalism has severely dented the initial impetus to probation and community-based corrections, and one can witness a clear move towards the recreation of the penal state. Despite these measures not impacting the rising crime statistics, the narrative continues to be one of calling for harsher laws and more imprisonment (Dornin, 2012).

It is in this context that the scope of community-based corrections needs re-evaluation. The solution may lie in widening the

---

[3] POs are Class III ranked officers, whereas the DWCDO is a Class I ranked officer, as are judicial officers, whereas as a prison superintendent is either a Class II or Class I officer, depending on the size of the prison they manage. This difference in their ranks creates problems relating to their confidence, credibility and status to be treated as equals, according to the POs interviewed in the TISS study.

probation net, community service programmes for first time and youth offenders, liberalising parole, de-institutionalising juvenile corrections and employing restorative justice for less serious offences. There is an urgent need to demonstrate the utility of probation and community service through evidence-based research and narratives of beneficiaries, for whom being on probation changed their lives (Srivastava, 1980). This question assumes significance in the context of a growing crime rate and an increasing trend of custodialisation of offender groups by the state to solve the problem of crime.

Six decades ago, at a seminar on probation services organised at TISS, Pardesi (1958) stated how probation started as a social work initiative and developed into a scientific and well-tried method in the field of correctional administration (cited in Panakkal & Dighe, 1961). Over the years, the centrality of the role of the PO in the correctional and rehabilitative context has been compromised in both the juvenile and adult CJS. The potential of the PO Act and the role of the PO in reducing custodial populations, diversion and rehabilitation need to be brought centre stage. In these neoliberal times, the introduction and strengthening of the role of the social worker in the CJS seems a difficult proposition. It is in this context that the probation system can play a lead role in re-establishing criminal justice social work, and the PO can be a key actor to demonstrate the role of the criminal justice social worker. This may have a salutary effect on reducing crime and victimisation of citizens.

References

Bauwens, A. (2009). Probation officers perspectives on recent Belgian changes in the probation service. *Probation Journal, 56*(3), 257–68. doi: 10.1177/0264550509337456

Burke, L., & Collett, S. (2010). People are not things: What new Labour has done to probation. *Probation Journal, 57*(3), 232–49. doi: 10.1177/0264550510373957

Cullen, F. T., & Gendreau, P. (2001). From nothing works to what works: Changing professional ideology in the 21st century. *The Prison Journal, 81*(3), 313–38.

Dave, A., Raghavan, V., and Solanki, D. (2012). Centrality of field action in social work education: A case for socio-legal work. *Social Change, 42* (4), 451–66.

Dornin, C. (2012). Sex offender laws are based on rage and fear. *Corrections. com*. Retrieved from http://www.corrections.com/news/article/30085

Durnescu, I., & Stout, B. (2011). A European approach to probation training: An investigation into the competencies required. *Probation Journal, 58*(4), 395–405. doi: 10.1177/0264550511420749

Ellis, T., Lewis, C., & Sato, M. (2011). The Japanese probation service: A third sector template? *Probation Journal, 58*(4), 333–44. doi: 10.1177/0264550511420750

Garland, D. (2001). *Culture of control: Crime and social order in contemporary society*. Chicago: University of Chicago Press.

Gough, D. (2011). Probation in the Republic of Korea: A compressed journal to public protection. *Probation Journal, 58*(4), 372–85. doi: 10.1177/0264550511422738

Harding, J., & Davies, K. (2011). Step by steppe: Progressing probation in Russia. *Probation Journal, 58*(4), 355–63. doi: 10.1177/0264550511421586

Harker, H., & Worrall, A. (2011). From 'community corrections' to 'probation and parole' in Western Australia. *Probation Journal, 58*(4), 364–71. doi: 10.1177/0264550511421517

Herzog-Evans, M. (2011). Probation in France: Some things old, some things new, some things borrowed, and often blue. *Probation Journal, 58*(4), 345–54. doi: 10.1177/0264550511420795

Nair, R., Mukundan, A., & Raghavan, V. (2008). *Status of the implementation of the Probation of Offenders Act: An insider's viewpoint*. Mumbai: TISS.

Panakkal, J. J., & Dighe, K. G. (1961). Probation. *The Indian Journal of Social Work, 22*(2), 143–62.

Prayas. (2002). *Report of the district level workshop on 'laws relating to rehabilitation of offenders in criminal justice'*. Mumbai: TISS. Retrieved from http://www.tiss.edu/TopMenuBar/field-action/publications/prayas-publications

Raghavan, V. (2012). Entry into crime and getting out: Male youth involved in criminal gangs in Mumbai. *Indian Journal of Social Work, 73*(3), 349–72.

———. (2013). Social work intervention in criminal justice: Field-theory linkage. In S. Singh (Ed.), *Social work and social development: Perspectives from India and the United States* (pp. 265–89). Chicago: Lyceum Books Inc.

Rosenthal, M. G. (2004). *The punitive (un)welfare state: U.S. penal policy in comparative perspective*. Retrieved from http://www.adelphi.edu/peoplematter/pdfs/Rosenthal.pdf

Srivastava, S. P. (1980). Community based corrections: A criminological perspective. *The Indian Journal of Social Work, 41*(2), 135–45.

Teague, M. (2011). Probation in America: Armed, private and unaffordable? *Probation Journal, 58*(4), 317–32. doi: 10.1177/0264550511421518

Wacquant, L. (2010). Crafting the neoliberal state: Workfare, prisonfare and social insecurity. *Sociological Forum, 25*(2), 197–220. doi: 10.1111/j.1573-7861.2010.01173.x

7

Social Work Intervention in Juvenile Justice

K. P. Asha Mukundan

Introduction

In India, the Juvenile Justice (Care and Protection of Children) Act 2015 (referred to as the JJ Act in this chapter) is the law designed to safeguard the rights of all children and protect them from abuse and exploitation as enshrined in the Indian Constitution[1] and the United Nations Convention on the Rights of the Children.[2] From the year 2000, the JJ Act categorises children into two broad groups, namely a 'Child in Need of Care and Protection' (a CNCP is also referred to as a 'child') and a 'Child in Conflict with Law' (a CCL is also referred to as a 'juvenile'). Correspondingly, it has established differential procedures for their functioning to be carried out by two competent authorities, namely the Child Welfare Committee (CWC) for the CNCP and the Juvenile Justice Board (JJB) for the CCLs. The rest of the key stakeholders which engage with the Juvenile Justice System (JJS) include the police, probation officers, counsellors, staff working

---

[1] The Indian Constitution was adopted in 1949, and came into effect in 1950.

[2] India has ratified the United Nations–Convention on the Rights of the Children in the year 1992.

in the residential home or custodial setting, civil society organisations, non-government organisations (NGOs) and other educational and vocational institutions.

A child or a juvenile is defined as any person who has not reached 18 years of age.[3] The minimum age of culpability for a juvenile is stated as seven years of age,[4] below which the actions of the child are not deemed to be an offence. The definition of a CNCP is kept wide in the JJ Act to include victims of every crime and societal circumstances, as well as those who could be potential victims. This definition can arguably be expanded to encompass a CCL, that is, even though an offender, the CCL is eligible to receive care and protection.

It is a known fact that children are amongst the most vulnerable in society. Within this vulnerable group, CCLs are an invisible subgroup—be it in society, within legal provisions or within the social and developmental sectors. The number of organisations that work towards the rehabilitation of CCLs from a holistic perspective of psychological, social, legal and economical spheres is limited.

The reason for this can be attributed to the misperception that working with juveniles requires primarily legal intervention with minimal social work intervention, whereas working with children requires primarily social work intervention with little or no legal intervention. Another reason for the lack of intervention in relation to CCLs can also be because of a lack of organisations wanting to fund such measures. The issues related to CCLs are seen as a state subject and not a matter falling within the arena of 'child protection'.

The documented text on intervention with respect to CCLs is limited to the analysis of various high courts and Supreme Court judgements on the subject, interpretation and critique of the JJ Act and the impact of the institutionalisation of children. There

---

[3] However, the recent JJ Act has permitted juveniles aged between 16 and 18 years who have been accused of a crime that carries a punishment of a prison sentence of at least seven years or more, to be prosecuted as an adult if the JJB finds that the offence was committed with their full knowledge and understanding of the consequences of their actions.

[4] Section 80 of the Indian Penal Code.

is, therefore, little written discourse available on social work intervention with CCLs in India.

Besides this, it is arguable that there are no accurate and reliable statistics, either at the national or state level, which reflect the true quantum of offences committed by juveniles. While the national crime rate is compiled by the National Crime Records Bureau (NCRB),[5] they too admit that 'the data supplied by most of the states/Union Territories/cities fail to satisfy various consistency checks prescribed by us' (Kumari, 2004). Another reason for the unreliability of data is because the NCRB uses 'Registration of First Information Report (FIR)'[6] as its source of information on crime (Government of India, 2011, p. 27). FIRs cannot be considered as an accurate source as they register the names of those accused in the crime. Those accused may eventually be found not guilty for the offence. So technically, the NCRB data must be read in the light of this important qualification. In this context, if the statistics of the NCRB are to be quoted, then the incidence of juvenile crime rate is as given in Table 7.1.

The statistics show that the percentage of juvenile crimes constitutes about 1.2 per cent of the total number of crimes in the country. There are no official figures to distinguish between serious and non-serious offences. The NCRB statistics also show that more than 95 per cent of these offences are committed by boys, and only the remainder by girls. Additionally, it shows that 53 per cent of juveniles hail from families earning ₹25,000 a year. Finally, the data reflect a dwindling number of cases registered when there is a corresponding increase in the economic status of the offender.

In the given context, this chapter will attempt to document the scope and relevance of social work intervention in the JJS, and the various challenges faced by the social worker at the ideological, administrative and procedural levels. It will look into the

---

[5] The NCRB, under the Ministry of Home Affairs, collects and publishes data on crime against children and juvenile delinquency on the basis of administrative records.

[6] The FIR is filed by the police when an offence is complained. It may name the suspects who are accused of committing a crime.

Table 7.1:
Incidence of Juvenile Crime Rate in India

Crime Head	2008	2009	2010	2011	2012	2013	2014
Total Crime	2,093,379	2,121,345	2,224,831	2,325,575	2,387,188	2,647,722	2,851,563
Total Juvenile Crimes	24,535	23,926	22,740	25,125	27,936	31,725	33,526
Percentage of Juvenile Crimes Against Total Crime in India	1.2	1.1	1	1.1	1.2	1.2	1.2

working of various Justice Delivery Systems (JDS)[7] and the apathy displayed in the delivery of justice. It will aim to project how justice should not be limited to positivist laws or legislative frameworks, but that it should contextualise the social-economic-cultural milieu of the individuals in question.

The JJS in India is a part of the larger adult criminal justice system (CJS). Except for the CWC and the JJB, the JDS for the JJ Act are a part of the CJS and do not exclusively work for juveniles. The problem related to this inclusive system is the difference in ideology between the two systems. The aim/goal of the CJS is rooted in the principle of punishment for the offender, while the ultimate aim of the JJS is to rehabilitate the offender. These two ideologies require a different mindset/perception, knowledge base and skill. Unfortunately, the JDS for the JJS are trained only for the CJS. These realities are a challenge for social work intervention which the author will try to flesh out in this chapter.

History of the 'Socio-legal' Journey in India

The seeds of the socio-legal approach can be traced to the legal doctrine of *parens patriae*, evolved in 1772, in the English Courts of Chancery. The philosophy of *parens patriae* was to get the juvenile court to adopt a paternalistic instead of an adversarial approach when addressing the issue of punishment, as well as the individual rehabilitative/reformative needs of the wayward youth brought before them. Stakeholders in the JJS were encouraged to look beyond a youth's alleged crimes and identify ways in which the juvenile could be rehabilitated in a manner which would help him/her be accepted in society.

With this approach, the Madras Children's Act, Bengal Children's Act and Bombay Children's Act came into existence in 1920, 1922 and 1924, respectively. Although the Madras and Bengal Acts came into existence before the Bombay Children's Act, it was the Bombay Children's Act which received significant

---

[7] This would include the stakeholder systems that involve the police, probation officers and residential home/custodial settings.

recognition because of its effective implementation. This Act mandated the constitution of juvenile courts to deal with children in difficult circumstances as well as with children who committed offences. A judicial officer headed the juvenile court and handled cases related to such children and juveniles. The probation officers assisted the court and worked to facilitate the rehabilitation process of juveniles, thus carving out the role of social work intervention in the system which had a strong legal underpinning given that the judiciary was its head.

The Children's Act of 1960 made provisions for the first time to set up separate machinery, that is, the Child Welfare Board and the Children's Court, to handle cases related to neglected and delinquent children, respectively. The judicial magistrate(s) headed the Children's Court, assisted by a panel of two social workers, while the Child Welfare Board comprised of social workers who were conferred with the powers of a Metropolitan Magistrate. This provision formally conferred a mandate for social work and social workers in the JJS, which earlier was limited to the judiciary and probation officer. However, this kind of constitution of the court and Board led to a perception that neglected children needed social work intervention with legal assistance, while those in conflict with law needed legal intervention with social work assistance.

To bring the operations of the JJS in the country in conformity with the United Nations Standard Minimum Rules for the Administration of Juvenile Justice, the Indian Parliament passed the Juvenile Justice Act 1986. The composition of the Juvenile Welfare Board and the Juvenile Court was the same as that of the Children's Act of 1960. During the period of the 1986 Act, there was an increase in the number of civil society organisations wanting to work on issues related to CNCPs. Those NGOs that provided services for CNCPs in the observation[8] and special[9] homes extended their services to the CCLs residing there as well.

---

[8] The Observation Home as a Home as per the 1986 Act is a transit home for CNCPs and CCLs, pending enquiry.

[9] The Special Home is a residential institution meant to house juveniles in conflict with law after being found to have committed the offence.

The 1986 Act was repealed with the advent of the Juvenile Justice (Care and Protection of Children) Amendment Act 2006, which was further amended to the Juvenile Justice (Care and Protection of Children) Act 2015 (previously referred to in this chapter as the JJ Act). This Act amalgamated the old and new concepts of juvenile justice, re-emphasising the spirit of *parens patriae*. It stressed the mandate of rehabilitation and reintegration of juveniles back into society with the full understanding that these objectives could be achieved only with the merging of the legal and social work approaches.

The CWC was constituted of five non-judicial members who were given magisterial powers. The JJB was constituted of one judicial officer and two non-judicial officers (social workers) who were empowered in the same capacity as a Judicial Magistrate First Class, and had to conduct sittings as a bench. The social workers were no longer given the task of 'assisting' the Board, but were a part of the constitution of the Board. The chairperson of the Board continued to be the Principal Magistrate (PM) appointed by the judiciary. The JJ Act nevertheless required the final order to be signed by at least two members. In other words, the signature of the social worker had to be present on the final order for the document to be valid, thus reiterating the importance of the role of the social worker in the system. This provision was made especially to ensure that the role of the social worker on the JJB was given due credit and that it would not become an ornamental position as it was during the period from 1960 to 2000.

Areas of Social Work Intervention in the JJS

In this chapter, the author distinguishes the scope of intervention with juveniles into two types. First, the role laid down by the law and second, the areas which need intervention but may not be explicitly stated to be so, by the law. The author primarily draws on her own experience in the field through the field action project (FAP),[10] 'Resource Cell for Juvenile Justice' (RCJJ)[11] and several research studies[12] done on CCLs and its JDS in various parts of the country.

1. *Social worker on the JJB:* The colloquial understanding of social work is to engage in any kind of charitable activity or work for a social cause. Unfortunately, professional social work in the country has yet to gain the recognition it deserves. In this context, the JJ Act specifies the qualification of the social worker to be appointed on the JJB as anyone who *possesses a degree in any one of the social sciences, law or medicine.*[13] The Act further acknowledges the

---

[10] FAPs are experimental and demonstration projects which have played a 'major role in piloting or pioneering new services' through social work intervention by its faculty, students and project staff' with the objective of demonstrating to the public, the need for such services. Further, these have emerged as a form of demonstration of new interventions and possibilities in order to test their efficacy, which then could be emulated by others; as a response to new needs, to changing realities, or from other social movements or campaigns; to enable faculty to develop academically and keep in touch with field practice, and to provide students opportunities for learning new interventions and formulation of creative strategy for greater relevance in practice. The matter was on the TISS website prior to February 2016 after which the website has been revamped.

[11] RCJJ is a field action project of the Centre for Criminology and Justice, School of Social Work, Tata Institute of Social Sciences. This project has been engaging and experimenting with social work concepts in the arena of CCLs and carving out the role of social work within the JJ system through a team of dedicated social workers. They have been engaging with the government departments and the judiciary to bring about systematic change in the working of the systems and increase their efficiency.

[12] Maharashtra study: An unpublished study done in 2008 and submitted to Mumbai High Court in 2009. This study has been successful in impacting the working of the JJS in Maharashtra and has led to policy level changes. Delhi study: An unpublished study done by RCJJ in 2010 which was commissioned by the Ministry of Law and Justice. The study was submitted to the Ministry and the Delhi High Court for its perusal.

[13] JJ Rule 13(2). Social Science such as Psychology, Criminology, Sociology, Social Work, Economics, Home Science, Education, Political Science, Women Studies, Rural Developments etc.

importance of appointing individuals having working experience with children and laid the onus on the state to provide specialised training to work on this issue. Thus, as per the Act, anyone with a heart to work with children can seek the post of a social worker on the JJB, which is broad enough to include doctors, paediatricians, and faculty members of colleges/schools with no relevant professional social work experience. Preference, however, is given to those having a legal background on the premise that people working on the JJB primarily should have a certain level of legal know-how, while the 'social-welfare' expertise may be garnered through experience over time. As a result, the training provided by the government is often limited to understanding the JJ Act with no focus laid on imparting the soft skills equally essential for the job.

In addition to adjudicating and disposing of cases involving juveniles, the role of the Board also

> involves, ensuring if the juvenile has been able to understand procedures, coordinate with the Child Welfare Committee if found that the juvenile is a child in need of care and protection, identify registered voluntary organization as a fit institution or any person as a fit person to receive charge of a specific juvenile for his further rehabilitation, seek and peruse progress reports of juveniles placed under the charge to parent, guardian, fit institution or fit person, and in appropriate cases modify the order in the interest of the juvenile, monitor institutions for juveniles, and recommend improvements and suggestions in case of lapses in the functioning of these institutions and ensure compliance of the same; bring to the notice of appropriate authority and to take appropriate action if it is noticed during the course of hearing that any offence is committed against the juvenile.[14]

It seems clear that these additional roles do not need a strong understanding of, or expertise in, the law.

---

[14] Rule 4A of the Maharashtra Juvenile Justice (Care and Protection of Children) Rules 2011 and Rule 10 of the Juvenile Justice (Care and Protection of Children) Rules, 2007 also known as the Model Rules.

Findings of the research done in Maharashtra and Delhi and other relevant studies (HAQ Centre for Child Rights, 2006) conducted showed that:

i. The JJB was predominantly run by the magistrate and he was in complete charge of taking and making all decisions with respect to the Board and juveniles.

ii. Social workers on the Board felt inadequate as they were unsure of their role. They had not read the JJ Rules. Those who had read the rules, continued to hold the opinion that the functioning of the Board required legal understanding. In most places, the role of the social worker was limited to 'counselling' or 'advising', and even then, was usually performed on a one-off basis.

iii. The social workers on the Board were so overwhelmed by the procedural legalities and legalese of the environment that they stopped attending the JJB.

iv. The role of the JJB was limited to looking at the offence committed and passing a final order. They worked towards closing the case rather than looking into rehabilitating the juvenile.

The social workers on the Board can play a crucial role in changing the mindset of judiciary by propagating the socio-legal practice which is the 'working' with cases approach rather than 'dealing' with cases. There have been a few enterprising social workers who, besides working on the mandate provided in the law, have expanded their purview to coordinate and engage with the various JDS, documented their roles, identified training needs of the system, and conducted training and capacity building programmes to the various stakeholders.

2. *Probation officer (PO):* The PO is considered to be a 'friend' of the Board and a guardian/mentor to the juvenile. Some of the duties of a probation officer as stated in the JJ Act and rules include:

i. Make inquiries regarding the home, school conditions, character and health of the juvenile.

ii. Prepare Social Investigation Report (SIRs).

iii. Prepare care plans.
iv. Protect the interests of the juvenile during police investigations.
v. Supervise juveniles on probation, supervision, and those given orders of community service.
vi. Facilitate group counselling.
vii. Be a friend and confidante to the juvenile and child and assist and advise him/her and also work towards their rehabilitation.
viii. Follow-up on the juveniles or children after their release from organisations and extend help and guidance to them.
ix. Network with voluntary workers and organisations to facilitate rehabilitation and social reintegration of the juveniles or children.

All of these activities require specialised skill and training in the methods of working with individuals, group work, community development and administrative related activities. Whiles such competencies do not all fall under legal education, they most certainly do under social work. With this understanding, many states in India now recruit those who hold a degree in a Masters in Social Work. The probation system is considered to be a backbone of the JJS, but given the lack of human resources, its role has been reduced to merely preparing Social Investigation Reports, mostly when called for by the JJB. That said, the holistic role of the PO has slowly been taken over by social workers associated with NGOs and voluntary organisations.

3. *Role of NGOs/civil society organisations/voluntary social workers:*

i. *Assisting the JJB:* The JJ Act and Rules make no mention of the administrative support required to assist the JJB in operationalising their orders. The magistrate of the JJB, is known to use the judicial clerk (JC) provided to him in the adult court to assist in the functioning of the JJB. Ideally, every JJB should be provided with an independent JC. For all other kinds of assistance, the JJB has to rely on available staff within Observation

Homes. The JJB seeks the assistance of NGOs and civil society organisations to assist them to prepare SIRs,[15] care plans, supervise and do follow-up of cases, which essentially is the role of the PO, as stated above. A few organisations/individuals have extended their role to include identification of long pending cases in Observation Homes or those out on bail, bring them to the attention of the JJB, identify reasons for pendency and coordinate with the various JDS to facilitate early disposition of the case.

ii. *Working with juveniles:* The general profile of juveniles interfacing with the JJS has been of school dropouts, those addicted to drugs, alcohol, tobacco or other kinds of substances, have behavioural issues and/or are highly influenced by their deviant peers. Many of these juveniles are legally in conflict with the law; but socially, could be argued to be a CNCP. For example, the national boundaries of India are quite porous. As a result, there are many immigrants who have been residing in India for years and earning a livelihood. However, when caught they are charged under the *Foreigners Act* and put in prison. As their parents have been booked for violating this law, their children, who are now victims of circumstances, are often considered by the authorities to be CCLs. Thus, these children have to deal with the dual trauma of separation from their parents, as well as needing to stay in an institution with other juveniles. The RCJJ has worked with many of such cases. In one particular matter, a small tribal boy of 10 years old was charged with killing a rare species of a bird under the *Wildlife Protection Act*. The boy hailed from a poor tribal family who used to hunt for food. He killed the bird as he was hungry and never knew it was

---

[15] This is a document drawn up to provide the court with background information on the child—above all, on all aspects of the family situation, as well as health and education status and highlighting any special problems or strengths—in order to help determine the most appropriate course of action regarding that particular child in response to the offence.

a crime. A report was submitted to the JJB by the social workers. The boy was placed under supervision with the social worker as per Section 15(1) (e) and (f) of the JJ Act.[16] Through the social workers intervention, the boy was admitted to a boarding school which helped secure his future.

Many juveniles are faced with several economic and social setbacks like expulsion from school by school authorities. The social worker has to negotiate and convince the school authorities to re-admit the juvenile. In cases where the juveniles do not want to enter mainstream education given the social stigma, the social worker has to work towards getting them enrolled in an alternative educational scheme. In cases of school dropouts who have no intention to continue with their education, the role of the social worker would be to identify the potential in the juvenile and help him/her select a trade or vocation which would help in earning a livelihood. In majority of cases however, such juveniles and their families will usually be forced to relocate their residences or for those juveniles to be sent off to a distant location (e.g., a familial relative's place or their native homestead), given the lack of community support, social stigma and police harassment.

Social workers also supervise juveniles given community sentences and ensure that they fulfil the conditions imposed on them by the JJB. Juveniles do cooperate with the social worker as they are aware of the importance of the social workers report which could affect their final order. Besides this, experience

---

[16] Section 15(1) (e) directs the juvenile to be released on probation of good conduct and placed under the care of any parent, guardian or other fit person, on such parent, guardian or other fit person executing a bond, with or without surety, as the Board may require, for the good behaviour and well-being of the juvenile for any period not exceeding three years; Section 15(1) (f) directs the juvenile to be released on probation of good conduct and placed under the care of any fit institution for the good behaviour and well-being of the juvenile for any period not exceeding three years.

has shown how the support of a social worker at this crucial juncture is valued by the juvenile and has prevented many from reoffending. De-addiction is another challenging area to work in given that there are very few drug and alcohol rehabilitation centres for children.

iii. *Assisting parents/guardians of the juveniles:* There are no written procedures to be followed by the JJB on such matters. In this context, the JJB generally follows procedures as set out in the Indian *Criminal Procedure Code*. This, of course, varies, and is subject to the understanding and sensitivity of the specific magistrate heading a particular sitting of the JJB.

As earlier stated, more than 50 per cent of the families involved in such processes are of low income status, and are not educated. Given the lack of official procedures and, arguably, the arbitrary functioning of the JJB, these juveniles and their parents are vulnerable to exploitation by lawyers, and police officers, who mislead them using adult criminal justice procedures. Those who barely earn ₹100/- a day are known to have paid exorbitant fees to private lawyers to get their children released on bail, or to draft various applications to the JJB, as the case may be. This happens because the parents are unaware of the JJ Act provisions, which states that the institutionalising of the juvenile should be the last resort, and that the juvenile would be released on bail irrespective of the nature of offence committed, unless there are reasons to believe that the community may harm the juvenile.

Social work intervention plays an important role here in making the juveniles and their parents/guardians aware of the intricate workings of the system. The RCJJ spearheaded an initiative of setting up a 'help desk' outside the JJB to be managed by two social workers. These social workers provide people with information on the workings of the JJS, provide free forms of the required templates, and if requested, also help to fill them out for the applicants. Periodic meetings of parents and children are held to discuss the challenges and problems faced while interacting with the JJS. Stakeholders like the police or a JJB member are invited to chair these sessions. Such interactions with officials in an informal setting enable the social workers' clients to discuss their problems; allows stakeholders to understand the difficulties faced by these clients; and explain to the clients the procedures and their limitations. Such interactions not only allay the fears that these social workers' clients hold about the system but also help them build trust in the system, and make them less susceptible to mental and economic exploitation by other stakeholders.

iv. *In police stations:* The police are the first point of contact for the juvenile within the JDS. Some of the provisions laid down in the JJ Act with respect to the constitution and role of police are:

- The setting up of Special Juvenile Police Units in every district of the state and Child Welfare Officers at every police station level respectively.[17]
- The police, at the time of apprehension, should inform the probation officer and the parent/guardian about the arrest/apprehension of the juvenile.[18] This is to help facilitate the PO's role to begin the process of home study/enquiry.[19]
- The juvenile is not supposed to be kept in a police lockup and has to be produced before the Board within 24 hours.[20]
- The police are supposed to prepare the Final Inquiry Report.[21]

Working experience and research studies reflect that while there are some within the police department

---

[17] Section 63 of the JJ Act.
[18] Section 13 of the JJ Act.
[19] Section 10 of the JJ Act.
[20] Section 10(1) of the JJ Act.
[21] Model Rules No. 28.

who genuinely go out of their way to facilitate the process of rehabilitating a juvenile, there is still a majority of them who view juveniles in a negative light. Cases have been formally and informally reported of children being picked up by police randomly under suspicion, parents not being informed of the 'pick up' as these children are not formally 'apprehended/arrested', use of violence during questioning, not informing the juveniles of their rights, and being placed in police lockups for more than 24 hours for questioning.

Juveniles have also complained of being forced by the police to make confessions based on what was stated in the FIR. Juveniles have also reported on how they have been told about the JJS being lenient and so 'advised' to confess to the offence as it would not have repercussions as an adult. This is, perhaps, based in part on the fact that children have the immunity from being disqualified if convicted of an offence that has been disposed of by the JJB.[22] Hence, the police have been known to "encourage" uninvolved/unrelated juveniles to confess to pending unsolved cases so as to reduce their own police stations' pendency case rates. Justification given by the police for keeping the juvenile under detention for more than the prescribed time was that once produced before the JJB, the police lose jurisdiction to interact/interrogate/question the juvenile. They would then have to seek the permission of the JJB if the juvenile is placed in the Observation Home—this permission was not always granted to them. In order to curb these unfair practises, the Rule 9 (11) of the Model Rules prevents the police from apprehending juveniles for offences which are non-serious in nature.

Furthermore, one of the reasons for long pendency of juvenile cases in the JJB has been due to the delay in the submission of the final inquiry report.[23] This delay

---

[22] Section 19 of the JJ Act.
[23] Better understood as the charge-sheet.

is attributed to the high workload of the police and the low priority accorded to such juvenile cases.

The role of the social worker/PO begins at the time of apprehension. Ideally, the PO should be present at the time of questioning by the police to ensure that the rights of the juvenile are not being violated. There is a need to build rapport with police stations to facilitate the follow up of cases. Social workers could positively assist the police in tracing the homes of juveniles and assisting the police in the escort process. They could identify training needs, design training modules and conduct/facilitate training programmes for the police on best practices on how to implement/enforce the JJS in 'Act' and in 'Spirit'.

v. *Intervention within institutional settings:* Juveniles are placed in an Observation Home[24] pending their enquiry (if not released on bail), and later placed in a Special Home,[25] post enquiry. As per the JJ Act, the enquiry of a juvenile should be done within 4 months and so the maximum period that a juvenile can reside in an Observation Home is 4 months. Their duration of stay varies from days to a few months depending on how soon their bail application is processed. Similarly, any final order that is passed by the JJB cannot exceed three years. Hence, the maximum period that a juvenile can reside in a Special Home is three years. Given traditional family cultural values, girls are rarely sent to an Observation Home and almost never sent to a Special Home. The aim of these residential institutions is to provide an environment and trained staff who would help facilitate the juvenile to reflect, learn normative behaviour, and unlearn behaviour which is considered socially and legally inappropriate. The Special Home is also mandated to provide skills and education to juveniles which would help him/her lead a productive life once out of the Special Home.

---

[24] Established as per section 8 of the JJ Act.
[25] Established as per section 9 of the JJ Act.

Though there are no official figures, the number of juveniles sent to a Special Home are hardly 1 to 2 per cent of the total cases being dealt with by the JJB. Similarly, more than 75 per cent and 99 per cent of juveniles are released out on bail in urban cities and semi urban/rural areas, respectively.

Given the infrastructure and the number of employees provided to staff these Observation and Special Homes vis-à-vis the small numbers of CCLs who are actually institutionalised in them—CNCPs are also placed there given the obvious availability of space and staff. Of the staff in the homes which include the superintendent, caretaker, cook, guard, probation officer, and teacher, only the probation officer is trained to deal with the child. The majority of staff and infrastructure in the Observation and Special Homes are not always equipped to deal with behavioural, developmental and legal issues faced by the juveniles and children. Therefore, they provide the basic provision of food, clothing and shelter and ensure that the children are safe, not up to mischief and run away.

Given this environment, the biggest problem faced by children within the Observation and Special Homes is boredom—there is a lack of space to allow them to vent their youthful energy. Besides this, there are also issues of physical, sexual and mental abuse committed by the staff and other peers, as well as homosexuality, and hygiene issues. Staff rely on assistance from other specialised agencies and personnel like counsellors, therapists, teachers, vocational trainers, and social workers to deal with such matters.

Social work intervention within such institutional settings involves working with individuals and groups of children, juveniles, and staff; coordinate/facilitate/network with agencies that offer services like education, mental and physical health services, recreation and other services which would help the juvenile utilise his/her time more constructively. Although the social worker is viewed as an outsider, this paradoxically results in the children find it safer to confide in him/her instead of the staff or peers. Evidently, the social worker has to play a different role of a mediator, negotiator, facilitator, and advocate, while working in such settings.

Besides this, the role of the social worker is extended to provide staff with periodic training, capacity building sessions and sensitisation programmes. Group sessions are also conducted with the staff on topics related to self, yoga, and recreation to boost their morale and energy.

vi. *Policy level advocacy:* The JJ Act was framed after calling for suggestions from all local and national level civil society organisations and individuals. Social workers today are a part of the framing of the juvenile justice rules developed at the state level. The government, in the making of such policies, also consults them so as to incorporate solutions to their ground level challenges and concerns. In recent years, the legal fraternity has begun to become involved and sought the expertise of social work professionals in the training and capacity building of judges on many social issues. The judiciary also now invites social workers for their comments and suggestions on certain legal issues that require social welfare considerations, especially those issues that involve women and children.

Conclusion

The JJ Act, and the CJS have made efforts to become child friendly by bringing about changes in its legal vocabulary which were stigmatising in nature, and through the composition of the JJB acknowledged the importance of social work intervention within its legal infrastructure.

The role of a social worker is still evolving and a lot is left to the skills and creativity of the personnel working there to identify and create a niche within the system. Nevertheless, social work intervention has come a long way in impacting individuals, JJSs and legislation relating to children. Although the scope for intervention in this arena of work holds potential, not many in the field have shown interest in engaging in this sector. This could be attributed partly to perceptions regarding the overt legal perception of the system and partly because funding to support work with this population is difficult to secure.

The unfortunate situation of CCLs not being included under the scheme of 'child protection' is an extremely disheartening development in the sector. However, the little interventions that have taken place in this field have proven beyond doubt that all CCLs require care and protection and it is only through the efforts of dedicated social workers that a juvenile can be rehabilitated and restored back into the community, which is the ultimate aim of any good JJS.

References

Government of India. (2011). *Report of the committee on crime statistics*. New Delhi: Ministry of Statistics & Programme Implementation. Retrieved from http://mospi.nic.in/mospi_new/upload/Report_crime_stats_29 june11.pdf

HAQ Centre for Child Rights. (2006). *Children's right to be heard in judicial processes, India*. Submission to the Committee on Rights of the Child, Day of General Discussion 2006, New Delhi: HAQ Centre for Child Rights. Retrieved from http://www.haqcrc.org/sites/default/files/ CHILDREN-RTBH-.pdf

Kumari, V. (2004). *Juvenile justice system in India: From welfare to rights*. New Delhi: Oxford University Press.

Legislation

Maharashtra Juvenile Justice (Care and Protection of Children) Rules 2011, (Maharashtra).

The Juvenile Justice (Care and Protection of Children) Amendment Act, 2006, (India).

The Juvenile Justice (Care and Protection of Children) Model Rules, 2007, (India).

The Juvenile Justice (Care and Protection of Children) Act, 2015, (India).

8

Supporting and Assisting Victims of Crime: The Indian Scenario

Pravin S. Khandpasole, Jyoti P. Khandpasole,
Mark David Chong and Katherine Hoffensetz

Introduction

Being victimised by crime is not an unusual occurrence and, in fact, people are touched by it in every section of society. It is a blight that is widely distributed in developed as well as developing countries. In layman's terms, crime denotes an unlawful act punishable by the state, and to that extent, every country has a criminal or penal code prohibiting undesirable acts, that is, crimes against either individuals or society as a whole (White, Perrone, & Gillespie, 2010). While this definition appears to be fairly simple, it is actually a very complex phenomenon that is socially constructed, that is, what constitutes a crime may differ in time, space and culture (Winfree & Abadinsky, 2010).

While criminologists such as Cesare Beccaria, Cesare Lombroso, Enrico Ferri, Raffaelle Garofalo, Edwin Sutherland, Hans von Hentig, Willem Hendrik Nagel, Henri Ellenberger, Marvin Wolfgang and Stephen Schafer all wrote extensively about 'victims' in their early works (as cited in Dussich, 2006, p. 116), it was Benjamin Mendelsohn who first coined the term 'victimology' in 1947

(Dussich, 2006, p. 116). Thus, the systematic study of victims or 'victimology' may now be understood as being

> an academic scientific discipline which studies data that describes phenomena and causal relationships related to victimizations. This includes events leading to the victimization, the victim's experience, its aftermath and the actions taken by society in response to these victimizations. Therefore, victimology includes the study of the precursors, vulnerabilities, events, impacts, recoveries, and responses by people, organizations and cultures related to victimizations. (Dussich, 2006, p. 118)

It is interesting to note that even though the criminological literature acknowledges or even privileges the 'victim' in its works on crime and deviance, the same cannot be said of the legal system of many countries. It has been pointed out, time and time again, that victims of crime have been deprioritised or marginalised by the criminal justice system (Chockalingham, 2003; Latha & Thilagaraj, 2013; Srinivasan & Eyre, 2007). Yet, it should always be remembered that it is the victim, as the complainant, who starts the whole prosecution process in the first place. Thus, upon receiving the complaint against an accused person, the police will then record the matter (usually called a First Information Report), and thereafter investigate the incident (especially if a cognisable offence is disclosed). If warranted, the police (or the prosecution) will then prosecute the alleged offender in a court of law. Throughout this process though, victim advocates have argued that the criminal justice focus is on ensuring that the accused is treated fairly through an application of his/her due process rights (White et al., 2010). Even if the offenders are convicted, there are still various laws and guidelines that seek to ensure that their punishments will be humane, their human rights will be respected, and, where possible, they will be given opportunities to rehabilitate (Ronel, Jaishankar, & Bensimon, 2008).

But what about the crime victims?

The victim's role normally ends after providing evidence as a witness, if at all needed. It is apparent that the criminal justice system views the acquittal or conviction of the accused person as the most important outcome of these prosecution proceedings (and of course, his/her sentence/punishment, in the latter event). This however fails to adequately address the loss suffered by the victim and his/her dependents. These victims, irrespective of the offenses committed against them or the ultimate punishments inflicted on their offenders, have to endure a lengthy and drawn-out wait for the conclusion of the trial and verdict, during which they will usually receive little or no support from the state (Goodey, 2005).

Types of Harm Suffered

Being victimised by crime thus leaves deep-rooted wounds or scars on the physical, spiritual, emotional/psychological, financial and social lives of the victims. According to Hans von Hentig's theory of victimisation (1948), offenders are what he considers to be the 'doers' of crime, whereas victims are unfortunately, its 'sufferers'. That said, while the individual victim is considered to be the primary sufferer/victim, it should not be forgotten that his/her dependants, extended family members and friends, are also victims, albeit secondary ones.

While Tables 8.1–8.6 are not meant to be exhaustive in its scope, they do however reflect, to some degree, what the first and second authors of this chapter have seen in their extensive field-work with victims of crime over the past few years in India.

It is arguable that the impact of crime may intensify considerably depending upon the victims' gender, age, caste, class, religious, socio-economic and/or political status. Lamentably, the pain and plight of such victims remain relatively unaddressed in many criminal justice systems around the world (Srinivasan & Eyre, 2007). Sadly, it is normally the most vulnerable of society who are going to be significantly impacted by crime and its aftermath (Wallace, 2007). It is the very old and young, women, working class or destitute youth, the poor, marginalised ethnic minorities, and the like, who will often find themselves violently victimised. Theirs is a world filled with dread, where the fear of

Table 8.1:
Physical Harm

Type of Harm	Description of Harm
Physical Impact	• Physiological anxiety • Physical injuries • Other medical emergencies • Permanent disability • Disfigurement • Immune disorders • Lethargy and body fatigue • Sleep disorders • Appetite or eating disorders • Decreased libido levels • Sexual dysfunction • Increased risk of future sexual dysfunction • Inability to work • Increased risk of future victimisation • Possible exposure to sexually transmitted diseases, and unwanted pregnancy

Table 8.2:
Spiritual Harm

Type of Harm	Description of Harm
Spiritual Impact	• Distrust of or anger against God/fate • Increased engagement in religious practice • Acceptance of suffering as punishment for present sins or for sins committed in past lives (reincarnation) • Acceptance of suffering as being part of God's Will

Table 8.3:
Emotional/Psychological Harm

Type of Harm	Description of Harm
Emotional/ Psychological Impact	• Shock • Terror • Feelings of unreality, numbness, out of control, vulnerability • Confusion • Helplessness • Shame • Fear • Anger or rage • Grief or intense sorrow

Type of Harm	Description of Harm
	• Anxiety/anxiety disorder • Difficulty trusting oneself or others • Depression • Panic symptoms • Inability to concentrate • Guilt and self-blame • Preoccupation with the crime • Concern about personal safety, being believed or being blamed • Problems with important personal relationships • Increased risk of drug abuse • Avoidance of things associated with the crime • Suicide ideation

Table 8.4:
Financial Harm

Type of Harm	Description of Harm

Financial Impact	• Medical bills
	• Medication and prescription drugs unavailable in government hospital/clinics
	• Personal belongings damaged, destroyed, or stolen
	• Costs for rehabilitative/restorative equipment, for example, wheelchair etc.
	• Loss of wages due to:
	   ○ incapacitation
	   ○ taking time off from work to repair damage
	   ○ participating in the criminal proceedings
	   ○ seeking medical or rehabilitative treatment
	• Loss of employment
	• Crime scene clean-up or repair costs
	• Child and elder care
	• Relocation expenses
	• Funeral and burial expenses

Table 8.5:
Social Relational Harm

Type of Harm	Description of Harm
Social Relational Impact	• Withdrawal • Isolation • Stigma • Blame

(Table 8.5 Continued)

(Table 8.5 Continued)

Type of Harm	Description of Harm
	• Unwanted sympathy • Others frequently wanting to discuss the crime • Interference with the crime incident • Gossiping • Non-acceptance • Avoidance by society • End of or upsetting personal relationships • Difficulty to find a marriage partner for rape victims

Table 8.6:
Harm to the Family

Type of Harm	Description of Harm
Family Impact	• Curtailing or eliminating the source of income for the family • Financial emergency • Forced to earn a livelihood • Disruptions in the education of the children • Increased risk of anxiety or related diseases in parents, spouse, or children • Increased vulnerability • Hardship to restart life • Increased risk to drug addiction • Hardship during investigation or prosecution process • Ignorance of legal rights leading to exploitation

crime diminishes their quality of life to such an extent that one wonders why they would even bother waking up each morning only to endure further suffering (Holtzhausen & Gxubane, 2012).

In fact, because many of them come from vulnerable groups within society, this vulnerability, coupled with being initially victimised, actually makes them ideal targets for re-victimisation! Re-victimisation is basically the recurrence of a crime (e.g., domestic or family violence, paedophilia, burglary and so on) to the same individual. Such re-victimisation tends to occur when situational factors of location (e.g., living in slum areas, being in close proximity to criminal gangs and so on), and lifestyle factors such as illegal drug use and excessive alcohol consumption, can expose such individuals to a greater risk of being victims of similar crimes again.

It is these crime victims who are in greatest need of assistance in order to recover from their horrific experiences. It is, however, an indictment against many societies that they are also the same people who have the most difficulty in accessing such assistance and compensation from the government or the community-at-large (Latha & Thilagaraj, 2013; Wallace, 2007). In many cases, this could be due to ignorance or a lack of information on the part of the victims, as well as on those who purport to help them. But sometimes, a more insidious reason lies behind this problem—one that is systemic in nature—where victims of crime undergo a secondary form of victimisation (Hall, 2012; White et al., 2010).

This chapter will, therefore, attempt to provide the reader with an overview of the relevant theories of victimology; an outline of the nature of criminal victimisation in India; an analysis of the way crime victims have been treated by the Indian criminal justice system (historical and current), and then finally, show how social workers can ameliorate these problems through a range of recommendations.

Theories of Victimology

Victimology began in earnest as a social scientific endeavour from only around the 1940s (Dussich, 2006, p. 116). Before this time, very little systematic scholarly consideration, if any, was given to victims of crime and the consequences of their experiences. As such, unlike criminological theories, theories of victimology have a rather recent history. Zaykowski and Campagna (2014) noted that these analytical frameworks fall within five broadly defined categories, and are as follows:

1. Victim precipitation theories
2. Exposure and opportunity theories
3. Social learning and cultural theories
4. Control theories
5. Critical theories

The first of these, that is, victim precipitation theories, and probably the most controversial, attempt to uncover 'what actions or characteristics of victims increase [their] risk for harm', which according to von Hentig, and Mendelsohn, will then allow us to distinguish between 'innocent victims', 'partially responsible victims' and 'guilty victims' (Zaykowski & Campagna, 2014, pp. 453–54). Although roundly criticised for essentially blaming the victims for their own suffering, there is nevertheless some empirical support to suggest that 'there is an "overlap" between victims and offenders ... and that "deviant" lifestyles are associated with greater risk of victimization' (Zaykowski & Campagna, 2014, p. 454).

Exposure and opportunity theories however broaden this inquiry from simply focussing on a victim's actions (as above), to looking for social structural risks in our surrounding environment that heighten the chances of us being victimised. Such theories examine how the way our neighbourhoods, industries, political system, schools, families, employment/workplace, gender relations, and peer groups are structured, and thereafter, analyse how these specific social arrangements and relationships increase or decrease, as the case may be, our vulnerability to crime (Zaykowski & Campagna, 2014, p. 454). So, for example, technological advances in mobile phones have allowed these items to become smaller, and hence, easier to steal, that is, improvements in technology has increased the product/target attractiveness.[1] In addition to this example, it could also be argued that residential properties are becoming more vulnerable to burglary these days because of the equalising of gender relations as well as the liberalising of employment practices—women now have more opportunities to work or seek jobs outside of the home, which has meant that during office hours (8.00 AM to 6.00 PM), homes are usually left without a capable guardian to protect the

---

[1] Staying with this illustration, affluent parents are increasingly giving their children these costly mobile phones to take to school in case of emergencies. These expensive mobile phones are then even more easily stolen from these relatively weaker young children by older and relatively stronger youth or adults.

contents therein.[2] Such product improvements and changed life-style patterns would fall under the consideration of the many modern crime prevention/crime opportunity paradigms, and, in particular, Cohen and Felson's routine activity theory would be particularly useful to employ in such circumstances (Zaykowski & Campagna, 2014, p. 454).

Other victimology theories include those that focus on social learning and culture. Here, deviant, anti-social, or criminal 'norms, values, and expected behaviours are transmitted through interaction between victim and offender, peer groups, family, or more broadly, society, including media exposure and other cultural influences' (Zaykowski & Campagna, 2014, p. 455). Thus, it is possible for victims to succumb to a form of 'learned helplessness' (a condition that some battered wives are susceptible to), or as seen in some violent sub-cultures where its members are so indoctrinated or socialised to accepting that being at the receiving end of a beating is as normal as being the one delivering the beating to another (Zaykowski & Campagna, 2014, p. 455).

Control theories, and in particular, those that concentrate on individuals who have low levels of self-control however, are quite different to the social learning and cultural paradigms discussed above. Here, it has been argued that 'characteristics of low self-control such as lacking future orientation, empathy, tolerance for problem-solving, diligence, preferring physical acts as opposed to mental thought and risk avoidance can plausibly be linked to victimization' (Zaykowski & Campagna, 2014, p. 457). Thus, because low self-control can lead to the adoption of risky life-styles, this then in turn can increase the likelihood of their victimisation (Zaykowski & Campagna, 2014, p. 457).

---

[2] Please note that there is no suggestion here that women working in the corporate world are to blame for any increase in the number of burglaries in the country! This is merely an example of how social structural changes in gender relations, and employment policies, can have unintended consequences. Rational choice offenders are constantly searching for opportunities to commit crimes, and will take advantage of any social/environmental changes that will make a target more vulnerable: for more guidance in this regard, please read about rational choice perspective, crime pattern theory and routine activity theory.

Finally, critical theories. Such analytical frameworks search for social systemic reasons for victimisation, arguing, for example, 'that victimization risk may be enhanced or explained through social marginalization (e.g., racism and sexism) and/or political forces such as state crime' (Zaykowski & Campagna, 2014, p. 457). Consequently, social structural oppression emanating from the patriarchy, capitalism, and ethnic or religious hegemony are key factors in understanding why some groups or segments of the population are more susceptible to victimisation than others.

The Nature of Criminal Victimisation in India

Uncovering the level of victimisation in any particular region in the world is generally sourced through several repositories including police records, victim and crime survey data, as well as self-reports (Goodey, 2005, p. 44). Unfortunately, actual crime and victimisation figures can be easily distorted through under-reporting and under-recording of offences, often referred to as the 'dark figure of crime'. This occurs when either the police decide not to record an incident that a victim has reported or when a victim decides not to report it at all. Universally, it is estimated that up to 60 to 70 per cent of crimes are not reported, and this is particularly so for sexual offences and assaults (Chockalingham, 2003). Victim and crime surveys record the responses of population samples regarding their experiences of victimisation and crime. These reports are free from official recording requirements and, therefore, potentially give a better indication of victimisation rates. Each of these methods has a different perspective from which their data is sourced. Consequently, when viewed in isolation from each other, they will necessarily have shortfalls. That said, when viewed together, however, they will provide a more comprehensive picture of the levels of victimisation in the country.

Victimisation levels in India are essentially assessed in the same manner and, hence, are greatly impacted by concerns over the 'dark figure of crime' due to issues involving caste discrimination, unclear or unreasonable police recording procedures and the minimal collection of victim survey data. The official crime figures annually produced by India's National Crime Records Bureau are collated into two categories: crimes against property and crimes against individuals. Victim surveys are relatively new in India, and those that have been conducted have shone a bright light on the stark difference between the number of unrecorded and unreported crimes as against the official crime statistics. As with most countries, the level of reporting in India is significantly lower than the actual occurrence of crime and victimisation. Many victims surveyed indicated that they did not report the crime for a number of reasons, including the victims' perception of the seriousness of the offence, the level of loss experienced and a lack of faith in the police service.

In the Indian Human Development survey conducted over 2004–05, 6.7 per cent of all households in India reported a crime which included burglary, theft or assault. The poorer rural areas reported 2.5 per cent higher levels than urban areas. The Dalits (a category within the *varna* (caste) system that is considered to be 'untouchable') reported 2.2 per cent more victimisation than those of higher castes. According to the National Crime Records Bureau, the Indian Penal Code crime rate increased by 6.2 per cent over the decade from 2000 to 2010 (Thilagaraj, 2012, p. 203).

Indian Victims of Crime through the Ages

Historically, disputes in India were dealt with by tribal law and through acts of retributive revenge. Ancient India saw the introduction of the concept of 'caste' and a division of laws and areas of jurisdiction into individual communities. Disputes within the community were settled in the *panchayat* system (village courts) by councils. The panchayat system consists of five respected elders from the village who would come to a collective decision regarding disputes. This adjudicative process would also include some notions of victim-offender mediation (Latha & Thilagaraj, 2013). This system was easily implemented and understood by all the villagers. It dealt with both criminal and civil cases. However, it was the king, his officials and his Brahmin advisors who oversaw disputes between communities or different groups, by enforcing the law and punishing those who broke it. In the *Sangam* period, the king was seen as the embodiment of justice, and hence the primary defender of the rights of victims, as well as a source for victim compensation (Bharti, 2002). That said, during these earlier societies, it was common practice to enforce payment by the perpetrator to the victim as a form of mandated restitution.

Medieval India gradually saw the decline of Hindu rule after numerous invasions by other cultures. This then led to a disintegration of the traditional justice systems outlined earlier. The new systems of governance, however, continued the practice of restitution. Restitution known as *diya* or 'blood money' was paid in the most serious of crimes to the deceased victim's next of kin (Ronel et al., 2008). An important and emphasised component of the *Smritis*, which is a specific section of Hindu scripture and codified customary law, is that the institution of kingship was designed to enforce *dharma* (law) as well as to provide protection and support to those afflicted. According to the *Smritis*, the severity of the punishment is determined by the crime as well as the varna system of the offender and victim (Bharti, 2002). This, in turn, often resulted in varied and inconsistent judgments.

From the early 1600s, the British East India Company started trade in the East Indies and was granted autonomy by the British monarch to self-regulate their business in the region. Over the next 200 years, the East India Company substantially expanded its holdings throughout India, and ultimately acted as if it were a colonial administrative proxy for the British Crown. By this stage, the Company was enacting laws and constitutions for India, and this continued until the Indian Sepoy Revolt of 1857. Subsequently, in 1858, the British Crown formally took rule, replacing the Company at the apex of Colonial India. During this British rule, the Indian criminal justice system was modified, with the *Dharmasastra Code* (also known as the *Manusmriti*) reintroduced (Ronel et al., 2008). This system formed the basis of the current Indian criminal justice system in which victims' rights lamentably continue to be overlooked. Macaulay's *Criminal Procedure Code* (revised in 1973) still lacked any significant protection afforded to crime victims, but did have some provision for monetary compensation to be made to them. However, these provisions were actually orders relating to restitution where compensation was specifically sought from the offender by the victim (Ronel et al., 2008).

The Current System

Before delving into more contemporary matters, it is important to remember that crime victims are often forgotten parties in the Indian criminal justice system. Immediately after the crime, the victim undergoes additional trauma, medical treatment and hardship brought about by a justice system that is, in theory, supposed to be their saviour (Chockalingam, 2010; Srinivasan & Eyre, 2007). The criminal justice system can be a very daunting process of rules, regulations and procedures that will be entirely alien to a non-legally trained victim. Consequently, without any institutional assistance, navigating this legal 'labyrinth' will be next to impossible for many. At the risk of being subject to further indifferent or unpleasant treatment, it is no wonder that some victims may opt not to report these crimes to the police, especially since the existing laws insufficiently protect the rights, concerns and psychosocial needs of crime victims in the criminal justice system. As mentioned earlier, this type of additional affliction has been termed secondary victimisation (Hall, 2012; White et al., 2010).

From an institutional point of view, this situation is quite untenable. Take, for example, the Constitution of India. It purports to guarantee the following fundamental rights of its citizens (Part III):

- Right to equality
- Right to freedom
- Right against exploitation
- Right to freedom of religion, cultural and educational rights
- Right to constitutional remedies

Accused persons frequently use these constitutional rights in order to ensure that they will not be taken advantage of by the state, and yet these are not reciprocal rights that victims of crime can similarly avail themselves to. It should always be remembered that the Indian criminal justice system, which applies these constitutional laws, was devised not only to punish the guilty but also to protect the rights of the innocent victims.

When analysing what crime victims really need from its government, a good starting point would be the United Nations' 'Declaration of Basic Principles of Justice for Victims of Crime and Abuse of Power' (as adopted by its General Assembly through Resolution No. 40/34 dated 29 November 1985). It defines 'victims of crime' as persons who, individually or collectively, have suffered harm, including physical or mental injury, emotional suffering, economic loss or substantial impairment of their fundamental rights, through acts or omissions that are in violation of criminal laws operative in member States, including those laws proscribing criminal abuse of power. According to this 1985 United Nations Declaration, victims of crime are in dire need of: (a) access to justice and fair treatment; (b) restitution; (c) compensation; and (d) assistance. This 1985 UN Declaration goes on to elaborate what these needs specifically entail:

1. Access to justice and fair treatment

   - Victims should be treated with compassion and respect for their dignity. They are entitled to access to the mechanisms of justice and to prompt redress, as provided for by national legislation, for the harm that they have suffered.
   - Judicial and administrative mechanisms should be established and strengthened where necessary, to enable victims to obtain redress through formal or informal procedures that are expeditious, fair, inexpensive and accessible. Victims should be informed of their rights in seeking redress through such mechanisms.
   - The responsiveness of judicial and administrative processes to the needs of victims should be facilitated by
     o informing victims of their role and the scope, timing and progress of the proceedings, and of the disposition of their cases, especially where serious crimes

are involved and where they have requested such information;

- allowing the views and concerns of victims to be presented and considered at appropriate stages of the proceedings where their personal interests are affected, without prejudice to the accused and consistent with the relevant national criminal justice system;
- providing proper assistance to victims throughout the legal process;
- taking measures to minimise inconvenience to victims, protect their privacy, when necessary, and ensure their safety, as well as that of their families and witnesses on their behalf, from intimidation and retaliation; and
- avoiding unnecessary delay in the disposition of cases and the execution of orders or decrees granting awards to victims.

- Informal mechanisms for the resolution of disputes, including mediation, arbitration and customary justice or indigenous practices, should be utilised where appropriate to facilitate conciliation and redress for victims.

2. Restitution
   - Offenders or third parties responsible for their behaviour should, where appropriate, make fair restitution to victims, their families or dependants. Such restitution should include the return of property or payment for the harm or loss suffered, reimbursement of expenses incurred as a result of the victimisation, the provision of services and the restoration of rights.
   - Governments should review their practices, regulations and laws to consider restitution as an available sentencing option in criminal cases, in addition to other criminal sanctions.
   - In cases of substantial harm to the environment, restitution, if ordered, should include, as far as possible, restoration of the environment, reconstruction of the infrastructure, replacement of community facilities and reimbursement of the expenses of relocation, whenever such harm results in the dislocation of a community.

- Where public officials or other agents acting in an official or quasi-official capacity have violated national criminal laws, the victims should receive restitution from the State whose officials or agents were responsible for the harm inflicted. In cases where the government under whose authority the victimising act or omission occurred is no longer in existence, the State or government successor in title should provide restitution to the victims.

3. Compensation
   - When compensation is not fully available from the offender or other sources, States should endeavour to provide financial compensation to
     - victims who have sustained significant bodily injury or impairment of physical or mental health as a result of serious crimes and
     - the family, in particular dependants of persons who have died or become physically or mentally incapacitated as a result of such victimisation.
   - The establishment, strengthening and expansion of national funds for compensation to victims should be encouraged. Where appropriate, other funds may also be established for this purpose, including in those cases where the State of which the victim is a national is not in a position to compensate the victim for the harm.

4. Assistance
   - Victims should receive the necessary material, medical, psychological and social assistance through governmental, voluntary, community-based and indigenous means.
   - Victims should be informed of the availability of health and social services and other relevant assistance and be readily afforded access to them.
   - Police, justice, health, social service and other personnel concerned should receive training to sensitise them to the needs of victims, and guidelines to ensure proper and prompt aid.
   - In providing services and assistance to victims, attention should be given to those who have special needs because of the nature of the harm inflicted or because of factors such as race, colour, sex and so on.

The 1985 UN Declaration represents a comprehensive approach towards achieving a holistic restoration of victims who have had their lives brutalised by crime. Thus, even though this UN General Assembly resolution is not legally binding on India, it nevertheless provides her policy makers, legislators and judges with an excellent guide to formulate safeguards and scaffolding structures for victims of criminal activity.

That said, what has India already done in this regard?

It should be noted that the Indian Penal Code 1860 did not originally define the term 'victim' specifically in its provisions, and it was only in 2008 that the Code of Criminal Procedure 1973 finally officially added the term 'victim' into the lexicon of Indian law, that is, 'a person who has suffered any loss or injury caused by reason of the act or omission for which the accused person has been charged and the expression "victim" includes his or her guardian or legal heir'. With this explicit recognition, victims of crime are now afforded certain protections and rights that they had hitherto been unable to rely upon. This would include, for example, victims being allowed to apply to the court to

1. avoid being asked indecent, scandalous or offensive questions (Section 151 of the Indian Evidence Act 1872);
2. be paid reasonable expenses (Section 311 of the Code of Criminal Procedure 1973); and
3. receive compensation (Sections 357 and 357A of the Code of Criminal Procedure 1973).

With regards to the issue of providing compensation to crime victims, a little more should be said about it, given its obvious importance. Under Section 357 of the Code of Criminal Procedure 1973, the power to award compensation is given to the trial, appellate or revision court, as the case may be. What is particularly interesting about this provision however is that Subsection (1) (b) specifically empowers the courts to apply the whole or any part of the *fine* recovered from the offender towards payment to any person as compensation for any loss or injury caused by the offence, when it is in the opinion of that court that such sums will be recoverable in civil proceedings. Furthermore, in order to strengthen this right, Subsection (3) empowers the court, in its discretion, to order the convicted offender to pay compensation to the victim even though the fine does not form a part of compensation.

Perhaps even more significantly, Section 357A(1) empowers the state government (in coordination with the central government), to set up a 'Victim Compensation Scheme' so as to compensate the victim or his/her dependents for loss or injury suffered as a result of the crime. Subsection (3) further empowers the trial court at the conclusion of the trial to recommend compensation to the administering body under this scheme if

- it is satisfied that compensation under Section 357 will not be adequate; or
- the prosecution's case ends in an acquittal; or
- the accused person is discharged.

In addition to this, Subsection (4) empowers the victim or his/her dependent to make an application for an award of compensation even if the offender cannot be traced or identified or where no trial takes place. The administering body (in this case being the State or District Legal Services Authority) has only two months to investigate the circumstances of the application or referral (as the case may be), and to award adequate compensation to the victim [Subsection (5)]. However, to cater for instances when the victims are in need of more immediate financial assistance, interim relief may also be provided to alleviate their suffering [Subsection (6)].[3]

It should be highlighted here that the Law Commission of India and other special committees like the Committee on Reforms of the Criminal Justice System (Government of India, Ministry of Home Affairs, 2003) under the chair of Dr Justice V. S. Malimath, have emphasised, inter alia, a need for greater witness protection and victim participation in police investigations. In this latter regard, recent special laws, that is, the Scheduled Castes and the

---

[3] Other pieces of legislation that likewise purport to provide compensation to victims of crime are as follows: Probation of Offenders Act 1958; Workman Compensation Act 1923; Fatal Accidents Act 1855; Motor Vehicle Act 1988; Protection of Women from Domestic Violence Act 2005; Protection of Children from Sexual Offences Act 2012.

Scheduled Tribes (Prevention of Atrocities) Act 1989, the Protection of Woman from Domestic Violence Act 2005 and the Protection of Children from Sexual Offences Act 2012 have attempted to redress this gap in protective provisions for victims.

The Scheduled Caste and Scheduled Tribes (Prevention of Atrocities) Act 1989 serves to provide acknowledgment and justice for the Dalits (untouchables) who live in fear of victimisation and retribution from the upper castes. It has been argued that with all investigations conducted and managed by the police, there tends to be a serious deficit in procedural regulation, which results in deficient outcomes and favouritism towards those of higher caste and social position. The Dalits have been, for many years, overlooked and excluded, by almost all aspects of Indian society, including the criminal justice system. This 1989 Act was therefore introduced to address some of these injustices perpetrated by and within the justice system (Sarkar, 2010).

The Protection of Women from Domestic Violence Act 2005 is designed to provide effective protection and rights to all women. The domestic violence definition encompasses abuse in all forms including verbal, emotional, sexual and physical, as well as a denial of access to all resources and facilities that are afforded to them in the context of the domestic relationship. This 2005 Act also includes regulations and obligations of the criminal justice stakeholders to provide information to the victim of their rights regarding assistance, services and legal options. Noncompliance by protection officers can result in financial penalties or imprisonment imposed on them.

The role of the Protection of Children from Sexual Offences Act 2012 is to provide children with protection from being victims to pornography, sexual assault and harassment. This 2012 Act also established special courts to examine and try such offences.

In order to improve the position of victims within the criminal justice system, the Malimath Committee made the following recommendations:

1. The right to participate in the criminal trial by being allowed to
   - produce evidence;
   - ask questions of the witnesses;

- be informed of case status;
- be heard in relation to bail and prosecution withdrawal;
- be able to move the court to pursue further investigation and
- advance arguments after submission of the prosecution arguments.

2. The right to an advocate, which will be provided by the State if the victim cannot afford it.
3. The right to appeal against lenient sentencing, acquittal, or inadequate compensation.
4. The State is obligated to compensate victims of serious crimes.
5. The right to legal services including medical and psychiatric help, interim compensation and protection from secondary victimisation.
6. The right to be impleaded as a party in criminal proceedings.
7. The right to have a voluntary organisation implead in court proceedings, in select cases.

These recommendations and Acts of Parliament should be understood as attempts to improve the plight of vulnerable victims of crime by trying to prevent them from being doubly victimised by the criminal justice system, that is, secondary victimisation (Chockalingam, 2010).

Shortcomings of the Existing System

While the above developments are certainly encouraging, the authors of this chapter would argue however that these are still sadly insufficient, particularly when you juxtapose them against the sorry plight faced by these victims (see Tables 8.1–8.6). Using the United Nations Declaration of 1985 as an investigative template to uncover the shortcomings of the Indian criminal justice system, the following questions will be instrumental in this regard.

Are Indian victims of crime given sufficient or adequate

1. access to justice and fair treatment?
2. restitution?
3. compensation?
4. assistance?

Each of these questions will be addressed in turn.

- *Are Indian victims of crime given sufficient or adequate access to justice and fair treatment?*
    i. The right to be informed: Generally speaking, the victim does not have a legal right to be informed of the status or the progress of the criminal case by the police or prosecution (Chockalingam, 2010). There is no specific application process for victims to avail themselves of, and usually they will only be informed of what is happening when they receive a summons to give evidence in court (Chockalingam, 2010; Sarkar, 2010). While crime victims have the right to oppose the release of an accused person applying for bail (Section 436 of the Code of Criminal Procedure 1973), he/she however, does not have the legal right to be informed when it happens or of any other key milestone events in the prosecution process. This lack of knowledge compounds feelings of victimisation and helplessness, which acts in concert to impede recovery, and, in fact, increases the potential to be doubly victimised (Holtzhausen & Gxubane, 2012).
    ii. The right to participate or be heard in the criminal proceedings: Usually victims of a crime are relatively emasculated when the police are investigating the complaint. There is no right for the victim to be involve in the investigation of the case (Chockalingam, 2010) nor is the victim empowered to be heard during the accused person's bail application. A crime victim is not considered to be a necessary party in a criminal revision, appeal or in any other court proceedings in which a writ is filed by the accused person for an order of court. The

only concession is that under Section 372 of the Code of Criminal Procedure 1973, the victim has a right to appeal against an order of a criminal court acquitting the accused, convicting the accused for a lesser offence or imposing an inadequate compensation order against the convicted offender.

- *Are Indian victims of crime given sufficient or adequate restitution?*
  i. The Code of Criminal Procedure 1973 has provision to instruct released offenders to pay restitution for loss or injury that is the result of the offence. However, the victim only receives this payment in cases where the offender is able to pay (Sarkar, 2010). There is little to no provision to supply or engage services that can provide restitution for the victim.
  ii. In Indian courts, the distinction between restitution and compensation is often lost, with the term compensation covering both concepts (Srinivasan & Eyre, 2007). Restitution is defined and interpreted differently throughout the world, but essentially requires the perpetrator to provide the means with which to help restore the victim of crime to a state that he/she was in before the crime had been committed. This includes any expenses incurred as a result of the crime such as loss and damage to property, loss of wages, medical expenses and any other costs resulting from the victimisation. This should not be limited to just financial restitution, but must likewise include gestures and actions that are ultimately symbolic to ensure that the victim feels emotionally and psychologically safe and whole again (Hall, 2012). As highlighted earlier, restitution should help to restore the victim to the same state as they were before experiencing the effects of victimisation.
- *Are Indian victims of crime given sufficient or adequate compensation?*
  i. The right to compensation: Compensation is recognised by Indian law under Section 357 of the Code of Criminal Procedure 1973, which states that part or all of the fine imposed on the convicted offender shall be used

to provide compensation to the victim, and in the case where no fine is imposed, the convicted offender may be ordered by the court to pay compensation directly to the victim. Unfortunately, this compensation is not disbursed to the victim until a conviction is recorded and the appeal process has been finalised, which can take quite a long time. However, in cases where an accused is not convicted or where no fine is imposed upon conviction or where the magistrate considers the convicted offender financially unable to pay a fine large enough for the victim to be adequately compensated from that sum or where the convicted offender defaults on paying either the fine or the compensation amount, the victim will not be able to receive any monetary assistance to make good their losses or injuries from the criminal court (Srinivasan & Mathew, 2007, pp. 53–54). Without a designated compensation fund which does not rely on the accused and changes to disbursement methods, the expectation of compensation cannot be guaranteed.

- *Are Indian victims of crime given sufficient or adequate assistance?*
  i. Victims are not used by the criminal justice system for any role other than as witnesses (Sarkar, 2010). Hence, it is in this context that very little consideration is given to their rights to receive assistance. Even when limited help is provided, victims are rarely notified of, or directed to, those sources.

Social Work Intervention

Thus, as the analysis shows, already vulnerable victims are primarily victimised by the criminal, and by the effects of the crime. They are then secondarily victimised by the criminal justice system. Perhaps most egregiously, for certain types of offences (e.g., rape), these poor victims are even victimised by society itself (Sarkar, 2010). There is therefore great scope for social workers and social service agencies to support victims by helping them to understand and navigate these complex legal procedures and processes, advocate for them if they have legitimate grievances against the agents of state, increase their visibility in a positive way and help them seek compensation from the criminal justice system. This is, of course, in addition to assisting them to address their mental/emotional trauma, as well as more immediate employment, housing, financial dependency and familial/social relationship issues.

These short-, medium- and long-term consequences of victimisation, particularly of the secondary kind, are thus a clarion call for society to provide crime victims with adequate protection and support throughout their journey within the criminal justice process and beyond (Srinivasan & Eyre, 2007). Their work at macro-, meso- and micro-interventional levels through casework, counselling of individuals and groups, advocacy and social action, community development and engagement and policy development, as well as research and professional education are precisely what is needed to address the shortcomings of the criminal justice system in relation to its treatment of victims of crime. It is in these areas that social workers will prove to be a valuable asset to leverage upon, given their professional structure, relevant expertise and empathetic disposition (Holtzhausen & Gxubane, 2012).

In a similar analytical scheme to that used in the previous section, the following recommendations will be conceptualised around the four key vectors outlined earlier by the United Nations through its 1985 Declaration.

1. *Access to justice and fair treatment:* The implementation and delivery of educational programs to inform all professionals involved in the victims' experience of the criminal justice system can significantly help enlighten them to the sensitivity, plight and situation of the victim. There is provision for social workers to facilitate victims' access to the justice system with information and explanation of the processes and procedures. This includes connecting victims to the services available for victims and their families.

2. *Restitution:* The Indian criminal justice system requires an emphasis and understanding of the benefits that restitution

can play in the recovery of the victim and potential to reduce re-victimisation. A distinction between restitution and compensation must be made. Greater attention paid to the needs of, as well as the delivery of services to, a victim for the purpose of restoration can be implemented through individual case management. This will provide an individually tailored intervention suitable for the specific requirements of a particular victim.

3. *Compensation:* As mentioned previously, the setting up of a state-funded compensation fund is critical so as to ensure that compensation can be provided regardless of the financial situation of the perpetrator. This should be put in place in tandem with allowing compensation to be disbursed prior to, and regardless of, any eventual conviction (although there should be a mechanism put in place to ensure only genuine victims of crime are compensated— this being a critical issue deserving of greater thought and research).

4. *Assistance:* Assistance by social workers can be delivered in the form of: (a) therapeutic assistance to help victims overcome their physical and emotional trauma and (b) supportive services to assist with the navigation and demands of the judicial system. The criminal justice system can be daunting and overwhelming particularly for those who have experienced the trauma of victimisation. Social workers are well positioned to demystify the formality and procedure of the victims' role as a witness, including helping them to construct and submit an impact statement to the court, if necessary, as this can be an overwhelming but empowering process for victims.

Conclusion

Victimisation can have very serious and lasting consequences on individuals, their families and society. It is important that we provide victims with the means to restore their lives and overcome the negative impact that has resulted from their experience with crime. Shifts in the way victims are perceived has seen changes around the world in relation to how they are viewed and treated. A good example of this would be the work done by the Delhi Commission for Women. This body was

> ...constituted with the aim to investigate and examine all matters relating to the safeguards provided for women under the constitution and other laws. The Commission functions in the manner of a Civil Court and strives to ensure aims envisaged in the Act through its various programmes like Sahyogini, Mahila Panchayats, Rape Crisis Cell, Mobile Help Line and Pre Marital Counselling Cell. The jurisdiction of the Commission is within National Capital Territory of Delhi. (Delhi Commission for Women, n.d.)

Unfortunately, such specific major initiatives are few and far between, and it is arguable that the Indian criminal justice system has neglected and overlooked the role and plight of victims, more generally. This has left victims in a position of not only being victimised by a criminal in the first instance but also being doubly victimised by the criminal justice system itself. With the inclusion of more comprehensive and specifically victim-focused policies and laws, these injustices can still be redressed.

An analysis of the current processes and procedures produces a clear picture of some of the current system's shortcomings that social workers are uniquely placed to ameliorate them. The specific skills set that social workers possess enable them to provide a range of services and assistance to victims, protecting their rights and supporting the process of recovery and restoration. The introduction of policies and laws that include protecting the rights of victims and ensuring that assistance is given to aid social workers in this regard, will have a significant and positive effect on the outcomes for victims of crime in India.

References

Bharti, D. (2002). *The Constitution and criminal justice administration*. New Delhi: A.P.H. Publishing Corporation.

Chockalingham, K. (2003). *Criminal victimization in four major cities in southern India.* Paper presented at the Forum on Crime and Society. Retrieved from http://www.unodc.org/pdf/crime/forum/forum3_note3.pdf

————. (2010). Measures for crime victims in the Indian criminal justice system. In M. Sasaki (Ed.), *UNAFEI resource materials series No. 81.* Tokyo: United Nations Asia and Far East Institute for the Prevention of Crime and the Treatment of Offenders.

Delhi Commission for Women. (n.d). *About us.* Retrieved from http://www.delhi.gov.in/wps/wcm/connect/lib_dcw/DCW/Home/About+Us

Dussich, J. (2006). Victimology—Past, present and future. In K. Sakai (Ed.), *The use and application of the United Nations declaration of basic principles of justice for victims of crime and abuse of power—Twenty years after its adoption* (Vol. 70) (pp. 116–29). Tokyo: United Nations Asia and Far East Institute for the Prevention of Crime and the Treatment of Offenders (UNAFEI).

Goodey, J. (2005). *Victims and victimology: Research, policy and practice.* Harlow: Pearson Longman.

Government of India, Ministry of Home Affairs. (2003). *Committee on reforms of criminal justice system report* (Vol. 1). Bengaluru: Ministry of Home Affairs, Government of India.

Hall, M. (2012). *Victims and policy-making: A comparative perspective.* Hoboken: Taylor and Francis.

Holtzhausen, L., & Gxubane, E. T. (2012). *Criminal justice social work: A South African practice framework.* Claremont, South Africa: Juta Limited.

Latha, S., & Thilagaraj, R. (2013). Restorative justice in India. *Asian Journal of Criminology, 8*(4), 309–19. doi: 10.1007/s11417-013-9164-4

Ronel, N., Jaishankar, K., & Bensimon, M. (2008). *Trends and issues in victimology.* Newcastle upon Tyn, England: Cambridge Scholars Publishing.

Sarkar, S. (2010). The quest for victims' justice in India. *Human Rights Brief, 17*(2), 16–20.

Srinivasan, M., & Eyre, M. (2007). Victims and the criminal justice system in India: Need for a paradigm shift in the justice system. *Temida, 10*(2), 51–62. doi: 10.2298/TEM0702051S

Srinivasan, M., & Mathew, E. J. (2007). Victims and the criminal justice system in India: Need for a paradigm shift in the justice system. *Temida,* (1), 51–62. doi: 10.2298/TEM0702051S

Thilagaraj, R. (2013). Criminal justice system in India. In J. Liu, B. Hebenton & S. Jou (Eds), *Handbook of Asian criminology* (pp. 119–211). New York: Springer.

United Nations. (1985). *Declaration on the basic principles of justice for victims of crime and abuse of power* (Resolution No. 40/34). Retrieved from http://www.un.org/documents/ga/res/40/a40r034.htm

Von Hentig, H. (1948). *The criminal and his victim: Studies in the sociobiology of crime.* New Haven: Yale University Press.

Wallace, H. (2007). *Victimology: Legal, psychological, and social perspectives* (2nd ed.). Boston: Pearson.

White, R. D., Perrone, S., & Gillespie, B. (2010). *Crime, criminality & criminal justice.* South Melbourne, Vic: Oxford University Press.

Winfree, L. T., & Abadinsky, H. (2010). *Understanding crime: Essentials of criminological theory.* Belmont, CA: Wadsworth Cengage Learning.

Zaykowski, H., & Campagna, L. (2014). Teaching theories of victimology. *Journal of Criminal Justice Education, 25*(4), 452–67.

SECTION III

Way Forward

9

The State of Criminal Justice Social Work Education and Professional Training in India

Sanjai Bhatt, Atul Pratap Singh and Digvijoy Phukan

Introduction

The study of criminology and victimology is not recent; in fact, crime and punishment have existed as concepts in parallel with the advent of civilisation. Crime and its punishment are among the oldest problems faced by humankind. Crime as a concept is dynamic, and it has evolved chronologically. While societies across the globe have responded in various ways to crime and offenders at different periods of history, punishing the accused has been the most common reaction to crime. Punishment and the institutions associated with it form an integral part of any orderly society (Marsh, 2004, p. 11). Chattoraj (1997, p. 43) has highlighted that an accused person may be motivated to commit crime for a range of reasons: (a) feelings of hostility and desire for revenge, (b) abstract philosophies, ideologies and religious beliefs and (c) prevailing theories of crime causation. Criminologists have identified three major categories of justification for punishing convicted persons. These justifications for inflicting punishment on criminals are as follows: (a) retribution, (b) deterrence and (c) reformation. The retributivist approach is grounded in the revenge (negative) or 'just deserts' (positive) motive. It is expressed in the logic of 'an eye for an eye and a tooth for a tooth'. It refers to the idea of deserved punishment in the penal context as retributionists emphasise the 'denunciation aspect of punishment' (Marsh, 2004, p. 12). As for deterrence, this can take at least two forms. Specific deterrence occurs when a particular offender is punished, and as a consequence, he/she refrains from committing crime in the future. General deterrence, however, occurs when other people watching how someone else has been punished for their crimes, thereafter refrain from committing similar offences for fear of being punished in like manner as well. Finally, the reformative approach attempts to change the behaviour of a criminal based on the underlying assumption that no person is born a criminal, and hence criminal violation is considered to be an outcome of the inadequate socialisation of the offender. Consequently, measures such as counselling and practical training may help to weaken or eliminate the stimuli that led the person to crime (Johnson, Wolfe, & Jones, 2008, p. 17).

The objectives of criminal justice administration can only be achieved through the reformation and rehabilitation of offenders (Chattoraj, 1997, p. 43). The primary objectives of criminal justice are the prevention and control of crime, maintenance of public order and peace, protection of the rights of the victims as well as persons in conflict with the law, punishment and rehabilitation of those adjudged guilty of committing crimes as well as the protection of life and property against crime and criminality (Thilagaraj, 2013, p. 199). Being political entities whose structure and function are lodged within the legislative, judicial and executive branches of the government, the criminal justice system (CJS) is 'society's instrument of social control' (Siegel & Worral, 2013, p. 7). The CJS aims to achieve the removal of dangerous people from society, deter others from indulging in criminal behaviour and transform the lawbreakers into law-abiding citizens. In its wider sense, the criminal justice process begins with 'social disorganization and ends in rehabilitation of criminals in society' (Sharma, 1998, p. 27). The rehabilitation of lawbreakers has been discussed virtually since the origin of the modern CJS as noted by Cullen and Gendreau (2000, p. 111). Owing to the recent shift in attention from crime to offender to convicts in penology, there is considerable emphasis on the need to change the deviant personality of offenders through rehabilitation, and reintegrate them into society for effective prevention of crime (Sharma, 1998, p. 19). Advocates of the rehabilitation perspective view the justice system as a means of caring for and treating people who have been the victims of social inequalities and are of the opinion that control of crime can be achieved by helping people overcome 'any personal and or psychological problems caused by their life circumstances' (Siegel & Worral, 2013, p. 17).

The Criminal Justice System in India: A Brief Overview

The history of crime in India is not new. In fact, crime as a concept in India has derived its historicity from the inequities of society where a majority of the population in India struggles every day for food, water and shelter. Incidentally, crime as a concept has also derived its origin from the existing deviancies in culture and the loss of morality as preached in the Ancient Vedas and Upanishads. The Constitution of an independent India provides for a quasi-federal system of government. Schedule VII of the Indian Constitution limits the law-making powers of the Union and state governments in what are known as the Union List, State List and the Concurrent List. Public order, police, officers and servants of the state high courts and prisons are subjects in the State List and the states have exclusive power to make laws on these subjects. Criminal procedure, the law of evidence and the criminal law are subjects in the Concurrent List and both Centre as well as states can make laws. However, Central law, if made, prevails over State law in case of any disparity between the two. The Indian Penal Code (IPC) (1860), the Code of Criminal Procedure (this Act was enacted in 1861 but was later repealed, and a new code came into effect in 1973) and the Indian Evidence Act of 1872, form the essence of India's criminal legislation, and are considered basic law. To supplement the provisions of this basic law and to deal with special matters or to meet local conditions, special laws are also made by both Centre and the states (Balakrishnan, 1979,

p. 116). India, like many other third-world countries, has inherited the systems of criminal law, procedures and rules which pertain to the three agencies of the CJS from its colonial rulers. These principal formal agencies of the CJS are the law enforcement agencies (e.g., the police), court agencies (e.g., the judiciary) and corrections agencies (e.g., the prisons). Each agency has a distinct task to perform. Detailing the functions of each agency, Siegel and Worral state that

> law enforcement agencies investigate crimes and apprehend suspects; court agencies, in which charges are brought, indictments submitted, trials conducted, and sentences formulated; and correctional agencies, which are charged with monitoring, treating, and rehabilitating convicted offenders. (2013, p. 8)

The functioning of all these agencies is interrelated and reforming any part of the CJS will necessitate a parallel change in the other parts and procedures of the administration (Sharma, 1998, p. 31). The correctional agencies which constitute the third agency of the CJS can be classified into institutional/residential corrections and non-institutional/community corrections (Gillespie, 2004, p. 17). Dassi (2012) has classified correctional interventions into three types, namely: (a) institutional treatment, (b) non-institutional treatment and (c) hybrid treatment (p. 1402). Under institutional treatment, the main agencies are the prison, the Observation Home, the Special Home, the Children's Home, the After-Care Organisation, the Protective Home for Women, the Short Stay Home and the Beggar Homes (Table 9.1). Non-institutional treatment includes probation and parole while community service and work release constitute hybrid treatment.

The Criminal Justice System and Correctional Social Work

The roots of crime and correctional administration are derived in the advent of social work practice in India. In fact, one of the earliest disciplines taught in the realm of social work was crime and

Table 9.1:
Correctional Agencies for Institutional Treatment

Nomenclature	Description
Prison	For adult offenders who are ineligible or inappropriate for non-institutional or community-based correctional programmes.
Observation Home	For the temporary reception of any juvenile in conflict with law during the pendency of a case before the Juvenile Justice Board. It is established under the Juvenile Justice (Care and Protection of Children) Act, 2015.
Special Home	For the reformation and rehabilitation of juveniles in conflict with the law. It is established under the Juvenile Justice (Care and Protection of Children) Act, 2015.
Children Home	For the reception of children in need of care and protection. It is established under the Juvenile Justice (Care and Protection of Children) Act, 2015.
After-Care Organisation	For the juveniles discharged from Special or Children Homes.
Protective Home for Women	Admits girls and women, who are rescued from brothels, are abducted and kidnapped, raped and are in moral danger. It is established under the Immoral Traffic (Prevention) Act, 1956.
Short Stay Home	For girls and women in the age group of 18–45 years, who are destitute, in distress, deserted or are in moral danger. It is established under the Immoral Traffic (Prevention) Act, 1956.
Beggar Home	For the reception of beggars. It is established under the anti-beggary laws of the state government.

Source: Dassi (2012).

how a positive change in socio-economic or psychological functioning can be brought about for criminals. The discipline of social work has been integral to the functioning of the CJS. The social work profession has a credible history in providing essential intervention and services to the criminal and juvenile justice populations to bring about meaningful change in the CJS (Wilson, 2010). Professional social workers act as key actors in the team of professionals and paraprofessionals working in the justice system. The engagement of social workers in the CJS is referred to as correctional social work. Social work has evolved as an essential component of the Indian CJS and the term criminal justice social work has recently been adopted. Social workers have had a defined role in providing services to the clientele group since soon after the expansion of the profession in the decade of 1960–70. Correction is a generic term covering a variety of functions carried out by government agencies that are concerned with punishment, treatment, supervision and management of individuals who have been accused or convicted of criminal offenses. These functions are carried out in secure institutions as well as in community-based correctional agencies like probation and parole departments (Stohr, Walsh, & Hemmens, 2009, p. 1). Siegel and Bartollas (2011) state that the correctional system has been developed to 'confine, manage, and provide rehabilitative programmes for those convicted of crime, all within a safe, secure, and humane environment' (p. 4). Harsh sentencing and punitive correctional philosophies were dominant in the major part of the twentieth century; however, the concept of rehabilitation has made a comeback and many correctional agencies are now focused on rehabilitation. Siegel and Bartollas note how a

> contemporary correctional system has emerged as an institution that serves to provide sufficient consequences to individuals convicted by courts for violating law so that the public will be protected, fear of crime will be reduced, and offenders are given a chance to reform. (2011, p. 19)

Srivastava (1969) traces the origin of the introduction of correctional services in India to 1836, when Lord Macaulay introduced reforms to the then existing prison practices (p. 118). After a decade of Indian independence, the following features of corrections were noticed: (a) a shift in emphasis of prisons being a punitive institution to one that is reformative; (b) design and construction of jails and reformatories to suit the implementation of corrective potentials and techniques; (c) a change in prison maintenance; (d) introduction of classification and segregation techniques among inmates; (e) a humane and liberal treatment of individuals; (f) expansion of educational and vocational training in prisons; (g) extension of probation and parole services and above all (h) a priority in appointment of social services trained personnel to supervisory posts in the prisons and reformatories.

The emphasis on reformation in corrections opened up positions for social workers in the correctional institutions in India. As a result, social workers were appointed to the posts of probation officer, liaison officer, child welfare officer, prison welfare officer and caseworker in these institutions. For social workers to be effective with criminal caseloads, they would need the following additional knowledge, skills and attitudes (Studt, 1959, as cited in Sikka, 1985): (a) knowledge of delinquent and criminal behaviour; (b) skills in identifying social and pathological factors in causation of particular delinquent behaviours and (c) attitude of acceptance of criminal behaviour and readiness to work experimentally and without undue discouragement.

While social casework is the most commonly used method of social work practice in dealing with correctional caseloads, there is also the scope for application of social group work in these settings (Sikka, 1985, p. 33). As noted by Champagne and Felizardo (2005), social workers employed within corrections have to constantly balance the needs and interests of the individual in conflict with the law, the directive and focus of the various correctional agencies, the standpoint of victims and commitments to the community, with an overriding emphasis on both public and personal safety.

Education and Training in the Criminal Justice System in India

Criminology in general, and the CJS in particular, are interdisciplinary sciences which involve knowledge from different academic disciplines such as sociology, political science, psychology, economics, natural sciences, law, social work etc. As an outcome of a national conference of higher level police officers in 1950, efforts were made to introduce criminology and forensic science as courses of study at university. The need for university teaching of criminology and forensic science was also stressed in various annual meetings of the Central Advisory Committee on Forensic Science (Tiwari & Ravikumar, 2000). In 1950, the United Nations Educational, Scientific and Cultural Organization (UNESCO) realised the significance of teaching criminal justice at college/university levels in Asia, and a consensus towards the same emerged in a symposium in London in 1955. Subsequently, in its 1957 report, the UNESCO strongly appealed for the teaching of criminology in universities throughout the world. The University of Sagar responded with the establishment of the Department of Criminology and Forensic Sciences in 1959. The introductory remarks about the Department of Criminology at the website of the University of Madras rightly mentioned that the size and urgency of the crime problem in India underscores the need for professional training. This provided a necessary impetus towards the formal teaching of criminology in the country (please refer to http://www.unom.ac.in/index.php?route=department/department/about&deptid=22).

The study of the nature, cause and treatment of crime is an area which deserves special attention with a separate academic curriculum. The University Grants Commission (UGC) set up a high level committee to advise the Commission on the steps to be taken for the introduction of criminology and forensic sciences in university education. This recommended that universities should be encouraged to introduce courses in criminology at the undergraduate level with postgraduate courses in criminology and forensic science. Consequently, three universities—Punjabi University, Patiala in the north; University of Madras and Karnataka University at Dharwad—started courses in the subject, followed by three more universities. The Gujarat Forensic Science University mainly has Departments of Forensic Science. In 2011, the School of Criminology and Criminal Justice in Rani Channamma University, Belgaum started imparting a complete set of training which equips students for any kind of employment in any of the allied and highly interrelated fields of criminal justice. So far, there are not more than a dozen departments offering postgraduate degrees with varying nomenclature serving the field of criminal justice. In the same year, India's premier open learning university—Indira Gandhi National Open University (IGNOU)—started a six-month certificate course in Social Work and Criminal Justice System (CSWCJS) in order to train a cadre of graduate professionals interested in working in correctional settings such as jails, family courts, beggar homes, special schools for boys and girls, observation homes, rescue homes etc. Despite the fact that criminological research and teaching seems to have a strong national bias in comparison to the British or American tradition of criminology, its growth remained too slow. While British criminology was initially more inclined towards a legalistic perspective, sociologists dominated American criminology for a long time. Indian criminology is largely oriented towards correctional social work with an emphasis on correctional administration and social defence programmes. It would not be inappropriate to note that the study of criminology and CJS was first integrated into courses of social work. Social work training in India, especially in the field of criminal justice, was in tune with the shift in penal philosophy from deterrence to reformation to rehabilitation of offenders. Juvenile delinquency as a subject of study was added at the Tata Institute of Social sciences (TISS) in a two-year diploma course in social work. TISS offered a six-month programme to prison officials in the early 1950s. In 1952, the United Nations (UN) experts played a crucial role in planning the specialisation in criminology and correctional administration as a course of study. Mr J. J. Panakal established the Department of Criminology and Correctional Administration in 1953. The training of correctional service professionals has remained a prominent area in Indian schools of social work. In 1990, Dr Sanober Sahni initiated the field action project called Prayas in the Mumbai Central Prison. Presently, the Centre for Criminology and Justice focuses on social pathology, social construction of crime and violence, as well as issues of prevention and access to justice.

Bhatt and Pathare (2005, p. 30) have previously outlined the five stages in the history of social work education in India, which are as follows: (a) initiation/inception (1936–46), (b) experimentation (1947–56), (c) expansion (1957–76), (d) moderation/stagnation (1977–86) and (e) explosion (1987 to date). Adding to this categorisation, the current phase of social work education in India can be termed as consolidation, with a diversification phase after 2005. There are a number of schools of social work that have been closed down for various reasons, though a number of schools, departments, allied courses (like human resource management, social entrepreneurs, disaster management, child protection etc.) have been initiated. There is now a realization, however, that more is needed to impart education for effective professional practice in most schools of social work. In the successive stages of growth of social work institutions (1947–76), 37 schools opened (Bhatt & Pathare, 2005, p. 30). It is interesting to note that most of these schools incorporated criminology and correctional services in their syllabi, and it emerged as one of the five most popular specialisations taught in schools of social work. The other four specialisations were labour welfare and personnel management, community development, family and child welfare and medical and psychiatric social work. It is clear that social work education in India has been actively responding to the need to engage with the CJS since the initial stage. Practical and academic training have been imparted to the social work students to enable them to work in various settings of the CJS and address the complex psychosocial needs of individuals who come into contact with any of the three agencies of the system (UGC, First Review Committee, 1965, p. 17).

In recent years, the problem of rehabilitation of certain maladjusted groups in society became important. The government has started taking an interest in this field and promulgated a number of legislation for the furtherance of preventive measures in respect of the immoral trafficking in women, juvenile delinquents, beggars etc. Steps have also been taken to set up rescue homes, Borstal schools, probation hostels and other institutions. The UGC appointed a second review committee to review social work education in India. The Committee emphasised that social work education should have a developmental thrust, but should not ignore rehabilitation and remedial tasks. Therefore, the Committee recommended making social work education relevant to the needs of the country, setting up programmes at doctoral, masters and bachelor degree levels (UGC, Second Review Committee, 1980, pp. 41–42). Despite this recommendation, not many universities opened programmes at bachelor and doctoral levels. In its third effort, the UGC provided the structure for social work education in the form of a model curriculum in 2001 which was developed by the UGC Panel for Social Work Education. The curriculum frame, and influences on the social work profession in India, is illustrated in Figure 9.1.

Figure 9.1 indicates the continued influence from other countries on social work education in India, especially in relation to the core domain of the profession which has been influenced by the American design. The suggested paradigm has three domains—the core, the supportive and the interdisciplinary; there is also a fourth domain that entails elective content which relates to the CJS, for example, criminology and correctional

Figure 9.1:
Social Work Profession—Curriculum Frame and Influences

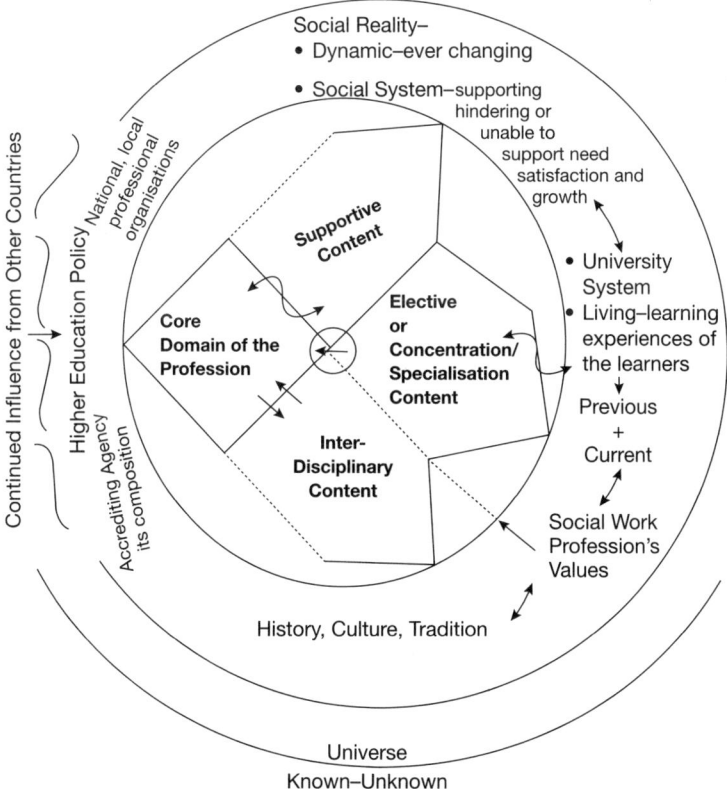

Source: UGC (2001, p. xiv).

administration or as seen in most social work schools: correctional services and social defence. The given curriculum framework demands educators to identify knowledge, values and objectives (UGC, 2001). Students at master's level are introduced to concepts from criminology, corrections and victimology, correctional administration, social defence, penology, criminal law and procedures, CJSs, juvenile delinquency, social legislation etc. The content of such curriculums are usually updated regularly to track pragmatic shifts, for example, from a welfare orientation to a rights-based perspective. Newer concepts are continually included: for example, environmental crimes, prevention of abuse of vulnerable senior citizens, drug addicts, beggars, sex workers, the homeless etc. This is to ensure that the students are kept abreast of recent developments in the field of criminal justice. Presently, correctional social work or criminal justice social work education is very popular in schools/departments of social work in various universities across India.

Training in Criminal Justice System

Training in the field of correctional social work is of great significance but unfortunately, critical 'on-the-job training' is often either inadequate or missing entirely. The work of reclaiming and reforming convicts or criminals, and of dealing with offenders of varied crimes can be done more effectively by trained personnel. Of particular importance is the training needed in social defence, this being an integrated concept for the protection of society against crime. According to the *Sage Dictionary of Criminology*, the penal philosophy of social defence focuses on the 'neutralisation' and 'resocialisation' of the offenders (Mclaughlin & Muncie, 2013, p. 425). This concept gained international recognition after it was accepted and used by the UN in 1948. The edifice of the modern concept of social defence is built around the following ideas: (a) a concern for the protection of society over and above the expiatory punishment; (b) a desire to bring about the amelioration of the offender beyond the infliction of retributive penalty and (c) an attempt to promote or to safeguard the concept of the human person to whom only humane treatment can be applied (Chattoraj, 1988, p. 50).

Srivastava (2000) is of the view that although the idea of social defence did reach India soon after it became popular in the Western countries, it was only in the first half of the twentieth century when, with the submission of the Report of the Indian Jail Committee (1919–20), that the era of social defence emerged. In view of the need to plan strategies to prevent crime and reform the offenders—in tune with the emerging philosophies in dealing with crime and criminals—the social defence approach found a place in the second Five-Year Plan (1957–62) of India. The Children's Act, 1960 passed by the central government does lay down that the rules made under the said Act may provide for the qualification and duties of probation officers as well as the recruitment and training of such employees. The Delhi School of Social Work, as the second school of social work in India, and the first school in Asia to offer a master's level programme within the university system, offered a specialisation in Social Defence and Correctional Services. The objectives of the specialisation was to enable students to gain an understanding of the concept and philosophy of social defence and correctional services, as well as to develop practice skills in prevention, correction and rehabilitation work from a social defence perspective. The Delhi School also organised training courses for government officials from the police, prison and social defence services to enable and sharpen practice learning. It is worthwhile to note that the shift from welfare to advocacy and empowerment in social work practice has brought about corresponding changes in training and capacity building exercises of social defence personnel. The trained social workers are employed by government and not-for-profit organisations working in the field of criminal justice and social defence.

Three centrally sponsored schemes operated by the state governments, thirteen posts of a welfare officer in the prisons and one hundred probation officer positions were created during the second Five-Year Plan. In addition to these, the government established remand homes, certified schools, protective homes, rescue homes and reception centres across the country (Chattoraj, 1988, p. 51). The third Five-Year Plan saw the launch of a government project offering non-institutional service for the prevention of juvenile delinquency and beggary. It was from the fourth Five-Year Plan that the social defence schemes were transferred to the state sector of the Plan. The administration of social defence services comes within the purview of State Government and Union Territory Administration. In the central government, there is a social defence division in the Ministry of Social Justice and Empowerment which caters to the requirements of the victims of alcoholism and substance abuse, as well as of senior citizens in India. The major focus areas of social defence in India are: (a) child protection, (b) welfare of prisoners, (c) probation and allied measures, (d) substance abuse prevention, (e) care of older persons, (f) beggary prevention and (g) suppression of immoral traffic in women and girls. In addition to these, social defence is also responding to emerging crime trends such as cybercrime, white-collar crime, terrorism, environmental crime etc.

A major landmark in the area of social defence in India was the establishment of the Central Bureau of Correctional Services in 1961 as per the recommendations of the All India Jail Manual Committee (1957–59) under the Ministry of Home Affairs. In 1975, the Central Bureau was reorganised into the National Institute of Social Defence which is the nodal agency for training and research in the field of social defence with the following main objectives: (a) to review policies and programmes in the field of social defence; (b) to anticipate and diagnose social defence problems; (c) to develop preventive, rehabilitative and curative policies in the field of social defence and (d) to develop and promote voluntary effort in the areas of social defence. The National Institute has, since its inception, collaborated with schools of social work in the country to advance research and training in the area of social defence. In addition, two national level organisations in India which have teamed up with social workers and the not-for-profit sector are the Bureau of Police Research and Development (BPR&D) and the National Institute of Criminology & Forensic Science (NICFS). While BPR&D was established in 1970 as a multifaceted consultancy organisation for researching issues related to police forces, NICFS was set up in January 1972 as a comprehensive facility for teaching, training, research and consultancy in the fields of criminology and forensic science so as to meet the ground level demand of criminal justice administration in the country. In-service training and other courses are being conducted by NICFS; these courses are meant for different categories of personnel such as judges, magistrates, senior police officers, defence officers, prosecution officials and prison/correctional/welfare administrators. NICFS also delivers the master's degree in forensic sciences.

The implementation of social defence programmes can face, however, several hurdles, such as the following: a lack of uniformity of institutional structure, policy declarations, administrative rules and practice; functioning of social defence institutions on traditional lines; an increased tendency to depend on institutional measures of crime prevention and treatment of offenders; the lack of much needed material and non-material resources and the lack of proper recognition of social defence personnel in terms of salary, conditions of service and growth opportunities (Srivastava, 2000, p. 9). The efficacy of these programmes in terms of protecting society against crime, and maintenance of social order, will increase with greater participation by the public (Gokhale, 1982, pp. 5–14). Concepts like community policing, which encourages police–community interaction so as to facilitate finding creative solutions for the various crime problems of the community (Chakraborty, 2003, p. 251), will also go a long way in the attainment of the ultimate objective of social defence. In the vision document submitted to the Planning Commission, Dr Hira Singh, the former director of National Institute of Social Defence (NISD), stated that the aim of the social defence approach on one hand, is to perfect the system dealing with the offender, and on the other hand, to forestall conditions that generate criminality (Singh, 2004, pp. 453–72).

Conclusion

Social work as a discipline has emerged and evolved through many facets of history. However, the prisons and their walls have more histories and secrets than the cases in courts reveal. Here, social work as a discipline plays an important role, especially in the rights-based approach. The discipline of social work, especially the bachelors and masters curricula in India, pays separate attention to correctional social work. Criminal justice social work is fraught with many challenges and contradictions. For example, the prison systems in India preach the idea of victimology to a considerable extent even though, an accused person (who is innocent until proven guilty) can remain undertrial (and sometimes in detention) for a lifetime because of the delays caused by court procedures. Further, the social work discipline plays an important role, not only for rights of the accused but also to ensure justice for imprisoned inmates. The juvenile justice system also poses a serious challenge for the discipline and its trainees. The complexities of crime and trials, especially to the under aged, and also the issues of exploitation of children in institutional care represent major hurdles for probationary officers who are mainly social work trained professionals. Training of social work professionals, therefore, needs to emerge from an integrated approach. Crimes committed within prisons, especially against women, and custodial deaths are issues which often remain behind the iron curtains of the prison, and consequently receive the least attention from the social work discipline, especially in research, and among the academia and activists. This, of course, must change. It has been re-emphasised by one and all that the key CJS stakeholders, probationary officers, police and correctional personnel, including the judiciary, require a social work orientation so as to meet these challenges head on. The emergence and adoption of social defence as a sub-discipline of the CJS is a positive development that brings with it the preventive aspects of crime and reinforces the rights of the accused, as well as victim. Incidentally, the list of successful projects on prisoners and after prison care is increasing. Such interventions are carried out by schools of social work and other organisations, and there are lot of field action projects aimed in this direction. The BPR&D often teaches police officers care and correctional methods in order to bring about positive rehabilitation of the undertrials and prisoners. The issue of women, and children of prisoners, has been addressed quite sensitively too. Training courses such as beautician, knitting, weaving, handicraft and computer applications are being imparted to female inmates so as to equip them with employable skills so that they can acquire a source of livelihood after being released from prison. In a nutshell, professional social workers have demonstrated their presence in the correctional justice system—from prevention, protection, education, reformation and rehabilitation—through innovative institutional and non-institutional programmes.

Social work as a practice–academic discipline is enriched by theories of social work, social sciences, humanities and indigenous knowledge. Social work is an essential/important qualification for the positions of probationary officers, child protection officers, family counsellors, superintendents of observation/juvenile homes and members of child welfare committees/juvenile justice boards. The unique practice-based services provided by social workers not only herald social change and social cohesion but also promote collective responsibility of the different stakeholders in the CJS. The weaknesses of the existing educational system with regards to criminal justice social work emanates from the fact that the courses related to the CJS are mostly taught at the master's level (as specific courses) in less than 1 per cent of the universities in India. The courses on forensic science are almost negligible within the university education system. The subject matter of criminology, human rights, forensic sciences and social defence are not being taught at the undergraduate level. Similarly, the paraprofessional courses are also missing. That being said, some of these gaps can be filled by designing needs-based short-term certificate/diploma courses for different categories of clientele. For example, these courses can be designed for house mothers, caregivers, social workers, counsellors, legal assistants, paralegal workers, office assistants, rehabilitation workers, housekeeping staff, vocational trainers etc. So far, these personnel neither have an orientation around the concept and philosophies of crime, offenders and reformations, nor do they have any integrated work approach. As a result, their reformative efforts get unintentional paralytic strokes and their major goals are crushed ignorantly. Such courses will create many jobs for the unemployed youngsters, and it will also minimise the gaps in delivery of requisite services. Further, it will improve the quality of manpower, reduce the cost of in-service training or capacity building programmes, as well as bring effectiveness to the system. To achieve a high quality of services, improving the quality of the personnel is a prerequisite.

Social workers employed in this area will have to emphasise the need to adopt a human rights-based approach when dealing with offenders or victims of crime. The need of the hour requires: (a) efficient management of the social defence projects; (b) increased collaboration between the national and state level organisations involved in research and training in the focus areas of social defence, and the schools of social work and (c) framing of policies with respect to job roles, remuneration and career growth of the social work professionals working in the field of social defence, and in the different agencies of the CJS, so as to ensure that they are encouraged to take up work in this challenging field of practice. The social work profession in general, and educators in particular, need to gear their advocacy efforts with the key stakeholder agencies—especially with government and higher educational authorities—in order to respond to the existing gaps and emerging realities in the field of criminal justice.

References

Balakrishnan, S. (1979). Recent innovations in criminal justice system in India. In W. Clifford (Ed.), *Innovations in criminal justice in Asia and the Pacific* (pp. 115–48). Canberra: Australian Institute of Criminology.

Bhatt, S., & Pathare, S. (2005). Social work literature in India: A critical review. In the *Proceedings of the National Seminar on Gender, HIV/ AIDS and Social Work* (pp. 29–45). New Delhi: National Institute of Public Cooperation and Child Development.

Chakraborty, T. (2003). Prospect of community policing: An Indian approach. *The Indian Journal of Political Science, 64*(3–4), 251–62.

Champagne, D., & Felizardo, V. (2005). *Social work practice in corrections.* Retrieved from http://www.casw-acts.ca/en/social-work-practice-corrections

Chattoraj, B. N. (1988). Social defence from an Indian perspective. *Indian Journal of Criminology and Criminalistics, V*(1–2), 50–55.

Chattoraj, B. N. (1997). Current penal philosophy. In N.K. Chakrabarti (Ed.), *Administration of criminal justice-1* (pp. 43–50). New Delhi: Deep & Deep Publications.

Cullen, F. T., & Gendreau, P. (2000). Assessing correctional rehabilitation: Policy, practice, and prospects. In J. Horney (Ed.), *Criminal justice 2000: Vol. 4. Policies, processes, and decisions of the criminal justice system* (pp. 109–75). Washington, DC: National Institute of Justice, U.S. Department of Justice.

Dassi, A. (2012). Social work in correctional setting. In S. Singh & S.P. Srivastav (Eds), *Encyclopedia of social work in India* (pp. 1397–1407). Lucknow: New Royal Book Company.

Gillespie, W. (2004). Crime and justice in the United States. In S. Stanko, W. Gillespie, & G. A. Crew (Eds.), *Living in a prison: A history of correctional system with an insider's view* (pp. 3–24). Westport: Greenwood Publishers.

Gokhale, S. D. (1982). Community participation in social defence. *Social Defence, 18*(70), 5–14.

Johnson, H. A., Wolfe, N. T., & Jones, M. (2008). *History of criminal justice* (4th ed.). Newark: LexisNexis Mathew Bender.

Marsh, I. (2004). *Criminal justice: An introduction to philosophies, theories and practice.* London: Routledge.

Sharma, P. D. (1998). *Criminal justice administration.* Jaipur: Rawat Publications.

Singh, H. (2004). *Social defence vision 2020 in India vision 2020: The report.* Report of the committee on India vision 2020, Planning Commission, Government of India. New Delhi: Academic Foundation.

Mclaughlin, E., & Muncie, J. (2013). *Sage Dictionary of Criminology* (3rd ed.). London: SAGE Publications Ltd.

Siegel, L., & Bartollas, C. (2011). *Corrections today.* Belmont, CA: Wadsworth.

Siegel, L., & Worral, J. L. (2013). *Essentials of criminal justice.* Belmont, CA: Wadsworth.

Sikka, K. D. (1985). Social work in correctional settings: An analysis. *Social Defence, XXI*(82), 25–41.

Srivastava, S. P. (1969). Corrections in India: Some issues. *The Indian Journal of Social Work, XXX*(2), 117–22.

———. (2000). Explaining the concept of social defence. *Social Defence, 49*(144), 1–12.

Stohr, M. K., Walsh, A., & Hemmens, C. (2009). *Corrections: A text/reader.* Thousand Oaks, CA: SAGE Publications.

Thilagaraj, R. (2013). Criminal justice system in India. In J. Liu, B. Hebenton, & S. Jou (Eds), *Handbook of Asian criminology* (pp. 119–211). New York: Springer.

Tiwari, R. K., & Ravikumar, K. V. (2000). History and development of forensic science in India. *Journal of Postgraduate Medicine, 46*(4), 303–08.

University Grants Commission (UGC). (1965). *Social work education in Indian universities.* New Delhi: Government of India.

————. (1980). *Review of social work education in India: Retrospect and prospect.* Report of the Second Review Committee, New Delhi: UGC.

————. (2001). *UGC panel on social work education.* National curriculum report for educational programmes of social work profession. New Delhi: Government of India. Retrieved from http://www.ugc.ac.in/policy/ug_pg/appendix.pdf

Wilson, M. (2010). *Criminal justice social work in the United States: Adapting to new challenges.* Washington, DC: NASW Center for Workforce Studies.

10

Human Rights in the Indian Criminal Justice System: Women and Children

Venkat Pulla, Mark David Chong,
Abraham P. Francis and Margaret Henni

Introduction

The fundamental rights in the Indian Constitution are meant to guarantee its citizens individual rights common to most liberal democracies, such as equality before the law, freedom of speech and expression, freedom of association and peaceful assembly, freedom of religion and the right to constitutional remedies for the protection of civil rights. In the most ideal context, while rights remain enshrined in the Constitution, the realisation of many of these is set out in the Directive Principles of State Policy (DPSP) as well as the fundamental duties contained in the sections of the Constitution of India that prescribe the obligations of the various states within the Union of India to its citizens, and the duties of the citizens to the state. Although, the DPSP sections are pivotal elements of the Constitution, they remain ironically unenforceable. These fundamental duties are sometimes described as the moral obligations of all citizens to help promote a spirit of patriotism, and to hold the country's unity. Writing on the ideas of justice, Nobel Laureate, Amartya Sen said

> there is no automatic guarantee of success by the mere existence of democratic institutions. The success of democracy is not merely a matter of having the most perfect institutional structure that we can think of. It depends inescapably on our actual behaviour patterns and the working of political and social interactions. There is no chance of resting the matter in the 'safe' hands of purely institutional virtuosity. The working of democratic institutions, like all other institutions, depends on the activities of human agents in utilizing opportunities for reasonable realization (2011, p. 1).

More recently, Justice Verma, Justice Seth and Mr Subramanium, in their 'Report of the Committee on Amendments to Criminal Law' (2013), referred to Amartya Sen's comments (as mentioned earlier), and further explained that '[i]nstitutional virtuosity by itself is not enough without "individual virtuosity." The most perfect laws would remain ineffective without the efficiency and "individual virtuosity" of the human agency for implementing the laws, namely, the law enforcement agencies' (Verma, Seth, & Subramanium, 2013, pp. 5-6).

Thus, having laws, in itself, is insufficient. It must be accompanied by a general obedience to those laws, and in particular, the fundamental duties articulated in Article 51A of the Constitution of India.[1] If the citizenry, more often than not, behaves

---

[1] Article 51A of the Constitution of India 1949 states that: Fundamental duties: It shall be the duty of every citizen of India (a) to abide by the Constitution and respect its ideals and institutions, the National Flag and the National Anthem; (b) to cherish and follow the noble ideals which inspired our national struggle for freedom; (c) to uphold and protect the sovereignty, unity and integrity of India; (d) to defend the country and render national service when called upon to do so; (e) to promote harmony and the spirit of common brotherhood amongst all the people of India transcending religious, linguistic and regional or sectional diversities; to renounce practices derogatory to the dignity of women; (f) to value and preserve the rich heritage of our composite culture; (g) to protect and improve the natural environment including forests, lakes, rivers and wild life, and to have compassion for living creatures; (h) to develop the scientific temper, humanism and the spirit of inquiry and reform; (i) to safeguard public property and to abjure violence; (j) to strive towards excellence in all spheres of

in contravention of the law, then the apparatus of the criminal justice system will only be a paper tiger—mere graffiti on the public walls and spaces in India. Justice clearly ought to be the first principle of social institutions and all social edifices (including the criminal justice system). Unfortunately, a surge in the number of complaints received by the National Human Rights Commission (NHRC) over the years, which has steadily grown from 496 complaints in 1993–94—the year the NHRC was set up—to 95,174 fresh cases in 2011–12, does not bode well at all (National Human Rights Commission, 2012, p. 4). That said, it could be argued that the phenomenal increase in the number of complaints is indicative of the growing awareness of rights among the people, and their growing faith in the Commission.

The same contention, however, may not be the case in relation to breaches of the criminal law. More than 5.7 million cognizable offences[2] were recorded under the Indian Penal Code (1.99 million) and Special and Local Laws (3.74 million)—equating to a rate of 504.5 (cognizable) crimes per 100,000 people in India in 2007 (Chockalingam, 2010, p. 97). The dismal police–population ratio in India (106 police personnel per 0.1 million of the population) has not only overburdened these key service providers but has also been negatively impacting upon their performance (Pandey, 2014). The underlying causes of many disputes that the police are expected to become involved in at the police station are intimately related to 'caste, class, ethnicity and gender' issues (Prayas, 2012b, p. 9). The Prayas Handbook explains that the presentation of aggrieved parties at a police station is usually a measure of last resort, often coming after 'ineffective or unjust interventions by social agencies such as the family, the community, religious or political institutions' (2012b, p. 10), and particularly when the original dispute is 'marked by power inequities' (2012b, p. 10).

It is axiomatic to state that no society can ever function properly without a responsible government and vigilant civil society

---

individual and collective activity so that the nation constantly rises to higher levels of endeavour and achievement; (k) who is a parent or guardian to provide opportunities for education to his child or, as the case may be, ward between the age of six and fourteen years.

[2] Cognizable offences are 'those for which a police officer can arrest a suspect without a court warrant' (Chockalingam, 2010, p. 97).

organisations. The protection of human rights in any society requires both the government and civil society to be in an indispensable partnership in the fight against human rights violations. Such a relationship is of course central to building an energetic and vibrant democracy. Governments ought to enshrine a strong human rights component in the policies and programmes that they devise so as to ensure a truly beneficial and equitable utilisation of national and human resources. As for members of civil society, it is the duty of every citizen to respect the rights of the 'other', particularly those who are the most vulnerable to the vagaries of social and economic forces. Unfortunately, the extent of the crime problem as well as human rights abuse in India present challenges at all levels of the criminal justice system. Lower caste and class women as well as children are particularly vulnerable in this regard.

India is a land of great contrasts. While significant strides have been taken in economic development, this sterling progress, however, has been blighted by a poor human rights record. Rape, sexual assault, eve-teasing (i.e., unsolicited sexual advances against a woman made in public) and stalking of women in public places have become a primary concern. Not a day passes without an innocent lass being raped or molested, and if these victims are from lower economic classes and/or castes, many have argued that it would be rare for any brave officer within the criminal justice system to even acknowledge the incident, much less to record and thereafter charge sheet the offender. India undeniably, and tragically, is a patriarchal society similar to its neighbours in Bangladesh and Pakistan. Commentators and activists alike note that the South Asian Association of Regional Cooperation (SAARC) nations (which includes Afghanistan, Pakistan, India, Bangladesh, Maldives, Nepal and Sri Lanka), have a long way to go in terms of respectful conduct in gender relations. Unfortunately, there is tremendous modernisation without the necessary attitudinal changes in the ethos of Indian society. In all the SAARC countries, there is rank violation of human values, and degradation sets in, for example, through social and illegal frameworks of honour killings. It hardly matters which country has small or large statistics in terms of uncharge sheeted killings of women and female children. Justice Verma, Justice Seth and Mr Subramanium more recently lamented that 'these practices are being tolerated by a society ostensibly wedded to the rule of law' (2013, p. 1). They further noted that '[t]he fundamental rights to life with human dignity, to equality, and to work in ones chosen profession or trade inherently include protection from sexual harassment. It is indubitably the position that the Constitution guarantees fundamental freedoms to women' (Verma, Seth, & Subramanium, 2013, p. 1).

Before delving more deeply into these egregious breaches and abuses against women and children, this chapter will now outline the relevant constitutional, criminal justice and human rights regimes that are applicable in India.

Human Rights in an International Context

Many of India's human rights are enshrined in the following municipal instruments: the Constitution of India (1949); The Protection of Human Rights Act (1993; Amendments) and the Code of Conduct for the Police in India (National Human Rights Commission, 2007, pp. 51–72). However, it should be noted that these human rights correspond closely with those articulated in the Universal Declaration of Human Rights (1948). For example,

- Article 3: Everyone has the right to life, liberty and security of person;
- Article 5: No one shall be subjected to torture, or to cruel, inhuman, or degrading treatment or punishment;
- Article 7: All are equal before the law and are entitled without any discrimination to the equal protection of the law;
- Article 8: Everyone has the right to an effective remedy by the competent national tribunals for the acts violating the fundamental rights granted to him by the constitution or law;
- Article 9: No one shall be subjected to arbitrary arrest, detention, or exile;
- Article 10: Everyone is entitled in full equality to a fair and public hearing by an independent and impartial tribunal in the determination of his rights and obligations and of the criminal charge against him;
- Article 11: (1) Everyone charged with a penal offence has the right to be presumed innocent until proved guilty according to

law in a public trial at which he has had all the guarantees necessary for his defence; and (2) No one shall be held guilty of any
penal offence on account of any act or omission which did not
constitute a penal offence under national or international law, at
the time when it was committed. Nor shall a heavier penalty be
imposed than the one that was applicable at the time the penal
offence was committed; and

• Article 12: No one shall be subjected to arbitrary interference with
his privacy, family, home or correspondence, nor to attacks upon
his honour and reputation.

(National Human Rights Commission, 2007, p. 51)

In addition to the Universal Declaration of Human Rights, other
important international instruments like the United Nations
Standard Minimum Rules for the Treatment of Prisoners 1955
are especially relevant because they include rules that prescribe
non-discrimination; separation of prisoners by sex, age, and
criminal record and so on; provision of minimum level, and quality, of facilities; special consideration of those who are undertrial;
and the need for adequate and appropriate rehabilitation services (Raghavan, 2013, pp. 268–69).

While this list is not meant to be exhaustive, the following
international regimes are likewise significant in this discourse.

• The International Covenant on Civil and Political Rights
1966
• The Convention against Torture and other Cruel, Inhuman
or Degrading Treatment or Punishment 1984
• The Convention on the Rights of the Child 1989
• The United Nations Standard Minimum Rules for the
Administration of Juvenile Justice 1980 (also known as the
'Beijing Rules')
• The United Nations Code of Conduct for Law Enforcement
Officials 1979

While United Nations resolutions represent guidelines for
appropriate treatment (e.g., the United Nations Standard
Minimum Rules for the Treatment of Prisoners 1955, United
Nations Standard Minimum Rules for the Administration of
Juvenile Justice 1980 and the United Nations Code of Conduct

for Law Enforcement Officials 1979), they are not, by themselves, legally binding. However, the Indian Constitution and many municipal human rights instruments of India also contain provisions that echo those laid down by the United Nations (Raghavan, 2013, p. 271).

Human Rights for Women and Children within an Indian Context: The Constitution

It is extremely important to remember that the equality of women and children is firmly entrenched in Article 14,[3] as well as Article 15(1)[4] of the Constitution.[5]

Other important constitutional clauses include (but are not limited to):

1. For women:
   - Article 39(a): The State shall, in particular, direct its policy towards securing—that the citizens, ... women equally, have the right to an adequate means of livelihood.
   - Article 39(d): The State shall, in particular, direct its policy towards securing—that there is equal pay for equal work for ... women.
   - Article 51A(e): It shall be the duty of every citizen of India—to promote harmony and the spirit of common brotherhood amongst all the people of India transcending religious, linguistic and regional or sectional diversities; to renounce practices derogatory to the dignity of women.
2. For children:
   - Article 21A: The State shall provide free and compulsory education to all children of the age of six to

---

[3] The State shall not deny to any person equality before the law or the equal protection of the laws within the territory of India.

[4] The State shall not discriminate against any citizen on grounds only of religion, race, caste, sex, place of birth or any of them.

[5] That said, Article 15(3) of the Indian Constitution does not inhibit the State from making special provisions for women and children.

fourteen years in such manner as the State may, by law, determine.

- Article 24: No child below the age of fourteen years shall be employed to work in any factory or mine or engaged in any other hazardous employment.
- Article 39(f): The State shall, in particular, direct its policy towards securing—that children are given opportunities and facilities to develop in a healthy manner and in conditions of freedom and dignity and that childhood and youth are protected against exploitation and against moral and material abandonment.
- Article 45: The State shall endeavour to provide early childhood care and education for all children until they complete the age of six years.
- Article 51A(k): It shall be the duty of every citizen of India—who is a parent or guardian to provide opportunities for education to his child or, as the case may be, ward between the age of six and fourteen years.
- Article 350A: It shall be the endeavour of every State and of every local authority within the State to provide adequate facilities for instruction in the mother tongue at the primary stage of education to children belonging to linguistic minority groups; and the President may issue such directions to any State as he considers necessary or proper for securing the provision of such facilities.

3. For both women and children:
   - Article 23: Traffic in human beings and begar [sic] and other similar forms of forced labour are prohibited and any contravention of this provision shall be an offence punishable in accordance with law.
   - Article 38: The State shall strive to promote the welfare of the people by securing and protecting as effectively as it may a social order in which justice, social, economic and political, shall inform all the institutions of the national life.
   - Article 39(e): The State shall, in particular, direct its policy towards securing—that the health and strength of workers, men and women, and the tender age of children

are not abused and that citizens are not forced by economic necessity to enter avocations unsuited to their age or strength.

In fact, the Preamble to the Constitution guarantees social, economic and political justice which, in the view of the Committee on the Amendments to the Criminal Law, would include gender justice, liberty of thought, expression, belief, faith and worship; equality of status and opportunity—these, of course, would reinforce the concept of equality; while fraternity enjoins citizens to treat each other with respect and dignity, regardless of gender. Justice Verma, Justice Seth and Mr Subramanium (2013) further clarified that

> [t]he right to be protected from sexual harassment and sexual assault is, therefore, guaranteed by the Constitution, and is one of the pillars on which the very construct of gender justice stands. This right is buttressed by the directive principles of State policy contained in Articles 38, 39 and 39A[6] of the Constitution, which are to be construed harmoniously with the fundamental rights in Part III; and these fundamental principles bind the State in performance of its task of governance of the country. (pp. 2–3)

Criminal Justice Rights for Women and Children

Indian criminal law also specifically protects women and children (as victims) from particular types of harm. For example, the Indian Penal Code, 1860 contains more than 20 provisions that are relevant to trafficking, as well as imposing punishments for offences like kidnapping, abduction, buying or selling a person

---

[6] Article 39A of the Indian Constitution stipulates,

> [t]he State shall secure that the operation of the legal system promotes justice, on a basis of equal opportunity, and shall, in particular, provide free legal aid, by suitable legislation or schemes or in any other way, to ensure that opportunities for securing justice are not denied to any citizen by reason of economic or other disabilities.

Table 10.1:
Main and Collateral Criminal Justice Instruments in India

Main Criminal Justice Instruments	Collateral Criminal Justice Instruments
• Karnataka Devadasis (Prohibition of Dedication) Act, 1982 • Child Labour (Prohibition and Regulation) Act, 1986 • Andhra Pradesh Devadasis (Prohibiting Dedication) Act, 1989 • Information Technology Act, 2000 • The Goa Children's Act, 2003 • The Juvenile Justice (Care and Protection of Children) Amendment Act, 2015	• Indian Evidence Act, 1872 • Code of Criminal Procedure, 1973 • Child Marriage Restraint Act, 1929 • Young Persons (Harmful Publications) Act, 1956 • Probation of Offenders Act, 1958; Criminal Procedure Code, 1973 • Bonded Labour System (Abolition) Act, 1976 • Indecent Representation of Women (Prohibition) Act, 1986 • Transplantation of Human Organs Act, 1994

for slavery/labour, buying or selling a minor for prostitution, importing/procuring a minor girl, rape and so on. The Immoral Traffic (Prevention) Act, 1956 (ITPA), initially enacted as the Suppression of Immoral Traffic in Women and Girls Act, 1956, remains the primary legislative tool for preventing and combating trafficking in human beings in India.[7] Other relevant statutes are listed in Table 10.1, along with pertinent collateral statutory instruments.

The quality and extent of victims' rights in India, however, have long been a source of disappointment for many academics and victim rights movements. That said, some positive developments have occurred over the past few years, and victims can now avail themselves to certain rights under the following pieces of legislation (note that this is not an exhaustive list):

- The Protection of Women from Domestic Violence Act, 2005
- The Maintenance and Welfare of Parents and Senior Citizens Act, 2007

---

[7] However, its prime objective to inhibit/abolish trafficking in women and girls for the purpose of prostitution as an organised means of living has been rather ineffective. The Act criminalises the procurers, traffickers and profiteers of the trade but in no way does it define 'trafficking' per se in human beings.

- Prevention of Caste-Based Victimization and Protection for Victims: The Scheduled Castes and the Scheduled Tribes (Prevention of Atrocities) Act, 1989

(Chockalingam, 2010, p. 104)

Offenders (including those who are women and children), are likewise afforded due process rights to protect them against the oppressive or unjust actions of formal agents of social control. And, even when they have been convicted, minimum standards must still be maintained for prison inmates under the Prisons Act of 1894, the Prison Manuals of each state, as well as the Model Prison Manual 1970 (Raghavan, 2013, p. 271).[8]

Breaches of Human Rights in the Indian Criminal Justice System

Before examining more closely some examples of human rights contraventions within the criminal justice system, it should be noted that such breaches are merely symptomatic of a much wider malaise afflicting the country. Patriarchal values at one level, and gender bias at the other, are arguably (though there are some notable exceptions) pervasive in South Asian countries. Even after six decades of planned development—women's human rights in general, and in particular their sexual and repro-ductive health rights—are still being violated for different motives by different sections of Indian society (Mamidi & Pulla, 2013). While the exploitation of poor rural women who are illit-erate has been amply recorded elsewhere, this chapter will high-light one particular egregious situation where illiterate women have become easy targets for 'forced' hysterectomies (Mamidi & Pulla, 2013), particularly when inhabitants of remote villages have little access to alternative health care institutions or advice, and hence, scope for making informed choices.

---

[8] For a fuller analysis of the human rights enshrined in the Indian Constitution and Indian Criminal Code, please refer to the National Human Rights Commission publication (2007).

Mamidi and Pulla (2013) reported that while female illiteracy of all ages constituted 49.71% in Andhra Pradesh in 2001, the illiterate hysterectomised women who were within the reproductive age category constituted more than three fourths. This startling statistic could be indicative of illiterate women being targeted for coerced hysterectomies. What sparked off this concern was the fact that most of these patients '... were from the Lambada tribal community, poor and illiterate' of the Medak district (Antony, 2012). In one study involving 728 hysterectomised women, many of them had little opportunity to approach any other physicians for a second opinion (Mamidi & Mamidi, 2005). Another study comprising of 171 hysterectomised women in the same district that was conducted by Life-HRG Group from 2009 to 2011 likewise arrived at similar results. The researchers there found that '[t]here was little consideration to the terms of consent given that the majority of women were from the lower income group and illiterate' (Kameswari & Vinjamuri, 2013). Similarly, women from marginalized sections of the community constitute a higher proportion among hysterectomised women, more generally. Lambada scheduled tribe women in Kowdipally mandal constituted 35.3% of hysterectomised women—significantly higher than their statistical presence of 17% of the total population (Mamidi & Mamidi, 2005). Ethnographic narratives from volunteers and other study participants highlighted the horrific suffering these victims underwent (Mamidi & Pulla, 2013):

'I am robbed of my life and my body. I did not know I was buying death. I thought the operation was going to relieve me from regular pain and the death from cancer. I am cheated and ruined. I suffer more now', complained Lakshmi, aged 35.

'They said you have sores on your ulcer. They asked us to come next day. They asked us for money and we took the money and went to them. Along with uterus they removed, the appendix also. I don't have children' told another woman.

'The reasons for surgery could be a small ailment from stomach pain to cyst. Normal problems like personal hygiene or white discharge is the most popular reason of the 728 affected women in Kowdipally mandal [who] were victims of human rights violations. After surgery results of these women make [sic] horrific stories with 72.94% of them had complaints of bleeding or white discharge, followed by stomach pain

(12.77%), cysts (4.26%), uterus erosion (3.12%), and other complaints (7.01%), explained a facilitator of a human rights campaign.

Justice Verma, Justice Seth and Mr Subramanium (2013) argued that the duty of the state, therefore, is to provide a safe environment at all times for its citizens and especially women, who constitute half of the nation's population; and failure to discharge this public duty renders the state accountable for the lapse. They additionally alluded to the fact that the state's role is not merely reactive, in the sense that the state only has to apprehend and punish the culprits for their crimes; its duty is also to prevent the commission of any crime to the best of its ability. This is particularly important because '[c]rimes against women are an egregious violation of several human rights demanding strict punishment with deterrence to prevent similar crimes in future by the likeminded' (Verma, Seth, & Subramanium, 2013, p. 3).

It must be said unequivocally that there is a great deal of violence perpetrated against women every day in India, much of this constituting rape and sexual assault. Should any sane society dismiss this as merely individual crimes of passion? No! It is arguable that these attacks are actually unwarranted and oppressive exertions of patriarchal power in India. Trafficking in women and children, both male and female, is also a serious violation of human rights on several counts. Nevertheless, such crimes are, to a certain degree, tolerated in a country with a baggage of inhuman yet culturally sanctioned practices such as the system of devadasis, jogins and bhavins and so on—some of which are ostensibly outlawed by the state but nevertheless still persist in villages and towns all over India.

It should be noted that this chapter does not intend to provide a comprehensive catalogue of every type of human rights abuse that occurs in this country. Rather, the following examples are designed to offer the reader a glimpse of the range of institutional breaches that are perpetrated against women and children by two of the most important institutions within the criminal justice system, that is, the police and the prisons.

1. Breaches committed by the Police
    The police are traditionally considered to be the gatekeepers of the criminal justice system and, coupled with being a

paramilitary force, can wield a great deal of coercive power over the population. According to Thilagaraj,

> [t]wo major issues in Indian Police system frequently raised are violence in the custody and undue political intervention in the police administration. In a number of judgments by high courts and also by the Supreme Court it has been spelt out clearly that every policeman must know that it is not permissible for police personnel to inflict even the slightest physical harm to anyone except in his own self-defense (Sunil Batra vs. Delhi Administration, 1980). Law places him on par with other citizens in that regard and he is entitled to use only that much physical force which is reasonably necessary to thwart any assault on him in the exercise of his right of self-defense. The National Human Rights has also many times intervened against this custodial violence. Despite all these interventions still there are reports on custodial violence and deaths in police custody. (2013, p. 201)

The following case studies will illustrate in greater detail some of the violence that has been perpetrated against women and children while in the custody of the police (please note, however, that these egregious acts of cruel brutality committed by a minority of police officers do not represent the otherwise benign actions of the police as a whole):

- Case Study No. 1: Torture and Gang Rape by Police Officers in Tripura—Case No. 5/23/2003–2004-WC

The National Human Rights Commission of India

> received a complaint from Shri Suhas Chakma, Director, Asian Centre for Human Rights, New Delhi alleging that a Reang girl was tortured and gang raped by a group of three Special Police Officers of the State Government of Tripura on 26/5/2003. The victim girl's family complained to the police station naming the three guilty SPOs but their complaint was not recorded. In response to the notice, a report received from the DGP, Tripura indicated that a case No. 6/2003 u/s 366 (A), 376, 326 and 34 IPC was registered in Police Station Raishyabari against the three named persons on 28/5/2003. The medical report confirmed that the victim, aged 17 years was sexually assaulted and raped. The three SPOs had been discharged from the service, arrested and sent to jail. In view of the gravity of the allegation of sexual brutality committed on a hapless girl by the three SPOS, the Commission directed to issue

a notice to the Chief Secretary, Govt. of Tripura to show cause why interim relief be not granted to the victim girl. The Govt. of Tripura informed the Commission that it had paid an amount of ₹15,000/- as compensation to the victim Ms. Mithirung Reang. However, the Commission observed that the offence of rape not only amounts to violation of the human rights of the victim, but it also tends to violate the mind and scar the psyche of a person permanently. Besides, it carries a social sigma for the victim and her family. The Commission, therefore, directed the Govt. of Tripura to pay an amount of Rupees fifty thousand as immediate interim relief to the victim after adjusting Rupees fifteen thousand already paid. As the State Government submitted its compliance report in respect of payment of an amount of Rupees thirty five thousand, the case was closed on 10/1/2005. (National Human Rights Commission, 2004–05a)

- Case Study No. 2: Illegal Detention of Two Adivasi Boys by Kerala Police—Case No. 208/11/97–98

The Christian Cultural Forum, Kollam, Kerala, submitted a complaint to the NHRC

alleging that police officials of Agali in Attappaddi in Palakkad district in Kerala arrested three Adivasis, Manikandan, Parameswaran and Kuppamma on 25.5.1997 and kept them in illegal custody for 23 days. During detention, one of the detenu Kuppamma, an Adivasi woman was beaten black and blue by the police and even chilli powder was stuffed into her vagina. According to the complainant, the Circle Inspector had falsely implicated around 100 adivasis in a fabricated case and as a result adivasis had left their houses. In response to the notice issued by the Commission, a report dated 18th December 97 was received from SP, Palakkad which revealed that an enquiry into the matter was conducted by SP, CB/CID and it was found on 27th May 1997 that police at Agali Police Station detained two boys Manikandan and Parameshwaran illegally till 17 June 1997, without any complaint having been registered against them. It was further mentioned that the Circle Inspector, ASI and two Constable who were involved in the incident had been suspended and criminal cases were instituted against them. The report also stated that Kupamma, the mother of Parmeshwaran did not make any allegations of torture, when she was produced before the Court in a criminal case. While considering the matter on 20th May 2003, the Commission directed to issue a show cause notice u/s 18(3) of the Protection of Human Rights Act, 1993 to the Chief Secretary, Govt. of Kerala to show cause as to why an immediate interim relief be not granted to Manikandan and Parameshwaran for their illegal detention. In response to the show cause notice a letter dated 26 June 2003 was received from Govt. of Kerala contending that the State Govt. is not in a position to make any payment till disposal of criminal cases, pending before the court, since the alleged delinquent officers are liable to pay compensation, if any, awarded by the court. The Commission considered the matter further on 20/5/2004 and while recommending a sum of ₹10,000/- to each of the victims as immediate interim relief, held that proceedings u/s 18(3) of the Protection of the Human Rights Act 1993 are independent and the pendency of criminal case is no impediment to the award of immediate interim relief. Pursuant to the directions of the Commission, the Govt. of Kerala vide their communication dated 14. July 2004 informed that the interim relief of ₹10,000/- each to Manikandan and Parameshwaran as recommended by the Commission has been disbursed to the incumbents on 2 July 2004. In view of compliance of the recommendations of the Commission, the case was closed. (National Human Rights Commission, 2004–05)

- Case Study No. 3: Stripping of Teenagers in Police Lock-up in Kerala

Based on the recommendation of the NHRC,

the Kerala Government has sanctioned payment of compensation of ₹10,000 to each of seven boys who were stripped and forced to spend two nights in the police lock-up at Tirunelli in Wayanad District. Necessary action has also been initiated by the State Government for recovering, through departmental proceedings, the total compensation amount of ₹70,000 from the delinquent police officers, who have been placed under suspension. The Commission took suo motu cognizance of press reports which stated that some tribal youths, mostly students, were picked up by the police when they were agitating against the opening of liquor shops in Appappara and who were treated in a very harsh manner. The Commission also subsequently received complaints in this regard from the Kerala Harijan Samajam, Centre for Human Rights, Legal Aid and Reserach [sic], Keralal and Madhya Pradesh Youth Organization, all of them being non-governmental organizations. In response to the Commission's notice calling for are port, the Kerala Government accepted that certain boys and girls, peacefully demonstrating in front of an arrack shop, were unnecessarily arrested and the the [sic] police constables behaved indecently with them. As the allegations were prima-facie found to be true, the State Government suspended four police personnel responsible for this incident and ordered a detailed enquiry. The Commission, after considering the State Government's report, termed the whole episode 'reprehensible' and as yet another case of the violation of human rights of the less fortunate in society. The Commission recommended that ₹10,000/- be paid as compensation to each of the victims and that the money be recovered from the errant personnel. In its reply, the Government of Kerala has stated [sic] that necessary [sic] compensation has been sanctioned and that efforts are on to recover it from the delinquent officers through Departmental or other appropriate proceedings. (National Human Rights Commission, 1995–96)

2. Breaches committed by the Prison Administration
   Given that imprisonment involves the deprivation of human liberty, it is no wonder that this form of punishment represents a critical human rights concern (Tiwari, 2013). Thus, decisions regarding imprisonment should not be taken lightly because once incarcerated, the prisoner is at the mercy of the state's interpretation of what constitutes fair treatment under the relevant human rights regime (Tiwari, 2013). It should be noted that prisoners are often not considered worthy of the same human rights as ordinary non-criminally convicted citizens. Many prisoners, sadly, are already from poor as well as marginalised communities— and hence, the stigmatisation associated with their imprisonment will further expose them to greater social exclusion (Tiwari, 2013). This same blighted population also has little access to advocacy or legal representation, rendering them particularly powerless to address human rights breaches and/or maltreatment (Tiwari, 2013). Overcrowding in both men and women prisons is often an underlying cause for human rights violations, and combined with the ageing infrastructure of the prison buildings, can lead to poor

living conditions that also constitute breaches of prison guidelines. A number of prisons inspected towards the end of 2013 and the beginning of 2014 were severely crowded, with evident associated problems with their living conditions. Some of the case studies below will outline these issues in more detail (please note, however, that these breaches committed by a minority of prison administrative officers do not represent the otherwise benign actions of the prison administration as a whole).

- Case Study No. 4: An Inspection of the Central Jails of Bhopal and Indore, and the District Jails of Indore and Harda

A Special Rapporteur for the NHRC visited the Central Jails of Bhopal and Indore, and the District Jails of Indore and Harda, in November 2013 (Narayan, 2013). The ensuing report listed multiple human rights violations, including, for example,

  o all the jails were overcrowded, with up to double the maximum number of inmates institutionalised there;
  o sanitation was unsatisfactory, with the water provided not of potable quality;
  o at night, there was only one toilet per 100 inmates;
  o the kitchens were unhygienic;
  o the medical centres were understaffed;
  o there were no female doctors available to treat female inmates; and
  o no mental health support was available (Narayan, 2013).

- Case Study No. 5: An Inspection of the Jodhpur Central Jail, Jodhpur, Rajasthan

A Special Rapporteur for the NHRC visited the Jodhpur Central Jail, Jodhpur, Rajasthan, in February 2014. The ensuing report noted that there was a history of custodial deaths in the prison, with 38 recorded, 16 of whom were between the age of 20 and 40 years old (Kumar, 2014). A further problem observed was the living conditions allocated to the staff of the prison. Given that only 100 staff quarters were provided for 313 prison officers, this was thought to have contributed to low morale levels among the correctional employees (Kumar, 2014). It is arguable that this low morale among the prison wardens could then have a knock-on negative effect on the way they then treated the inmates in the course of their work.

- Case Study No. 6: Escape of Inmates from Juvenile Homes, etc. (Case No. 497/13/97-98 & other 86 cases)

According to the NHRC,

> the attention of the Commission was drawn to the escape of several inmates from the Beggars' Homes/Juvenile Homes/ Remand Homes situated in different parts of Maharashtra. The Commission pointed out that it was the State Government's duty to take appropriate measures for the safe custody of the inmates. The escape of such a large number of inmates was indicative of the fact that there were either serious infrastructural deficiencies or that security arrangements were faulty. The Commission directed that the Chief Secretary, Government of Maharashtra should review the functioning of the Beggars' Home/Juvenile Homes/Remand Homes with a view to ensuring better care in these institutions and avoiding the recurrence of circumstances leading to such instance.

COMMENT

Progressive criminology propagates the use of non-institutional treatment of offenders. The loss of liberty, separation from the family and the social environment in institutions often results in unwanted consequences. Considering this, Rule 19 of the UN Standard Minimum Rules for the administration of Juvenile Justice (1980) aims at restricting institutionalisation in quantity and in time. Rule 19 lays down that the placement of juveniles in an institution shall always be a disposition of last resort and for the minimum necessary period. Art. 3 of the Convention on the Rights of the Child (CRC) mandates the state to ensure that the institutions responsible for care or protection of children shall conform with the standards established by competent authorities. Art. 19 of that Convention further mandates that the state shall take all appropriate legislative, administrative, social and educational measures to protect the child in all respects, while in the care of parents and so on or any other person. Art. 40 of that Convention recognises the state's duty to treat the child offender in a manner consistent with the child's sense of dignity and worth, which reinforces the child's respect for the human rights and fundamental freedoms of others. Rule 26 of the Beijing Declaration [i.e., the Beijing Rules] says that the juveniles shall receive care, protection and all necessary assistance, for example, social, educational, vocational, psychological, medical and physical, which they require due to their age, sex, personality and in the interest of their wholesome development.

The order of the Commission sought to review of conditions in the institutions for children, in order to bring them into conformity with acceptable standards. (National Human Rights Commission, 1998–99).

- Case Study No. 7: A Case Study of Jaipur Central Prison for Women

As stated earlier, traditional Indian society is deeply patriarchal, where women are regarded as inferior and expected to adhere to their gendered role. In this regard, traditional social norms dictate that a female should be a 'self-sacrificing, ever-serving, docile woman with no desires and needs of her own' (Kaushik & Sharma, 2009, p. 254). Thus, any assertion by a woman of her human rights is not considered to be a socially acceptable behaviour. In fact, research would suggest that many women (a majority of whom are illiterate or barely literate) are unaware that they even have a right to humane treatment while incarcerated in prison. Kaushik and Sharma (2009) studied some of the problems that women inmates were experiencing in the Jaipur Central Prison for Women. Of their sample of 150 women, 144 of them had no knowledge of their human rights while in prison. Despite rules that prescribe (minimal) payment for work undertaken in the prison factories and kitchens, not one of those questioned reported being paid for their work.[9] This is a clear violation of rights as contained in Article 23 of the Constitution which requires

---

[9] This finding is substantiated by an official report into the Rajasthan prisons completed by Lal (2004, p. 23).

that 'payment has to be equivalent to the services rendered, otherwise it would be forced labour' (Srinivasan, 2013). Furthermore, very few women inmates were achieving any additional educational qualifications while in prison, and because there are very few female-only gaols in India, these prisoners are generally (geographically) isolated from their families. Both these factors will ultimately increase their likelihood of recidivism and social dislocation post-release.

The above case studies indicate writ large just how much needs to be done in order to protect the human rights of women and children within the criminal justice system. With less than two police officers per 1,000 residents in India (Sandhu, 2011/12, p. 64), as well as constant prison overcrowding and appalling living conditions (Sivagnanam, 2012), it will be argued here that an increased use of social workers employed in, and working with, the criminal justice system, can be an effective method of improving human rights for women and children, they be offenders or victims of crime. For example, Prayas, a non-governmental organisation (NGO) based in Mumbai, has established a joint intervention model of social workers and police officers, so as to better resolve problems associated with police–community relations (2012b, p. 24). In this regard, police social work is emerging as an important speciality within criminal justice social work, and complements well the efforts of their colleagues involved in the more established correctional social work profession.

The Role of Criminal Justice Social Workers

Interactions between women, children and the police, are of special concern for Prayas. The reason for this is,

> [t]he social and economic status of women in our country gives them little autonomy in decision-making processes. In times of need, when they approach the police station, many women are scared, apprehensive and non-communicative. In such circumstances, the presence of a social worker may be seen as essential for effective communication between the women and the police. (Prayas, 2012b, p. 13)

To address these issues, police social workers must 'make the police station environment more empathetic and approachable. She has to put in the effort to explain the procedures, thus helping the women to shed their inhibitions and talk confidently about their problems and the kind of help required'. (Prayas, 2012b, p. 14)

Given that '[t]he children who reach the police station may be delinquents, runaways from homes or residential institutions, children with alleged behavioural problems, and lost children, etc.', police social workers '… must be able to provide the emotional support necessary for the child, and to suggest suitable alternatives for its rehabilitation' (Prayas, 2012b, p. 14).

Srinivasan and Mathew (2007) have noted that many victims of crime have been marginalised by the state, and hence receive little, or no, support from the criminal justice system. This lack of recognition, often occurring at the first presentation at a police station, can further exacerbate feelings of helplessness, thereby inflicting a form of secondary victimisation on them.[10] Thus, Srinivasan and Mathew (2007) emphasised that there was a need to provide all victims with assistance throughout the criminal justice process, and beyond. To address this issue, Prayas recommended that

> a social worker placed at a police station can exclusively work with cases of victims and families of victims of violent crimes such as murder, attempted murder, assault, sexual crimes, marital dispute, alcohol abuse, burns etc. where the bread winner or an equivalent family member has been killed or seriously injured. In such cases, the services offered could include counseling, home visits, hospital visits, identifying organizations/medical trusts for medical assistance, guidance and support towards gaining the benefit of government schemes, etc. (2012b, p. 15)

Thus, to make a real difference in the lives of these women and children, police social workers should be on-hand to provide them with the following services:

---

[10] Please note that the primary suffering of the victim occurred as a result of initially being victimised by the offender.

- counseling of clients and family members;
- giving information and guidance about the police station, citizens' rights and welfare services available in the community;
- making home visits to give information, assess the family situation, counseling and follow-up;
- provide medical help with regard to admission to hospital and reimbursement of bills in case of extreme poverty;
- providing financial assistance in case of emergencies, extreme poverty, etc.;
- referring of cases to institutions/agencies for shelter, legal aid, etc.; and
- legal guidance to families in criminal and family matters. (Prayas, 2012b, p. 16)

In addition to its partnership with the police, Prayas (2012a) has also done a lot of work with the prisons, and in particular expressed its concern at the lack of classification and segregation of prisoners due to overcrowding, with first-time and minor offenders being housed alongside hardened criminals. In addition, undertrial prisoners (i.e., those who have been detained while awaiting their trial, and hence not on bail) are housed with convicts (those who have been found guilty of their crimes). This can lead to a number of problems, not least the initiating of non-career criminals into a criminogenic learning environment. Furthermore, although undertrial prisoners are in the majority in such detention centres, they appear to be relatively powerless within the prison system, and are often led further astray or manipulated by the more hard-core criminal inmates (Prayas, 2012a).

To prevent first-time and minor offenders (including those who are undertrial detainees) from being socialised into this criminal subculture, correctional social workers are normally assigned to them as soon as they are institutionalised. In practise, a significant proportion of their caseload involves the provision of counselling and guidance (including post-release scaffolding), and legal support (e.g., helping them to access legal aid, and explaining the various criminal procedures that they have to comply with, as well as the paperwork that they will need to complete). These social workers are also involved in initiating or encouraging support from the inmates' families, as well as liaising with the various tiers of the criminal justice system, including prison staff, police, health authorities, the judiciary, lawyers and probation officers, so as to maintain their psycho-social well-being while incarcerated, and to the extent that funding allows, after they have been released as well (Prayas, 2012a).

The correctional social worker's overall objective is to counteract the criminalising effect of imprisonment, and provide the best chance of rehabilitation and reintegration into the community post-release. This can be achieved by providing positive experiences during the time of incarceration; such as education, vocational training, and recreational opportunities that facilitate higher levels of self-esteem and self-control in the prisoner. Careful planning of the post-release and reintegration period with ongoing support can also help prevent recidivism and promote pro-social goals within the newly released prisoner (Prayas, 2012a).

Criminal justice social workers are also involved in trying to improve conditions for women prisoners. Due to their relative lack of numbers within the prison system, their specific gender needs are often overlooked, particularly when housed in a female section of a predominantly male prison. Problems experienced by female prisoners are exacerbated when they are pregnant or have young children to care for. The welfare of the children of imprisoned females is an area of particular concern, requiring different types of interventions by correctional social workers, depending upon whether the children are housed with their inmate mothers, or are cared for by others outside of the prison compound (Prayas, 2012a).

Conclusion

Various sectors of the criminal justice system, legal fraternity and those working alongside the criminal justice system have made recommendations that will enhance the human rights of victims and offenders within the criminal justice system in India. What is now needed is the will and commitment of all involved, including frontline workers, to implement these changes. The Vice President of India, Mr Hamid Ansari (2013) in his speech at the commemoration of the International Human Rights Day, stated that India should

> take pride, with justice, in the fact that we have put in place the requisite intellectual, legal and institutional framework for the protection and promotion of human rights as a national responsibility. Questions however continue to arise with regard to their efficacy in actual implementation. Violations are widespread, discrimination based on religion, caste, language, ethnicity, creed, work, descent and economic status continue to occur with disturbing frequency. These violations relate to denial of rights by State agencies, by individuals and groups. The weaker party is the invariable victim.

In his reflections over justice and human rights in India, Mr Ansari (2013) suggested that

> [t]he dilemma is a real one and while improvements and correctives to the existing mechanism continue to take place, perhaps the question needs to be raised differently, conjointly from the perspectives of justice and human wrong, meaning by the latter term any act by a human agency that transgresses on the right or dignity of a human being.

He further argued that

> [t]he conclusion is unavoidable that notwithstanding considerations of convenience or statecraft, human conscience and societal practice is conditioned by the dichotomy of expressions like good–bad, right–wrong, just–unjust, moral–immoral and human beings cannot avoid the impulse to invoke morality and justice in support of acts undertaken. The impulse may be a dormant one; it nevertheless exists and, like other human faculties, can be cultivated and induced to perform better. (Ansari, 2013)

Mr Ansari (2013) continued by asking all of us two questions: '[D]o human rights as perceived today address human wrongs? Can a human wrong be considered virtuous?'

Unfortunately,

> [t]he victims of human wrongs operate between the polarities of suf-
> fering and the desire for relief and justice. It is the voice of the victims
> that needs articulation. But between the suffering and enunciation of
> human rights falls the shadow of state sovereignty. This necessitates
> a relook at the traditional approach. (Ansari, 2013)

While human rights for offenders and victims have been articulated in various United Nations instruments, and subsequently
incorporated into municipal Indian legislation, their application
on the ground is clearly lagging. Many of the violations appear to
be caused by high crime rates, low staffing in the criminal justice
system, problems of prison overcrowding, the accompanying
inhumane living conditions, as well as ageing prison infrastructure. Notwithstanding these causes, improved education of the
employees within the criminal justice system, as well as greater
use of criminal justice social workers, will go a long way towards
alleviating current conditions. Recommendations to reduce the
prison population by changing bail conditions, for example, could
conceivably provide the 'breathing space' needed for further
reforms to be implemented.

India's democracy, including its sovereignty, is contingent on
the realisation of the tenets of social justice, and therefore the
existing gender oppression and inequality in India is contrary to
the central principles of democracy. No amount of enshrining
within the Constitution of fundamental human rights will guarantee their translation until effective attitudinal changes occur
concerning the inappropriateness of maintaining a patriarchal
mindset among the powerful and the average Indian alike.

Given the high crime rates in India, and with only two police
officers per 1,000 residents, the role of the police can be both
thankless and wrought with danger (Sandhu, 2011/12). Bearing
in mind the inevitable performance targets imposed by senior
management on ground-level officers, as well as the public's
unrealistic expectation that all crime should be solved, it is of
little surprise that human rights are not always the foremost consideration in police stations. As Sandhu explicated, '[w]hen the
"ends" become important and the "means" are not questioned.

[sic] Human Rights become first casualty followed by the "Rule of Law" and "Due Process established by Law"' (2011/12, p. 64). In addition, the diversity of problems that are presented at the police stations may be outside the police officer's scope of work, or training. In this latter regard, Prayas dismally explained that 'the police station often becomes the theatre where power dynamics and the inter-play of caste, class, ethnicity and gender decide who gets justice and at what cost' (2012b, p. 9). Notwithstanding this bleak assessment, it is nevertheless the contention of this chapter that criminal justice social workers are ideally positioned and equipped to ameliorate these very tensions and conflicts, not only in police stations but in our prisons as well. Furthermore, with research and advocacy training embedded within their educational and professional curriculums, police and correctional social workers will also be able to act as the 'voice of the victims that needs articulation' (Ansari, 2013)—to speak on behalf of those who do not have sufficient social capital to fight for themselves.

References

Ansari, M. H. (2013, December 10). *Human rights and human wrongs.* Speech presented at the Human Rights Day function organized by the National Human Rights Commission, Vigyan Bhawan, New Delhi, India. Retrieved from http://nhrc.nic.in/disparchive.asp?fno=13052

Antony, K. R. (2012, August 22). Put errant doctors on the mat. *The Hindu.* Retrieved from http://www.thehindu.com/opinion/op-ed/put-errant-doctors-on-the-mat/article3804283.ece

Chockalingam, K. (2010). Measures for crime victims in the Indian criminal justice system. In M. Sasaki (Ed.), *UNAFEI resource materials series No. 81* (pp. 97–109). Tokyo: United Nations Asia and Far East Institute for the Prevention of Crime and the Treatment of Offenders.

Kameswari, S. V., & Vinjamuri, P. (2013). *Medical ethics: A case study of hysterectomy in Andhra Pradesh.* Retrieved from http://kicsforum.net/kics/setdev/hysterectomy-ethics-in-S-T-for-setdev-final-1.pdf

Kaushik, A., & Sharma, K. (2009). Human rights of women prisoners in India: A case study of Jaipur Central Prison for women. *Indian Journal of Gender Studies, 16*(2), 253–71. doi: 10.1177/097152150901600205

Kumar, A. (2014). *Report on the visit of Ajay Kumar, special rapporteur, NHRC, central west zone, to Jodhpur Central Jail, Jodhpur, Rajasthan, on 11 February 2014* (Report No. 81). Retrieved from http://nhrc.nic.in/Reports_prison.htm

Lal, C. (2004). *Report on the visit of Shri Charman Lal, special rapporteur to jails, in Rajasthan from 16–18 February 2004* (Report No. 15). Retrieved from http://nhrc.nic.in/Reports_prison.htm

Mamidi, M. B., & Mamidi, S. C. (2005). *Hysterectomies in Kowdipally Mandal, Medak district of South India* (Discussion Paper No. 8). Hyderabad: Centre for Action Research and People's Development.

Mamidi, B. B., & Pulla, V. (2013). Hysterectomies and violation of human rights: Case study from India. *International Journal of Social Work and Human Services Practice, 1*(1), 64–75. doi: 10.13189/ijrh.2013.010110

Narayan, S. (2013). *Report of the visit of Prof. S. Narayan, special rapporteur, NHRC, of MP, from 11 to 21 December 2013* (Report No. 74). Retrieved from http://nhrc.nic.in/Reports_prison.htm

National Human Rights Commission (NHRC). (2007). *Human rights best practices relating to criminal justice in a nutshell.* New Delhi: NHRC.

———. (2012). *Annual report 2011–2012.* New Delhi: NHRC. Retrieved from http://nhrc.nic.in/archive.htm

National Human Rights Commission (NHRC). (1995–96). *Cases related to children/women.* Retrieved from http://nhrc.nic.in/ChildCases.htm#no6

———. (1998–99): *Cases related to children / women.* Retrieved from http://nhrc.nic.in/ChildCases.htm#no11

———. (2004–05a). *Torture, illegal detention/unlawful arrest, false implication etc.* Retrieved from http://nhrc.nic.in/PoliceCases.htm#43

———. (2004–05b). *Torture, illegal detention/unlawful arrest, false implication etc.* Retrieved from http://nhrc.nic.in/PoliceCases.htm#44

Pandey, V. (2014). Community policing for conflict resolution and community resilience. *International Journal of Social Work and Human Services Practice, 2*(6), 228–33. doi: 10.13189/ijrh.2014.020604

Prayas. (2012a). *Initiating work in prison settings.* Mumbai: Prayas.

———. (2012b). *Social work intervention at police stations.* Mumbai: Prayas.

Raghavan, V. (2013). Social work intervention in criminal justice: Field-theory linkage. In S. Singh (Ed.), *Social work and social development: Perspectives from India and the United States* (pp. 265–89). Chicago, Illinois: Lyceum Books Inc.

Sandhu, H. S. (2011/12). Obligation of the police leadership in the protection of human rights. *The Indian Police Journal, LVIII*(4), 63–68.

Sen. A. (2011). *The idea of justice.* Cambridge, MA: The Belknap Press of Harvard University Press.

Sivagnanam, T. S. (2012, February 24–26). *Rights of prisoners and convicts under the criminal justice administration.* Paper presented at the

National Judicial Academy Regional Judicial Conference, Tamil Nadu State Judicial Academy, Chennai, India. Retrieved from http://www. tnsja.tn.nic.in/article/Role%20of%20Prisoner%20and%20 Conv%20TSSJ.pdf

Srinivasan, R. (2013). Internalizing international human rights on prisoners in India: An analytical study. *The Indian Police Journal, LX*(2), 110–35.

Srinivasan, M., & Mathew, E. J. (2007). Victims and the criminal justice system in India: Need for a paradigm shift in the justice system. *Temida,* (2), 51–62. doi: 10.2298/TEM0702051S

Thilagaraj, R. (2013). Criminal justice system in India. In J. Liu, S. Jou & B. Hebenton (Eds.), *Handbook of Asian criminology* (pp. 199–211). New York: Springer Publishing.

Tiwari, A. (2013). Human rights approach to prison management. *The Indian Police Journal, LX(2),* 41–78.

Verma, J. S., Seth, L., & Subramanium, G. (2013). *Report of the committee on amendments to criminal law.* Retrieved from http://www.prsindia. org/parliamenttrack/report-summaries/justice-verma-committee-report-summary-2628/

11

Cybercrime Victims in India: Responsibilities, Reactions and Issues of Criminal Justice Social Workers

Debarati Halder and K. Jaishankar

Introduction

Cybercrime generates a typical group of victims who need special healing treatment due to the peculiar nature of the offence as well as its growing number of variations—due to rapid technological developments as well as its increasingly pervasive use within modern society. Even though cybercrimes can be targeted at three groups of victims—the government, corporations and individuals (Jaishankar, 2013)—this chapter will concentrate on the problems of the third group, that is, the individuals. Based on the motive of the offender, cybercrimes targeted at this group can further be divided into three clusters as follows: (a) crimes targeted against children, (b) identity-related crimes and (c) defamatory crimes. The first group of crimes in cyberspace is specifically targeted against children, whereas men, women and children can become victims of the other two types of crimes. Crimes targeted against children may include online grooming, cyberbullying, and production and distribution of child pornography.

While these are conventional offences of cybercrimes against children, there have been cases where children have been adversely affected from accessing particular gaming sites. Although not specifically targeting children per se, many young persons are able to access such sites, which in some instances requires these children to adopt avatars and thereafter to engage in simulated adult life activities. For example, playing 'The SIMs' (a strategic life simulation video game series) potentially allows impressionable children to 'virtually' act out real-life scenarios, including getting pregnant, delivering babies, etc. In some more liberal jurisdictions, such genres of games are considered to be socially acceptable, given the fact that many of the game scenarios may include normal real-life experiences of these adolescents. However, in other more conservative jurisdictions like India or Pakistan, such activities among children may not only raise questions regarding the legality of the sites, but also challenge the morals and values inculcated in their children through orthodox upbringing styles. Engaging in such online gaming activities, these children risk exposure to age-inappropriate content, and they may emulate such activities in real life, for example, sexual activities at an early age as well as risky health life choices, such as drinking alcohol, smoking cigarettes and consuming illegal drugs.

Identity-related crimes, on the other hand, may include financial crimes like phishing[1] and privacy infringement offences like hacking and cracking.[2] While identity-related crimes can often target individuals through these two types of cybercrimes, online terrorist activities may also include such offences, although the

---

[1] Google (2014) defines 'phishing' as "a form of fraud in which a message sender attempts to trick the recipient into divulging important personal information like a password or bank account number, transferring money, or installing malicious software. Usually the sender pretends to be a representative of a legitimate organization'.

[2] 'Hacking is gaining unauthorised access to a computer system and, as such, is conceptually analogous to real-world trespassing. Cracking, which consists of gaining unauthorised access to a computer system for the purpose of committing a crime "inside" the system, is conceptually analogous to burglary' (Brenner, 2006, pp. 11–12).

scale of victimisation will be much greater, perhaps even to the extent where mass populations are tragically affected (Halder, 2011). Further, identity-related crimes may also result in the creation of fake avatars (Halder, 2011), which may then be used to cause harm to a woman's reputation (all under the 'protection' of a pseudonym). In this regard, defamatory crimes may or may not be directly associated with identity-related offences. That said, there is certainly evidence of many victims complaining that they have been defamed through false allegations spread through numerous modes including the circulation of emails, messages, hacking and modifying (without authorisation) documents and subsequently circulating the same, leakage of private photographs through multimedia messaging service (MMS), YouTube and Facebook profiles, trolling, etc. Many of these activities were conducted through fake identity avatars. Thus, it is arguable that such defamatory crimes can involve identity-related crimes in a very significant way.

In the present authors' capacities as cybercrime victim counsellors and researchers, a range of threats have been encountered in the course of their work that impact not only upon the existing social culture but also their physical and virtual security. Thus, this chapter intends to forewarn its readers of the pitfalls of being cybercrime victim counsellors, as well as to provide some solutions to these problems. There are therefore two core questions that need to be asked at this juncture: First, what sorts of problems can arise when counselling the victims of cybercrime? Second, how does one deal with such problems without harming the 'victimhood' status of these victims?

The structure of this chapter will entail two sections that will address in detail these two concerns. In the first part, an explication will be given of the holistic trend of 'demands' made by victims, and the practical difficulties that they face as a result of being cyber victimised. This will lead readers to better understand the core of the first question cited earlier. The second part will then examine the multifaceted role of counsellor(s) in counselling victims of cybercrime, as well as to emphasise the necessity and importance of the role played by women counsellors in such cases.

Problems and Issues in Counselling Victims of Cybercrimes

Forms of Cyber Victimisation

Cyber victimisation by Digital Communication Technology (DCT) or Internet Communication Technology (ICT) may in some cases involve the participation of both the offender and the victim. The involvement of the victim can be seen more in cases such as phishing, online grooming, trolling or even cyber stalking. Victim involvement may occur due to several reasons: the victim may be fraudulently made to believe the possibility of winning a fortune, or the victim may give away vital information to the offenders which may then be detrimental to his/her privacy, physical security, reputation or even profession, if that data are subsequently misused and/or presented in a different form, by the criminals. When the victim is a minor or a teenager, the problem arises because of his/her curiosity to explore and experiment in dangerous or risky activities before sadly falling into the offenders' trap. Among school students, the most notable and probably greatest researched area in cases of cyber victimisation, however, is cyberbullying (Jaishankar & Halder, 2009). Such bullying often occurs on the social media profile page of the victim or in group chats. The risk of victimisation increases when the potential victim provides the virtual space to the online bullies to victimise him/her. For example, the victim either makes his/her profile open to the bullies or shares their email address with them. The bully may also initiate the harassment by posting intimidating or hurtful messages on his/her profile page, a school page or his/her/common friend's profile page. The victim is deliberately provoked to view the bullying messages or hear about the bullying. As a result, he/she often becomes depressed. The bully is successful when the victim either loses control over his/her emotions and thereafter responds in an extreme way, for example, by committing suicide, going into severe depression or fighting back, which will only make the situation worse for him/herself as this may be what the bully wants in the first place.

The other issue concerning teenagers and young adults in the cyber world is revenge porn[3] (Halder & Jaishankar, 2013). It has become a trend among teenagers as well as young adults to partake in sexting (Jaishankar, 2009). Young girls occasionally take 'selfies'[4] in sexy attire, or even nude, and convey the image via text to their male friends. Many young couples also record their first date, physical intimate moments and passionate kissing sessions only for them to be misused later by either of the partners when he/she is dumped. Revenge porn includes not only the illicit use of consensual sexted images/videos but also non-consensual private images of the victimised partner taken without his/her permission. Revenge porn may be interconnected with bullying and may be an independent form of online victimisation. This is definitely a current trend where many jilted lovers take their revenge on their partners or ex-partners in cyberspace.

In addition, teenagers also often face the problem of being victimised by online groomers. This happens when the victim extends virtual friendship to strangers or falls into the trap of identity-related crimes, whereby the groomer poses as a known person of the victim and thereafter reacquaints him/herself through cyberspace. The victim, in such cases, may give away vital information about him/herself, thereby facilitating his/ her groomer as a potential consumer of porn materials or a potential contributor to child pornography. If the victim refuses to cooperate, he/she can then become a victim of stalking and online blackmail.

Adults can also be victimised in a range of ways similar to those crimes suffered by children or teenagers. Cyber stalking is

---

[3] Revenge porn is defined as 'an act whereby the perpetrator satisfies his anger and frustration for a broken relationship through publicizing false, sexually provocative portrayal of his/her victim, by misusing the information that he may have known naturally and that he may have stored in his personal computer, or may have been conveyed to his electronic device by the victim herself, or may have been stored in the device with the consent of the victim herself; and which may have been done to publicly defame the victim essentially' (Halder & Jaishankar, 2013, p. 83).

[4] A photograph that one has taken of oneself, typically one taken with a smart phone or webcam and uploaded to a social media website (Oxford Dictionary, 2014).

a significant problem for adult women in cyberspace. Other forms of victimisation that may initially stem from cyber stalking include online bullying, creation of fake avatars, online harassment, trolling[5] and online sextortion.[6] It may also result in physical threats being made against the families of the victim(s). Voyeurism is another form of offence which may target adult women or even couples. Many such cases involve victims who discover images of their private moments leaked onto adult networking sites due to surveillance cameras placed in public places, or because of theft from their electronic devices (for example, laptops and mobile phones), and subsequent misuse of that data by the offenders. Men and women may also become victims of threatening and blackmailing communication by their ex-spouse. Apart from adult men and women being victimised, transgender bullying also occurs in cyberspace; some cases are as serious as abetting the victim to commit suicide.

While the offences mentioned above tend to be of a personal, sexual or reputational nature, adult victims may also suffer from financial fraud, for example, the victim may be groomed to believe that they have won the lottery or bequeathed a portion of a fortune by helping a wealthy patron who is dying. The victim may then voluntarily give away his/her banking information or may pay a sum of money to particular accounts in anticipation of getting back much more funds than what was initially given. Financial crimes may also involve consumer fraud, for example, failure to deliver goods after payment was made in e-commerce cases.

In addition to the above personal, sexual, reputational and financial offences, the exercise of freedom of speech in cyberspace

---

[5] 'Trolling is a common phenomenon in online discussion groups where an individual baits and provokes other group members, often with the result of drawing them into fruitless argument and diverting attention from the stated purposes of the group' (Herring, Job-Sluder, Scheckler, & Barab, 2002, p. 371).

[6] 'Sextortion is a form of sexual exploitation where people are extorted with a nude image of themselves they shared on the Internet through sexting (from the words: sex and texting) *or by stolen images* (our emphasis). They are later coerced into performing sexual acts with the person doing the extorting, and are coerced into performing hard-core pornography' (de la Cerna, 2012, para 1).

has created unexpected dangers for the users of ICT and DCT. In such incidences, users may intentionally play the 'stop me if you can' role, defying Internet safety rules to establish their points of view. This can lead them to be 'flamed' by trolls or to have their personal privacy infringed or hacked.

Cybercrime Victims and the Irrational Demands That They Make on Their Counsellors

The most crucial part of counselling victims of cybercrimes is to know what the victims want. Their demands vary from case to case. However, generally speaking, many victims want public support from their online followers. This support can take the form of supportive posts, for example, publicly defending the victim or denouncing the negative claims or statements made by the victims' stalkers or trolls. Often the victims even expect their counsellors (many of whom are social workers) to step in the shoes of their 'supporters' and defend them against these cyber criminals or to 'attack' the credibility or reputation of these offenders in a similar way. The demands made on their counsellors can take the form of quite irrational coping mechanisms (Halder & Jaishankar, 2012) including accessing the offending profile and hacking and removing the offending posts, contacting the harasser to warn him/her of dire consequences, asking the media to step in and report the whole harassment, tracking the mails to get information about the original harasser, and even requesting the counsellor to contact the online fraudsters so as to ask for their money back.

In some cases where the victim is a female, the responsibility of the counsellor becomes more to relieve the victim of the psychological and emotional trauma as well as to encourage her to bravely face the often disapproving gaze of a deeply patriarchal society. Women who have been victimised through the creation of their own fake avatar/s feel particularly vulnerable about complaining the matter to their immediate family members, or to reporting the crime to the police, because of the anticipated ensuing humiliation (Halder, 2013a), and even forced confinement to their houses. In these cases, the majority of such victims demand their counsellors to help them immediately remove their fake avatars through hacking. The fear of reporting the matter to the police stems from the anticipation that the police will not only humiliate them due to their involvement (especially if the fake avatar is the result of a jilted love affair) with the harasser, but also due to the assumption that reporting the crime will make the matter public by way of media reports. Many female victims also fear that such infringement of privacy by the police, as well as by the media, may damage their reputation in the marriage market or in their profession. Sometimes quite contrasting views are held by these victims: the victims refuse to believe that their reputation has already been damaged by the harasser who may have already spread malicious rumours about them to a wider audience. Contrarily, they believe that the reporting of the crime may do more harm to them since society, more generally, and their acquaintances, in particular, can physically see them going to the police station or even to court.

In the case of cyber stalking by anonymous identities where the modus operandi is restricted to offensive messages communicated privately to only the adult victims, the latter often want their counsellors to track the offending emails/messages in order to discover from where the harasser was contacting them, as well as the identity of the criminal. This may include wanting the counsellor to not only block the harasser from continuing to cyber stalk her, but also to hack the ID/profile of the harasser as well!

These demands may be quite similar in cases where the victim is a teenager too. While most teenagers above the age of 16 prefer to reach out to the counsellors themselves, younger teenagers may seek help by sharing their concerns with friends or parents. When parents are involved, most of them demand that the offensive posts be removed in the ways discussed above. Some teenage victims adopt quite rational coping mechanisms to deal with their emotional/psychological wellbeing as well as security. Parents, however, are often interested in questions as to how they can limit their child's exposure to the sexual content over the Internet that he/she may have already accessed. Unfortunately, the role of the counsellor becomes challenging when the victim wishes to adopt irrational coping mechanisms to deal with the situation. In this context, irrational coping mechanisms refer to actions that are not authorised by law and the established policies of Internet safety rules and guidelines (Halder & Jaishankar, 2015). Such a response is often born out from the emotional distress suffered and the urge to end the victimisation faster than that by employing rational coping methods like reporting the matter to the police or avoiding communicating with the harasser (Halder & Jaishankar, 2015).

Counsellors have a duty to make the victims understand the privacy rules followed by the ICT and DCT websites, as well as the legal consequences of breaking those rules. For example, almost all of the US-based ICT and DCT websites are bound by Section 512 of the Digital Millennium Copyright Act, through which 'safe harbour' policies are created (Edwards, 2011). This gives these websites the power to develop their own rules for preventing an infringement of the copyright of the users (Edwards, 2011). Such websites are further bound by 'due diligence' laws which give users the power to report any infringement of their privacy to the website moderators or administrators. Based on the users' complaints, action can be taken against those infringers. The websites are also covered by immunity cloaks which make them immune from third-party liability (Edwards, 2011). While these are beneficial for any victim of online harassment, these have also proved to be beneficial for the harassers since the harasser gets immediate privacy protection from the websites. Consequently, moderators and administrators can only be compelled to provide any information about the harasser when that information is sought by the police (as part of a formal investigation) or through a court notice or warrant. This implies that to seek relief from the victimisation, the victim must choose from three options. These include reporting the harassment to the website, reporting the matter to the police and, if this fails, seeking relief directly from the courts. The counsellor's main duty is to persuade the victim against taking up irrational coping mechanisms and instead select a rational coping method such as those cited earlier. Sadly, however, the victim's frustration is exacerbated when none of these prove personally beneficial for him/her.

Challenges before the Counsellors

Studies have shown that many ICT and DCT websites refuse to pay any heed to a victim's report of abuse (Halder & Jaishankar, 2011). At this juncture, the victim needs constant emotional support from the counsellor to gain maximum emotional strength to report the matter to the police. If the counsellor fails to convince the victim about the necessity and benefits of police reporting, the victim may immediately leave the counselling session to take up an irrational coping mechanism. However, if the victim does make a report to the police, he/she is vulnerable to threats from the society, for example, she may be socially ostracised, and even her harassers may threaten her. The victim may also be refused help due to a lack of proper infrastructure within the specific local police organisation to deal with cybercrime cases or due to jurisdictional issues. This is particularly worthy of mention since the laws in different jurisdictions may vary in regard to the powers of investigation, when it involves an online crime perpetrated outside of its geographical jurisdiction (Halder & Jaishankar, 2011). The victim may also be told by the police that no crime has been committed against him/her, and consequently assistance from them would not be forthcoming (Halder & Jaishankar, 2011). At this juncture, it becomes the duty of the counsellor to guide the victim to seek intervention from more senior officials or to ask for help from a lawyer. Sadly, many victims may refuse to proceed further due to the humiliating treatment received from the police as this adds on to the existing humiliation that they already experienced as a result of being a victim of the online crime.

Here, the role of the counsellor becomes extremely challenging, especially if the police official taunts the victim about the counselling process that the victim receives, such as asking the genuineness of the counselling, and the reasons why the victim went to a third party rather than reporting the matter to the police. Further, in the case of online counselling, the counsellor's role becomes crippled due to the limitations of the interaction with the victim through the communication mode of the ICT or DCT. Furthermore, the counsellor can only guide the victim to seek assistance from the relevant authority or to make him/her understand the therapeutic role of the laws and procedure but cannot ensure that the victim will follow that advice. In addition, the counsellor's role also becomes limited when attempting to make the victim understand the situation while encouraging him/her to break their fear of society which may have been created due to the presence of an orthodox culture in the victim's home.

The legal/criminological background of the counsellor(s) would also prevent him/her from implementing any irrational coping mechanism to help the victim, for example, by reaching out to the harasser and threatening or warning him/her, unnecessarily interfering in the police enquiries and giving exaggerated evidence of the harasser's misdeeds to the authorities. It becomes the duty of the counsellor to make the victim acutely aware of the thin line between reporting the crime in a proper fashion and bringing false allegations against the harasser as the latter conduct may result in the offender being successful in a potential defamation action against his/her victim.

When handling cases involving children and teenagers, the counsellor(s) has to shoulder a double responsibility of counselling the parents as well as the victim. It has been noted on many occasions that teenage victims are quite willing to report the crime or to abide by the advice given by the counsellor. The parents, however, tend to remain extremely protective and may oppose that the matter be reported to the proper authorities. This is not an unreasonable position to take, notwithstanding the fact that many nations have taken preventive steps to secure the privacy of child victims in online sexual crimes cases. Nevertheless, the reality is a little less reassuring, and as seen in many prominent cases of cyberbullying, revenge porn or sexting in the United States, vital identifying information about the minor victim was actually disclosed in the media. A prominent example of this would include the Megan Meier cyberbullying case,[7] where the

---

[7] Megan Meir committed suicide after being bullied by an impersonated profile created by a woman. After her death, cyberbullying became a major concern for law makers and the Megan Meier Cyberbullying Prevention Act was introduced in 2008 (Lidsky & Garcia, 2012).

victim was immortalised by the creation of a preventive law on cyberbullying in the United States. There is no suggestion that there was an insidious motive behind this disclosure as such attempts by the government were clearly taken for the welfare of society. Nevertheless, the unintended consequences of such disclosure can negatively impact the decisions that future minor victims and their parents will take in this regard. This is especially true for orthodox societies like India where parents concerned about the safety and reputation of their family name, as well as their children, may not want to report the matter to the authorities for fear of public embarrassment or worse, ridicule. Alternatively, they may discourage their children from accessing the Internet altogether, thereby limiting their opportunities to take advantage of modern communication tools such as the ICT and DCT in order to connect with their friends, fellow students or even teachers. In such cases, first, the counsellor has to advise the parents to make them understand the domestic laws that protect the privacy of child victims, as well as the investigation process of online crime cases involving children. Thereafter, the counsellor will have to explain to the primary victim (the child) and the secondary victims (the parents), the positive and negative aspects of the Internet and, in particular, how they can use it to good effect (Halder & Jaishankar, 2015) while preventing or minimising the negative features.

Multifaceted Role of Counsellors in Handling Cybercrime Victimisation Cases

The role of the counsellor is not limited to only conducting counselling sessions with victims of online crimes. Internet and digital technology are Frankenstein creations of mankind which can do both good and bad to society depending upon how it is handled. Hence, it becomes a necessity to continuously learn and research the trends of crimes online as well as the reasons why such trends are occurring. Cybercrime is an example of an offence where some of its variations are situations where the victim may have contributed to his/her victimisation (Jaishankar, 2013). Knowing this is essential as it will make the counsellor more competent in handling a case where a contributor-turned victim seeks help from him/her. Along with researching the psychological aspects of the offender and the victim, as well as the sociological reasons behind any escalation of these cybercrimes, the counsellor/researcher(s) needs to learn the laws governing the Internet as well as the physical handling of the computer or electronic device (i.e., becoming computer literate). The laws in this regard are proliferating all over the globe, so is the confusion among states when confronted with having to accept each other's laws while dealing with cross-jurisdictional cases. While in India making satirist comments about a particular religion on the Internet or making any indecent remarks targeting women can attract penal sanction straightaway, it is not the same for website developers in the United States who, in their policy guidelines, exhibit a wide use of the 'Free Speech Guarantee'. Further, the criminal procedure laws and judicial understandings of the same in relation to the rights of the offenders and victims, as well as the duties of the police in regard to offences committed online also differ from country to country (Halder, 2013b). The counsellor needs to be aware of these issues so that he/she can better facilitate the victim adopting the best possible remedial measure offered by the laws of a particular country. The counsellor may also play the role of a whistle blower or an awareness creator by way of his/her research publications through blogs, social media updates, journal articles, book chapters, conference presentations, etc. so as to alert the society of the growing trends of online crimes, and the consequent need for better policies and laws.

The impact of the gender of the counsellor on counselling victims of online victimisation also needs to be highlighted here. The lead author of this chapter, being a female counsellor, especially found that women victims of interpersonal crimes involving ex-girlfriends of their husbands or boyfriends, or male victims who had been targeted by their wives' ex-boyfriends, felt freer to discuss their issues with her. It needs to be remembered that mediation requires empathy and a skill to establish a connection with the relevant parties, and many times female counsellors prove excellent in this task (Center for Substance Abuse Treatment, 2000). Counselling victims of online crime is no exception. It is arguable that female victims will feel connected to a woman counsellor more quickly, and, hence, they feel confident enough to share private emotional moments which may have motivated them to contribute to their own victimisation. Such empathetic communication may also lead to the building and growing of confidence in the counsellor, and this may finally motivate the victim to take the advice seriously. Being a female counsellor, it may be easier to channel a caring mother-figure persona so as to more effectively explain the positive aspects of the situation to women, children as well as men. At the same time, through the counsellor, the victim can grow a circle of positive friends, including police officers, lawyers as well as other victims who may have suffered like her/him. Teenage victims especially may feel more close to a female counsellor since they can discuss not only their own experiences of online victimisation, but also how their parents and teachers are motivating or demotivating them to take up a positive course of action towards relief. Further, the lead author has also experienced the solidarity between the victim and the counsellor when the victim is from an LGBT (lesbian, gay, bisexual and transgender) community. From a transgender community, victims who have newly acquired 'womanhood' may feel more relaxed when sharing the pains of online bullying or trolling with a woman counsellor. A female counsellor should also anticipate the creation of fake avatars of herself created by frustrated victims or even by the perpetrator when he/she comes to know that the victim is being helped by the counsellor.

It is important for a counsellor, whether male or female, to maintain clear professional boundaries between themselves and the victims. Being physically present in the counselling sessions and witnessing the sudden eruption of emotions of the victim or the harasser may bring secondary trauma to the counsellor (Center for Substance Abuse Treatment, 2000); this is no exception in cases of online counselling. In online counselling, the counsellor must be ready for secondary trauma since the victim may expect a chain of responses from the counsellor through emails/messages almost every hour of the day. The victim may also hurl abusive comments when he/she feels that they are not being heard or helped properly. Here it becomes necessary for the counsellor to maintain a necessary distance from the victim, as well as the harasser, as should be the case in a face-to-face counselling case. It needs to be noted that in the case of online counselling, the usage of language plays a significant role in mediating the problem and counselling the victims. Hence, even if the victim crosses the free speech limits by abusing the counsellor or posting comments of frustration about the counsellor in the social media, the counsellor should not step into the shoes of a victim-turned offender (Halder & Jaishankar, 2012), but to immediately handle the situation by contacting the victim directly and making him/her understand the situation, by contacting the police and making them understand the victim's situation so that he/she is not doubly harassed by the police, or by reporting the matter to the website so that the offending posts may be removed, if possible, through normal procedural channels. There may also be a chance that a frustrated victim or perpetrator may become dangerous trolls in the social media, targeting the counsellor or the organisation to which the counsellor is attached. Even though such U-turns of the victim (i.e., from initially being a victim to now being an offender) may prove disastrous for the counsellor's career, the counsellor needs to have patience to negotiate a way out of the situation. It needs to be understood that such disastrous defamatory comments may stay afloat on the Internet for a long time, but the counsellor should try his/her level very best not to publicly blame the victim or the offender, but to make this a positive experience of learning and sharing of thoughts on the issue.

Conclusion

Cybercrime and the remedial measures as offered by private and public stakeholders through websites, as well as the law and justice machineries, are ever-changing. Concepts of online crimes change rapidly due to vastly developing technology and trends of usage and mis-usage of the same; such changes are also influenced by legal developments. Counsellors are not protectors of victims or crime-prevention experts like the police. Rather, they are a small part of the preventive machinery. In India, some counsellors, however, tend to be overly proactive when highlighting the experiences of a victim or of the cybercrime trends, in general. This may be seen when such counsellors encourage the victim to report the matter to the media before seeking remedial measures from the police. That said, such actions may become detrimental not only to the victim but also to the general law-and-order process involved in the investigation of such cyber offences. It is, therefore, arguable that such an approach should, unless extreme circumstances prevail, be eschewed from by any competent and professional counsellor.

The Right to Information Act (2005) in India has proved to be extremely beneficial for whistle blowers, including those who availed this law, in providing help for victims of various sorts of human rights abuses. Similarly, the parliament has tried to regulate net-etiquette through various preventive laws, including laws curtailing the freedom of speech which may prove annoying, misleading, insulting, etc.[8] Laws are also made to curtail child abuse on the Internet,[9] prevent the sexual harassment of women on the Internet, cyber stalking of women,[10] financial frauds, etc. Nevertheless, it should be noted that these laws are not exhaustive and contain more loopholes than expected. Further, the lack of theoretical as well as practical knowledge surrounding the need to provide remedial measures to victims exhibited by many police, lawyers and sometimes judges, also proves extremely frustrating. But the existence of such laws and constant efforts by the relevant stakeholders to upgrade them on par with global standards must still be acknowledged and encouraged. It is therefore the counsellor's duty in cybercrime-related cases to continue to highlight these existing loopholes and advocate for improvements. Hence, it can be said that the role of the social

---

[8] Section 66A of the Information Technology Act, 2000 (amended in 2008).

[9] This has been ensured through the Prevention of Children from Sexual Harassment Act, 2013.

[10] See Section 354D of the Indian Penal Code, inserted by the Criminal Amendment Act, 2013.

worker/counsellor is a combination of a friend, a learner, a teacher, a whistle blower, an advocate, as well as a resource person. Once the social worker understands the scope of each of these roles and executes the same in their own limits, escalation of the crime rate may be reduced.

References

Brenner, S. W. (2006). Cybercrime: Re-thinking crime control strategies. In Y. Jewkes (Ed.), *Crime online* (pp. 11–28). Collumpton: Willan.

Center for Substance Abuse Treatment. (2000). Therapeutic issues for counsellors. In *Substance abuse treatment for persons with child abuse and neglect issues* (Treatment Improvement Protocols [TIP] Series, No. 36). Rockville, MD: Substance Abuse and Mental Health Services Administration (US). Retrieved from http://www.ncbi.nlm.nih.gov/books/NBK64902/

De la Cerna, M. (2012, April 15). Sextortion. *Cebu Daily News.* Retrieved from http://newsinfo.inquirer.net/177037/sextortion

Edwards, L. (2011, June 22). *The role and responsibility of internet intermediaries in the field of copyright and related rights.* Geneva: World Intellectual Property Organization. Retrieved from http://www.wipo.int/export/sites/www/copyright/en/doc/role_and_responsibility_of_the_internet_intermediaries_final.pdf

Google. (2014). *About phishing.* Retrieved from https://support.google.com/accounts/answer/75061?hl=en

Halder, D. (2011). Information Technology Act and cyber terrorism: A critical review. In P. Madhava Soma Sundaram & S. Umarhathab (Eds), *Cyber crime and digital disorder* (pp. 75–90). Tirunelveli: Publication Division, Manonmaniam Sundaranar University.

———. (2013a). Examining the scope of Indecent Representation of Women (Prevention) Act, 1986, in the light of cyber victimization of women in India. *National Law School Journal, 11,* 188–218.

———. (2013b). *Cyber socialising and victimisation of women: A comparative analysis of laws in India, UK and Canada* (Unpublished PhD thesis). National Law School of India University, Bengaluru.

Halder D., & Jaishankar, K. (2011). Cyber gender harassment and secondary victimization: A comparative analysis of US, UK and India. *Victims and Offenders, 6*(4), 386–98.

———. (2012). *Cyber crime and victim turned offenders: An analysis of impact of victimisation and coping mechanisms of women victims.*

Paper presented at the Stockholm Criminology Symposium, June 11–13, 2012, Stockholm, Sweden.

———. (2013). Revenge porn by teens in the United States and India: A socio-legal analysis. *International Annals of Criminology,* 51(1–2), 85–111.

———. (2015). Irrational coping theory and positive criminology: A frame work to protect victims of cyber crime. In N. Ronel & D. Segev (Eds), *Positive criminology* (pp. 276–91). Abingdon, Oxon: Routledge.

Herring, S., Job-Sluder, K., Scheckler, R., & Barab, S. (2002). Searching for safety online: Managing 'trolling' in a feminist forum. *The Information Society, 18*(5), 371–84.

Jaishankar, K. (2009). Sexting: A new form of victimless crime? *International Journal of Cyber Criminology, 3*(1), 21–25.

———. (2013). Cyber victimization: New typology and novel trends of interpersonal attacks on the internet. In Korean Institute of Criminology (Ed.), *Information society and cybercrime: Challenges for criminology and criminal justice* (pp. 31–47). Seoul: Korean Institute of Criminology.

Jaishankar, K., & Halder, D. (2009). Cyber bullying among school students in India. In K. Jaishankar (Ed.), *International perspectives on crime and justice* (pp. 579–98). Newcastle upon Tyne: Cambridge Scholars Publishing.

Lidsky, L., & Garcia, A. P. (2012). How not to criminalize cyberbullying. *Missouri Law Review, 77* (Summer 2012), 693.

Oxford Dictionaries. (2014). Selfie. *Oxford Dictionary.* Retrieved from http://www.oxforddictionaries.com/definition/english/selfie

Conclusion: The Future of Criminal Justice Social Work—Reflections

Abraham P. Francis and Mark David Chong

Introduction

Sadly, this is the last chapter of the book—a text that we hope you have found to be both informative and inspiring, in equal measure. Each of the chapter contributors has tried their best to provide you with a clear picture of how important criminologically-trained social workers are to the effective and affective running of almost every facet of the criminal justice system. While a range of new ideas and recommendations have been incorporated into this book based on the available literature, it should be noted that criminal justice social work is still in a state of relative flux. While that may be disconcerting for some, this is also an opportunity for many of you to make a meaningful difference in the lives of so many, whether offenders, victims or their respective families. This text is intended for such matters to be kept at the forefront of criminological as well as social work discourses where both disciplines can come together (as has the first author being a social worker and the second author as a criminologist) to not only engage but also collaborate for the betterment of some of the most marginalised of communities within India. This final chapter will therefore not only refresh your minds and hearts of what was previously written in this book, but also more importantly provide you with a glimpse of the exciting vistas that await you in this regard, as well as some pertinent questions to ponder over while you embark upon that journey. This will offer you direction and guidance in your passage to becoming a more effective and empathetic criminal justice social worker.

As has been amply illustrated in the preceding chapters, even though social workers play key roles in the criminal justice system, criminal justice social work, however, has been diminishing due to the many factors that the chapter authors have described in the book. For many social work practitioners, the criminal justice system, with its complex policies and procedures as well as its focus on retribution, deterrence, incapacitation, reformation and rehabilitation, can be a difficult institution to understand and practise. Hence, this book has been written with the aim of demystifying some of these aspects so that a climate of genuine appreciation of what social workers can do in the field is engendered, and to reposition the profession's response to this field of work through quality academic education and evidence-based training.

Unfortunately, we are living in very troubled times. Safety and security have become serious concerns for most people. No matter where we live, just a mere glance at the local newspaper, television or internet reveals the extent of crimes and violence that permeate in our society. Are we all affected by it? Certainly, the answer is yes! In fact, much more than in the past, as we now live in a digitally and technologically controlled world that provides instant news and world views at our fingertips. How can we not be sad about reading, listening or watching some of these issues unfold before us—issues like violence against women, brutal killings, acts of terrorism, corruption, robberies, bomb threats, cybercrimes and so on? The world has never seemed a more dangerous place to live in (Raghavan, 2013). But does that mean we should run and hide? Or, should we instead boldly face these fears, gird ourselves and fight the 'good fight'?

If the latter is the option you would choose, then this book is here to provide you with a strong theoretical and evidence base upon which to arm and fortify yourself with knowledge, and vicarious experience, garnered from years of academic research and professional practice.

To recap:

What has already been covered in this book?

The various chapter contributors have discussed a range of aspects involving the criminal justice system, and its intersection with criminal justice social work. This would include, for example, the Indian criminal justice process, the causes of criminal behaviour, the impact mental illness has had on prison inmates and victims of crime, a critical overview of criminal justice social work in India, police social work, probation, correctional social work, the plight of victims of crimes, juvenile justice, human rights abuses, social work education/training and cybercrime victim counselling. Each of these chapters focuses on a specific theme, and provide not only an overview but also specific explanations concerning the theories or concepts used therein, as well as how they have been applied in practice (e.g., through case studies). These chapters also encourage the readers to adopt a critical view of the status quo, so that the readers will not simply be satisfied with 'what is' but rather strive to conceptualise 'what should be'. These chapters will therefore challenge the readers to revisit their knowledge base and application skills. By demystifying criminal justice social work in India, the authors hope that this will ultimately strengthen the role of the profession in designing a more effective criminal justice social work curriculum/training programme as well as criminal justice policies.

These, of course, will not be easy tasks to accomplish.

What are some of the challenges that social workers face in the criminal justice system?

It should be noted that this section is not intended to be exhaustive, but will nonetheless attempt to capture some of the more salient challenges that have echoed throughout this book. To aid in initiating greater critical analysis of these issues, a number of *specific* thought-provoking questions will pepper the content, and readers are encouraged to pause and ponder over them first before moving on to the succeeding paragraphs. Some of the more *general* questions, however, are as follows:

- *What are the origins of the Indian criminal justice system? What was the context in which it developed through the years? To what extent has this development affected the role of social workers in the criminal justice system (adult and juvenile)?*
- *What roles do you think a social worker should play in the criminal justice system?*
- *Have you read or heard of any exciting criminal justice social work initiatives going on in your village, town or city? If so, would you like to get involved in them? What expertise or experience do you think you can bring to them?*
- *Are you a criminal justice social worker? If so, what motivated you to embark on this journey of service? If not, do you know why you decided against it? What would you need in order to reconsider your decision? For example, specific educational and/or training opportunities, scholarships/bursaries, employment incentives, security of tenure, public/professional recognition and so on?*
- *What are the ideological, philosophical and political issues that you think would affect the effective delivery of services provided by a criminal justice social worker?*

In India, criminal justice social work got off to a head start in the postcolonial period, especially between the 1950s and 1970s. However, with the gradual withdrawal of the welfare state, the roles played by criminal justice and correctional social work have been reduced to mere tokenism. This is a serious concern which has led to the shrinking of jobs in the welfare sector, and this has consequently shifted the focus of the social work profession from one of working in or with the criminal justice system, to one of augmenting (due to its perceived deficiencies) and confronting (due to its perceived weaknesses) the system. As Professor Raghavan made clear in his chapter here, the situation has come to pass whereby the onus of keeping alive the rehabilitative objective of the criminal justice system is now left to civil society organisations and an activist judiciary. This is indeed a systemic challenge that needs to be addressed as soon as possible.

+ *Question* +

What can be done to re-instate the original focus of criminal justice social work within the Indian criminal justice system?

Another significant challenge confronting criminal justice social workers is the state's efforts to relinquish its responsibility of facilitating the reasonable well-being, rehabilitation and reintegration of custodial populations. Here, the responsibility of caring for custodial populations seems to be at risk, evidenced by a decline of jobs for correctional social workers, as well as provision of services to needy prison inmates and undertrials, as well as their respective families. There is sufficient literature to show that criminal justice social work which emerged to facilitate the social re-entry of institutionalised populations, has been turned on its head to protect the rights of victims and ordinary citizens in the neoliberal West (Burke & Collett, 2010; Cullen & Gendreau, 2000; Harker & Worrall, 2011; Herzog-Evans, 2011; Teague, 2011).

Earlier efforts of rehabilitating offenders are now seen 'as permissive, uncaring about crime victims, and committed to a rehabilitative ideal that ignores the reality of violent, predatory criminals' (Petersilia, 1997, p. 150). Caring for the interests of crime victims is certainly a justifiably appropriate position to take. What may be less defensible, however, is to forget that: first, many offenders are themselves victims of social inequality and injustice (which are significant criminogenic risk factors) and second, by ensuring that they are successfully rehabilitated and reintegrated into society, that will decrease the likelihood of recidivism as well as increase the chances of them making up for the misdeeds to their victims, as well as the communities that they had previously brutalised.

+ *Question* +

How can we articulate a balanced position that shows support for both the victim, and the offender, without marginalising the former or demonising the latter?

The incidence of mental illness in victims of crime and offenders is relatively high when compared to the general population,[1] and the detrimental effects on their well-being and social functioning are significant. To address such psychological disorders within offender and victim groups (and in particular, the consequent effects these illnesses have on their social lives), social work intervention and support is arguably essential for their successful rehabilitation and/or reintegration into the community. Fortunately, there are comprehensive and robust models of intervention that social workers can employ in order to achieve these objectives. Lamentably however, encouraging social workers to become more involved in matters pertaining to criminal justice, more generally, is difficult. Correctional social workers often find themselves particularly troubled, not least because many of their clients are mandated ones. Consequently, social workers often find balancing the needs of their mentally ill offender clients, with that of community safety—an onerous task to achieve. Nevertheless, it is arguable that criminal justice social workers, with their professional ethos, temperament and training, are ideally equipped to positively influence the lives of mentally ill offenders and victims of crime, many of whom feature significantly in the socio-economically marginalised strata of Indian society.

+ Question +

How can criminal justice social workers create an institutional space for themselves to assist with the mental health needs of their clients, whether criminals or victims, when there are already other professions, for example, mental health nurses, psychologists and psychiatrists, who purport to perform similar roles?

There is also a need to know how to appropriately respond to the rise of relatively new types of crimes, for example, self-radicalised terrorism and cybercrime (including, cyberstalking, cyberbullying, revenge pornography and so on).

---

[1] As the introductory chapter and chapter 3 highlight, however, Indian government *prison* data does show a lower morbidity rate as compared to comparable data from other studies.

+ Questions +

What roles can criminal justice social workers play in address-ing such novel crimes?

What educational and training needs will have to be provided to criminal justice social workers in order for them to perform those roles effectively and efficiently?

Police social work in India is lamentably struggling for official recognition. According to Associate Professor Ruchi Sinha in her chapter here, this official endorsement remains strongly con-tested by both the state (which is reluctant to integrate social workers in the criminal justice system) and by the profession (due to limited competencies and motivation existing in most schools of social work across India to integrate criminal justice social work as part of their core curriculum). Even the more established correctional social workers are also increasingly marginalised. And yet, this is not because the Indian criminal jus-tice system is beyond reproach. In fact, the criminal justice system in India has been the target of severe criticism from numerous quarters due to the exponential increase in criminal cases that are pending, resulting in delayed justice for all concerned. The correctional institutions in the country have likewise been severely chastised by human rights advocates for overcrowding, prolonged detention, unsatisfactory living conditions, lack of treatment programmes and allegations of an indifferent and/or inhumane approach taken by prison staff against the inmates. Unlike other advanced countries, professional social workers in India have still not really made its presence felt in the criminal justice system. It would appear to some that the profession has deviated from its original mission which had embedded its cher-ished value of service to humanity, to a more mundane role of supplying administrative or functionary manpower to meet the market-driven economy's demands for such employees. It is, however, the contention of this book that such a position should be reversed, and that the profession of social work must endeav-our to realise its mandate once more, re-set its course and boldly meet head-on all of these humanitarian concerns within the criminal justice system.

+ Question +

What can social work's professional bodies do to encourage its members to not only pursue criminal justice social work as their chosen speciality but to also embed in their everyday practice the core social work values of caring, empathy and empowerment?

A great deal has already been written about correctional social work, an area of practice that deals primarily with offenders. Unfortunately, much less has been done in relation to victims of crime. That said, in recent years, this emphasis has shifted somewhat due in large part to the successes of various victim rights movements, particular in the West. Sadly, the Indian criminal justice system has not reached that stage of development and, to a large extent, still neglects and overlooks the role and plight of crime victims. This has left victims in a position of not only being primarily victimised by the initial criminal act but also by being doubly victimised (or secondarily victimisation) by the criminal justice system itself. Many criminal justice social workers, however, are mindful of this imbalance, and through increased advocacy for more comprehensive and specific victim-focused policies and laws, it is hoped that these injustices will be overturned sometime in the near future.

+ Question +

Explain how social work interventions (for example, clinical, research and policy analysis, as well as advocacy) can be employed to assist victims of crime overcome or avoid the trauma of both primary and secondary victimisation?

The acute need for criminal justice social workers is accentuated by the fact that over the years, government officials without the requisite educational or training qualifications to handle cases requiring psycho-social intervention continue to function in many criminal justice institutions in India. It is arguable that social work[2]

---

[2] Other relevant degrees would also include criminology, psychology, counselling, law, human services, sociology, nursing, health/allied health, education or community services, to name a few.

should be an essential qualification for the positions of Probationary Officer, Child Protection Officer, Family Counsellor, Superintendent of Observation/Juvenile Homes, as well as a Member of Child Welfare Committees/Juvenile Justice Boards. This could be attributable to the existing university social work curriculum because specific courses (e.g., majors or specialisations) related to the criminal justice system are mostly taught at the masters' level, and only in less than 1 per cent of the universities in the country. Sadly, the subject matters of criminology, human rights and social defence are not generally taught at the social work undergraduate level. Thus, to improve the competencies of criminal justice social workers who only have an undergraduate degree, more should be done to encourage social work schools to revise their subject content and professional training at this foundational level.

+ Questions +

What do you think are the impediments preventing the formal incorporation of criminal justice social work modules / majors / specialisations as a core element of an undergraduate social work degree?

What can be done to overcome those obstacles?

These are of course questions, both specific and general, that many of you may have already pondered over many-a-time—and while these challenges are certainly difficult to overcome, they must not, however, defeat your sincere resolve to address them through additional study, professional practice, academic research and teaching, as well as advocacy and critical policy analysis. This book is specifically designed to help you in all of these critical tasks.

Nevertheless, where do we go from here though? What exciting opportunities do we see in store for criminal justice social work in the future? To that end, we have made a deliberate choice of introducing in the next section, the virtues of employing a strengths-based perspective in the criminal justice system. This is, in part, our response to the challenge raised by Professor Raghavan in this book for 'a different breed of professionals to intervene in the system, instead of the earlier heavy reliance on personnel who were trained to ensure safety, security and discipline amongst the offending population'. We believe criminal justice social workers trained to deliver services that are underpinned by a strengths-based perspective will be Professor Raghavan's 'different breed of professionals'.

Strengths-based Practice

Francis, Pulla, Clark, Mariscal and Ilango, in their 2014 book entitled *Advancing Social Work in Mental Health through Strengths Based Practice*, advocated the idea of employing this paradigm in the field of mental health. This perspective emerged in the early 1980s at the University of Kansas under the leadership of remarkable scholars such as Dennis Saleebey, Charles Rapp and Ann Weick, to name a few. They were able to articulate a set of notions that had held so much promise for multiple client populations, in multiple settings and systems, and using a broader range of methods. This exciting development was amply documented in Dennis Saleebey's *The Strengths Perspective in Social Work Practice*, first published in 1992, and thereafter in its succeeding five editions, with the 6th edition being published in 2013. It has been largely through their initial and ongoing efforts that a wide variety of applications have been initiated. Strengths-based is essentially a practice that is premised by a philosophy which shows us how to work more effectively with individuals, families, groups, organisations and communities (O'Neil, 2005). As Steven Onken explained, '[w]hen you change the way you look at things, the things that you look at changes' (2014, p. 146). Notwithstanding the term 'strengths' in its title, it does not discount problems or weaknesses, but rather concentrates on offering possibilities, promises and hope to those who often lack such optimism in life by focussing and leveraging on their existing positives (Francis, 2014, p. 27). As Stalker, Levine and Coady noted, every person contains 'untapped and often unconscious resources' (1999, p. 470). By analysing their circumstances through a strengths-based perspective, a path is created towards the exploration of future positive possibilities for the client and his/her family (Saleebey, 1997). This is done by ensuring that all the relevant facts are seen in the light of … [the offenders'] capacities, talents, competencies, possibilities, visions, values, and hopes, however dashed and distorted these may have become through circumstance, oppression, and trauma. The strengths approach requires an accounting of what people know and what they can do, however inchoate that may sometimes seem. (Saleebey, 1996, p. 297)

This, however, is more easily said than done, and as Clark (2014) has lamented, the criminal justice system, and in particular, the prisons, is essentially premised on 3 'C's, that is, Control, Correction and Compliance (Clark, 2013, p. 147)—aims that tend to accentuate the offenders' weaknesses and marginalise their strengths. Nevertheless, while cognisant of the need for control and compliance within correctional settings, Clark (2013) asserted that using the strengths-based model of social work practice, lasting positive changes can still be effected in the lives of the offenders.

In the specific context of addressing the needs of mentally ill offenders, Francis and Chong (2015) proposed a further three 'C's that represent how strengths-based practice (SBP) can be usefully employed alongside the existing, and many might say, necessary fundamental aims of control and compliance. These would be: Climate, Compassion and Commitment (Francis & Chong, 2015, p. 95). The authors made it amply clear that the use strengths-based social work in this regard does not discount 'the existing problems of the mentally ill offenders but rather is an approach to view things differently through a lens of positivity and an attitude of optimism and hope' (Francis & Chong, 2015, p. 90). A key plank in successfully implementing a strengths-based approach could lie in the initiative's capacity 'to look at motivation to change from an offender's point of view' (McMurran, 2002, p. 5). What better way to motivate an offender to change his/her wayward ways than by initially helping them to uncover and/or recognise that they have particular strengths, and thereafter to assist the offender to leverage upon them in a way that increases the likelihood of their living a pro-social life in the future. More particularly, Francis and Chong explained that

it is only by forging a genuine cooperative relationship and being willing to listen to the lived experiences of their clients, can practitioners establish trust and develop a *'climate of guided self-healing'* (where the offender's own strengths are enhanced so as to facilitate the meta-phorical 'body' to heal itself of its illnesses). Unfortunately, a '*compassionate approach*' to practice (where positive action on the part of the criminal justice practitioner is driven by a strong sense of empathy, and a desire to share in the suffering of the client), together with an unwavering '*commitment to such self-healing and compassion*' are concepts that are often challenged or marginalised in an ideologically charged environment where police enforcement (control), legal compliance and strict correctional justice often prevail. (2015, pp. 94–95)

Rapp and Goscha further reminded us that there is only so much that this approach can do, and as such

a focus on strengths should never ignore that there are economic and social conditions that affect the wellbeing of those with a mental illness. Poverty, unemployment, discrimination, social exclusion, disparities in health care, etc., can be far more disabling for people than symptoms associated with a mental illness. The Strengths Model was never intended to serve as a comprehensive social, economic, and political agenda. Economic and social policy will continuously need to be evaluated to determine its effect on the wellbeing of those with disabilities. But we cannot wait for economic and social justice to occur before we help people use the power of their own strengths and existing strengths of the community to impact their life. This would be an equal injustice. (2014, p. 35)

But are criminal justice social workers ready to embrace such a paradigm shift—from one that is characterised by control, correction and compliance—to that which engenders a *climate* of guided self-healing, a *compassionate* approach and a *commitment* to such self-healing and compassion?

Conclusion: Are We Ready to Embrace This Shift in Practice?

There is some evidence to suggest that a strengths-based approach is gaining prominence in contemporary social work practice in India. In recent years, there have been a number of papers published that reflect this change in the practice context in the country (Francis, 2012; Francis et al., 2014; Ilango, Francis, & Udhayakumar, 2012; Pulla, 2012; Shekhar, Ilango, & Francis, 2014). The challenge before criminal justice social workers is to constantly seek out opportunities at micro (clinical), meso (institutional) and macro (governmental) levels to put into practise their strengths-based philosophy—to devise, implement and evaluate measures that empower and heal by leveraging on the offenders' and victims' strengths—a rigorous process that will demand from them far more than simply acquiring new techniques, vocabulary or protocols (Francis & Chong, 2015). This perspective will require a deep transformation of the practitioner's beliefs and worldview. A criminal justice social worker will now have to look and listen for potentiality, possibility, promise, skills, experience, wisdom, assets, knowledge and even the smallest sparkle of hope in the eyes of their client, be they an offender or a victim.

As Saleebey (2001) asserted, to embrace a strengths-based approach involves 'changing one's heart and mind—a personal paradigm shift' (p. 13). The question, however, is: Are we ready to embrace such a shift in practice? This will of course have significant implications for social work education, teaching and practise especially in the context of criminal justice social work. As Pulla explained,

> [s]ocial workers interested in the strengths perspective need to engage in a personal process of analysis and transformation, recognizing that this will be a continuous process, recognizing signs of the traditional framework in their practice, becoming aware of themselves and their attitudes, biases, and limitations, and defining a new position for themselves in the helping relationship, that is, removing their 'expert' hats and acknowledging the client's expertise, knowledge, and capabilities. (2012, p. 15)

It is arguable that adopting such an approach will pave the way for a positive change, in and of, the system. That said, this transformation will not occur overnight nor will it happen in a vacuum. It will take time, hard work, courage and a spirit of cooperation and engagement with a range of key stakeholders. Unfortunately, this may not be as easy as it sounds given the vested interests of other professions and agencies already entrenched in the criminal justice system. Police officers, correctional officers, lawyers, prosecutors, judges, psychologists and psychiatrists are powerful actors that have already staked their claims over the criminal justice process for many years, and as such have built substantial reputations and evidence-based practices. Disappointingly, criminal justice social workers, as compared to these agents of social control, have a less established reputation and repository of evidence-based practice. Consequently, the role of criminal justice social workers must be revisited and prioritised in this regard. The connection between research, practice and a credible reputation is fundamental to the practise of all professions. Harvey, Plummer, Pighills and Pain, observed that '[p]ractitioner research is potentially the most useful and relevant source of new knowledge for social work and service innovations' (2013, p. 2). Bender and Windsor, however, lamented that the social work profession, more generally, has struggled

> to demonstrate its value to the public and define the field as contributing distinct knowledge and services. Creating a social work knowledge base is critical in the development of guidelines that inform social workers' effective and efficient interventions to clients. A strong social work knowledge base, moreover, enables social workers to more effectively inform public policy and services for vulnerable and disadvantaged populations. (2010, p. 148)

Furthermore, Ilango, Francis and Harris encouraged social workers to remember that

> [t]hrough writing and publishing we are able to increase professional recognition of our practice and create evidences that demonstrate a commitment to excellence in social work practice. It is the responsibility of all of us to engage in this process, (students, academics, social work institutions, social work practitioners and researchers) and together we can create a change in this field. This is both a challenge and an opportunity for social work fraternity in India. (2013, p. 11)

This encouragement is particularly apt for criminal justice social workers in India, and more must be done to encourage both aspiring as well as seasoned practitioners and researchers to focus on improving the depth and width of their knowledge base via peer reviewed studies, projects and publications. Through such endeavours, the profession will be able to re-claim its space and legitimacy within multidisciplinary teams of practitioners in the criminal justice system. As Raghavan (2013) stated: '[t]here is a need to revive some of these institutions or build new institutions to sustain the development process. Social work and social science institutions with a sense of history and hope for the future are required' (p. 286).

In order to make positive changes in this area of work, there is a need to renew the existing partnerships, create new ones, as well as establish novel ways of working with the staff and the community, so that work can be directed towards 'healing at the individual and family level but also at the community level, achieving a more just society' (Raghavan, 2013, p. 286). In this context, the Association Schools of Social Work in India, the National Association of Professional Social Workers in India and other regional and professional organisations could play vital roles in promoting the role of social work in this sector and advocate for a change in the system. This is indeed a great opportunity for the profession. As Francis and Chong (2015) reminded us before: '[l]et strengths-based practitioners trust in their *own* strengths, just as they trust in the strengths of their clients' (p. 100).

We acknowledge that this field of SBP may not be suitable for everyone. Only those who have open minds, questioning intellects, as well as passionate and compassionate hearts will find themselves faced with a great opportunity to make a huge difference in the lives of so many, both sinners and saints alike, who have been forgotten or marginalised by Indian society. While we can only give you guidance and encouragement, the exciting choice to undertake this task using strengths-based principles lies squarely on your shoulders. Should you decide to embark on this arduous but rewarding journey, we anticipate that your SBP will ultimately pave the way for positive change within the criminal justice system. That said, it should be noted that this transformation will not happen immediately nor will it occur in a vacuum where there is no resistance. Rather, you must cultivate patience as well as a spirit of cooperation and engagement with the various multidisciplinary stakeholders. Will this be challenging? Yes, it will. Will you experience disappointments? Probably.

But do not despair.
+ Remember +
The glory of Rome was neither built in a day.
Nor was it accomplished by just one person.

References

Bender, K., & Windsor, L. C. (2010). The four Ps of publishing: Demystifying publishing in peer reviewed journals for social work doctoral students. *Journal of Teaching in Social Work, 30*(2), 147–58.

Burke, L., & Collett, S. (2010). People are not things: What new labour has done to probation. *Probation Journal, 57*(3), 232–49.

Clark, M. D. (2013). The strengths perspective in criminal justice. In D. Saleebey (Ed.), *The strengths perspective in social work practice* (6th ed., pp. 129–48). Boston, MA: Pearson Education Inc.

————. (2014). The strengths perspective in criminal justice. In A. P. Francis, V. Pulla, M. Clark, E. S. Mariscal & P. Ilango (Eds), *Advancing social work in mental health through strengths-based practice* (pp. 229–42). Brisbane: Primrose Hall Publishing Group.

Cullen, F. T., & Gendreau, P. (2000). Assessing correctional rehabilitation: Policy, practice, and prospects. In J. Horney (Ed.), *Policies, processes, and decisions of the criminal justice system: Criminal justice 2000* (Vol. 3, pp. 109–75). Washington, DC: US Department of Justice, National Institute of Justice.

Francis, A. (2012). Journey towards recovery in mental health. In V. Pulla, L. Chenoweth, A. Francis & B. Stefan (Eds), *Papers in strengths based practice* (pp. 19–33). New Delhi: Allied Publishers.

————. (2014). Strengths-based practice: 'Not about discounting problems but offering possibilities, promises and hope'. *Adelaide Journal of Social Work, 1*(1), 27–44.

Francis, A. P., Pulla, V., Clark, M., Mariscal, E. S., & Ilango, P. (2014). *Advancing social work in mental health through strengths-based practice.* Brisbane: Primrose Hall.

Francis, A., & Chong, M. D. (2015). Application of strengths-based principles in addressing mental health issues in the criminal justice system. In A. Francis, P. L. Rosa, L. Sankaran, & S. P. Rajeev (Eds), *Social work practice in mental health: Cross-cultural perspectives* (pp. 90–102). New Delhi: Allied Publishers.

Harker, H., & Worrall, A. (2011). From 'community corrections' to 'probation and parole' in Western Australia. *Probation Journal: The Journal of Community & Criminal Justice, 58*(4), 364–71.

Harvey, D., Plummer, D., Pighills, A., & Pain, T. (2013). Practitioner research capacity: A survey of social workers in Northern Queensland. *Australian Social Work, 66*(4), 2–15.

Herzog-Evans, M. (2011). Judicial rehabilitation in France: Helping with the desisting process and acknowledging achieved desistance. *European Journal of Probation, 3*(1), 4–19.

McMurran, M. (2002). Motivation to change: Selection criterion or treatment need? In M. McMurran (Ed.), *Motivating offenders to change: A guide to enhancing engagement in therapy* (pp. 3–15). New York: John Wiley & Sons.

O'Neil, D. (2005). How can a strengths approach increase safety in a child protection context? *Children Australia, 30*(4), 28–32.

Onken, S. (2014). Realising recovery: A strengths based practice framework. In A. Francis, V. Pulla, M. Clark, E. S. Mariscal & P. Ilango (Eds). *Advancing social work in mental health through strengths based practice* (pp. 145–75). Sydney: Primrose Hall Publishing Group Aus.

Petersilia, J. (1997). Probation in the United States. In M. Tonry (Ed.), *Crime and justice: An annual review of research* (Vol. 22, pp. 149–200). Chicago, IL: University of Chicago Press.

Ilango, P., Francis, A. P., & Harris, N. (2013). Scientific writing and publication in social work: Issues and concerns. In P. Ilango, A. P. Francis & N. Harris (Eds), *Scientific writing and publishing in social work* (pp. 3–12). Bangalore: Niruta Publications.

Ilango, P., Francis, A., & Udhayakumar, P. (2012). Strengths-based approach to social work practice with older persons. In A. Pulla, L. Chenoweth, A. Francis & S. Bakaj (Eds), *Papers in strengths-based practice* (pp. 150–61). New Delhi: Allied Publishers.

Pulla, V. (2012). What are strengths based practice all about? In Pulla, V., Chenoweth, L., Francis, A. & Bakaj, S. (Eds.), *Papers in strengths based practice* (pp. 1–18). New Delhi: Allied Publishers.

Raghavan, V. (2013). Social work intervention in criminal justice: Field-theory linkage. In S. Singh (Ed.), *Social work and social development: Perspectives from India and the United States* (pp. 265–89). Chicago, IL: Lyceum Publications Inc.

Rapp, C., & Goscha, R. (2014). Three decades of strengths: Reflections of the past and challenges of the future. In A. Francis, V. Pulla, M. Clark, E. S. Mariscal & P. Ilango (Eds), *Advancing social work in mental health through strengths based practice* (pp. 39–53). Sydney: Primrose Hall Publishing Group Aus.

Saleebey, D. (Ed.). (1992). *The strengths perspective in social work practice.* New York: Longman.

———. (1996). The strengths perspective in social work practice: Extensions and cautions. *Social Work, 41*(3), 296–306.

Saleebey, D. (Ed.). (1997). Introduction: Power in the people. In D. Saleebey (Ed.), *The strengths perspective in social work practice* (2nd ed., pp. 3–19). New York: Longman.

———. (2001). *Human behavior and social environments: A biopsychosocial approach*. New York: Columbia University Press.

———. (Ed.). (2013). *The strengths perspective in social work practice* (6th ed.). Boston, MA: Pearson Education Inc.

Shekhar, R., Ilango, P., & Francis, A. (2014). Efficacy of strengths-based practice in engaging with children with behavioural problems: A case study from India. In A. Francis, V. Pulla, M. Clark, S. Mariscal & P. Ilango (Eds), *Advancing social work in mental health through strengths based practice* (pp. 31–38). Sydney: Primrose Hall Publishing Group Aus.

Stalker, C., Levine, J., & Coady, N. (1999). Solution-focused brief therapy: One model fits all? *Families in Society, 80*(5), 468–77.

Teague, M. (2011). Probation in America: Armed, private and unaffordable? *Probation Journal, 58*(4), 317–32.

About the Editors and Contributors

Editors

Mark David Chong is currently a Senior Lecturer in Criminology and Criminal Justice Studies as well as the Criminology Major Coordinator for the Bachelor of Arts programme at the College of Arts, Society and Education, James Cook University (JCU), Australia. He was also formerly the Director of Research Education for the School of Arts and Social Sciences, JCU, from 2012 to January 2015. In 2015, he was recognised for his 'exceptional support for students with a disability' through the university's Inclusive Practice Award. He was thereafter invited by the Vice Chancellor and the Students Association to deliver JCU's annual public 'Last Lecture for 2015', entitled 'A Humanistic Approach to Educating our Next Generation of Crime Fighters'. He is also an external assessor (grant applications) for the Social Sciences and Humanities Research Council of Canada.

He graduated with a PhD in law from the University of Sydney, where he received his Law School's Longworth Scholarship (2003), the Cooke, Cooke, Coghlan, Godfrey and Littlejohn Scholarship (2004), the Longworth Scholarship for Academic Merit (2006) and the Longworth Scholarship once again in 2007. He was initially trained as a criminal defence lawyer and later secured an LLM (Merit) in Criminology and Criminal Justice from Queen Mary, University of London. Thereafter, he was appointed as a Judicial Referee by the President of the Republic of Singapore on the recommendation of the Chief Justice to the Small Claims Tribunals' bench. However, given his deep interest in criminal justice issues, Mark subsequently taught the Singapore Police Force and the Central Narcotics Bureau at Temasek Polytechnic, Singapore, under a joint academic programme with Queensland University of Technology, Australia. He was also an adjunct lecturer and tutor at SIM University, Singapore, where he designed a criminology subject specifically for students from the Singapore Police Force. Of late, Mark has begun to develop expertise in converging criminology and social work through the specialisation of criminal justice social work in India. In this regard, he has published works that pertain to human rights, mental illness and strengths-based practice.

Abraham P. Francis is an Associate Professor in Social Work and Human Services at the College of Arts, Society and Education, JCU. With international exposure and extensive experience in community development and mental health, he taught social work at the University of Delhi in India and also worked as a senior mental health social worker with Country Health in South Australia, before moving to Townsville to join JCU. He held a stint in Queensland Health as Assistant Director of Social Work. He is associated with many voluntary organisations, associations, professional bodies and developmental projects, in both Australia and India. He has established international partnerships and research collaborations with universities and non-governmental organisations (NGOs) in Asia. He is passionate about working and researching in strengths-based practice in mental health. His other research interests are in the field of communities, criminal justice, international social work and gerontological social work.

His excellence in teaching has likewise been recognised on a number of occasions. For example, in 2010, he was a recipient of JCU's Inclusive Practice Award for his 'exceptional support for students with a disability'. More recently, in 2016, he received the university's 'Citation for Outstanding Contributions to Student Learning' for his 'leadership and expertise in social work education in mental health that inspires and nurtures students to be competent, confident and compassionate practitioners'.

Contributors

Sanjai Bhatt is presently the senior most Professor at Department of Social Work, University of Delhi and President of National Association of Professional Social Workers in India. He joined the University of Delhi after serving the University of Lucknow; Kashi Vidyapeeth, Varanasi; Kurukshetra University and Chitrakoot Gramodaya Vishwavidyalaya.

His areas of interest are social work education, social development, social security, occupational social work, climate change and corporate social responsibility (CSR). He has authored/edited eight books, namely *Social Work Education in India: A Resource Book; Social Work Practice: The Changing Context; Social Justice and Social Work Profession in India: Challenging Responses and Responding Challenges; Social Work Education and Practice Engagement; Social Work Response to Environment and Disasters; Social Work Response to Social Realities; Patterns of Mobility, Migration and HIV Risk in India; and Democracy in Trade Unions.* He has contributed a dozen book chapters and around 80 research papers on various themes. His thesis '4 W's (Water, Work, Waste and Women) in Development Paradigm' is widely accepted in academic fraternity. He has conducted varied research/consultancy work which includes benchmark survey, social assessment, need assessment, desk review, organisational review, programme evaluation, capacity building, programme designing, human resource management, manpower planning, team building, participatory research and so on. He has initiated many innovative projects such as the University for Development Action and Integrated Learning (UDAI-I) for rehabilitation of earthquake-affected persons in Bhuj, Gujarat (2001), and UDAI-II for relief and rehabilitation of flood-affected people in Supaul, Bihar (2008). He is a member of various government committees, including Bureau of Police Research and Development, Ministry of Home Affairs, Delhi Urban Slum Improvement Board, Juvenile Justice Board, 12th Five-Year Plan for Social Justice and so on, and is in Board of many NGOs and CSR Foundations. He has been part of campaigns such as Chipko Movement, Voters' Education Movement, Child Right, Reform in International Financial Institutions, and has founded an advocacy group PAIRVI.

Jamie Fellows is currently a Lecturer of Law at JCU (2009–present). He lectures and researches in the areas of public law, including public international law, administrative law, legal ethics, criminal law, Australian legal history, governance, sovereignty and colonialism. He has had extensive industry and professional experience in Australia and North East Asia, where he held several roles in finance and commercial property. Prior to entering academia, he worked as a Compliance Analyst with the Australian Securities and Investments Commission in Sydney and later as a Director with CB Richard Ellis in Tokyo, where he was responsible for corporate compliance, acquisition/disposition of foreign assets and commercial leasing. He holds undergraduate and postgraduate degrees from James Cook University (LLB Hons, BA), University of Sydney (MA), Australian National University (Graduate Diploma of Legal Practice) and University of New South Wales (Graduate Diploma in Education). He is currently pursuing a PhD from JCU.

Debarati Halder is an advocate by profession and the Honorary Managing Director of Centre for Cyber Victim Counselling (CCVC), an online non-profit organisation meant for helping and counselling the victims of internet and digital communication crime victims. Currently, she is Research Officer at Unitedworld School of Law, Ahmedabad, Gujarat. She has served as a lawyer in Madras High Court and Tirunelveli District courts. She is also the founding secretary of the South Asian Society of Criminology and Victimology (SASCV). She received her PhD degree in Law from the National Law School of India University, Bengaluru, ML degree from the University of Madras and LLB degree from the University of Calcutta. She is also an independent legal researcher and author. She has authored three books and published many scholarly articles on online victimisation of women, children and laws, therapeutic jurisprudence, human rights, prison rights of women and so on in many national as well as international peer-reviewed journals including the *British Journal of Criminology*, *International Annals of Criminology* and *Journal of Law and Religion*. She has also been an invited speaker in the Stockholm Criminology Symposium, 2012, and International Conference on Social Media, 2015, Istanbul, Turkey.

Margaret Henni is a graduate of the College of Arts, Society and Education at JCU. She majored in Criminology and Psychology, and received the prestigious University Academic Medal (Bachelor Coursework) '[f]or excellent academic achievement in coursework studies undertaken at undergraduate level'. She was later awarded a Class One Honours degree for her thesis 'Youth Crime in Townsville: Moral Panic or Regional Crisis', which examined the response to youth crime by the media and the subsequent legislative changes to the youth justice system. She has worked in a variety of research and support roles across the disciplines of criminology, sociology, social work, and political science; tutors first-year criminology students, and holds the position of Student Support Officer at the university.

Katherine Hoffensetz was selected as the inaugural JCU–Queensland Victim Assist Intern in 2014 and graduated from JCU with a Bachelor of Psychosocial Science in 2015, with a heavy focus on criminology and the plight of victims. Currently, she is working in the domestic violence sector, whereby she helps empower victims of domestic violence to build new lives with security and support. Through the work at Sera's, women are provided with counselling, guidance, information as well as emotional and practical support to engender opportunities to break the cycle of domestic violence.

K. Jaishankar is presently the Head of the Department of Criminology at the Raksha Shakti University, Gujarat. Earlier to the present position, he was a faculty member at the Department of Criminology and a Professor in Criminology and Criminal Justice, Manonmaniam Sundaranar University, Tamil Nadu. He has published more than a hundred publications, including peer-reviewed articles in journals such as *British Journal of Criminology*, editorials, book chapters and books. He is the recipient of the prestigious 'National Academy of Sciences, India (NASI)–SCOPUS Young Scientist Award (2012)–Social Sciences' and ISC–S. S. Srivastava Award for Excellence in Teaching and Research in Criminology (2013). He is the founding Editor-in-Chief of the *International Journal of Cyber Criminology* and Editor-in-Chief of *International Journal of Criminal Justice Sciences*. He is also the founder President of SASCV and the founder Executive Director of CCVC. He was a Keynote Speaker at the 15th World Society of Victimology Symposium held during 5–9 July 2015, Perth, Western Australia. He is recently appointed as an International Ambassador of the British Society of Criminology.

Sonny Jose is the Head of Social Work, Loyola College of Social Sciences, Thiruvananthapuram. He is a Linneus-Palme Scholar, Ersta Skondal University. He did his undergraduation in Mathematics (1989), Masters in Social Work (1991) and Masters in Psychology (1997). He started his career as a business manager (1991), later trained and practised as psychotherapist-cum-counsellor prior to venturing into teaching at Loyola College of Social Sciences in 1999. He is a popular academic trainer, engages in research and has 34 publications in peer-reviewed journals— national and international—to his credit. He has authored two books, *Perspectives on Mental Health* and *Women in Tourism*, and 24 chapters in other books. He is on the Editorial Board of peer-reviewed journals such as *IJSWHR (USA), Adelaide Journal Educere, Teens and the Loyola Journal of Social Sciences*, and is a consultant for World Bank, Kerala Women Development Corporation, Kerala Public Service Commission, Child Development Center (CDC) research projects, and State Council of Educational Research and Training (SCERT) as well as Indira Gandhi National Open University (IGNOU) for academics. He is a Member of Board of Studies for various universities—Manipal University, Mangalore University, Mahatma Gandhi University, Calicut University and the University of Kerala—and a Member of the Research Review Committee for Sree Sankaracharya University and M.G. University. He is the Founder Director of LiveLab, a self-sustaining NGO propagating Life Skills Education. He is the life member of Indian Association of Schools of Social Work, Indian Council of Social Welfare, Indian Association of Life Skill Educators, Kerala Association of Professional Social Work and National Association of Professional Social Workers in India. His innovations for quality assurance include STeF-04, MFS07 and SAPv.4.

Jyoti P. Khandpasole is working as a Project Manager in Resource Cell for Juvenile Justice (RCJJ). It is a field action project

(FAP) of the Centre for Criminology and Justice (CCJ), Tata Institute of Social Sciences (TISS), Mumbai. The RCJJ introduced the concept of a 'Help Desk' on the lines of a 'May I Help You'/'enquiry' desk in 2010. The Help Desk functions from Observation Homes on all days to impart information, guidance on juvenile justice issues and assisting juveniles, parents on case-related matters. Prior to this, she has served as a Research Officer in the CCJ, TISS, Mumbai, for one year. She started her career by helping to rehabilitate prisoners in central prisons of Maharashtra.

Pravin S. Khandpasole is the Director of DISHA since 2009. DISHA is a registered NGO working for the rights and restoration of victims of violent crimes such as murder, sexual offences in Maharashtra. A 24-hour telephone helpline (07666102103) is being run to provide free information, socio-legal guidance and outreach support services to needy and poor people interfacing with criminal justice system (CJS). DISHA has been instrumental in focusing the government attention on the victim's plight and the furnishing of the Victim Compensation Scheme (Section 357A of Criminal Procedure Code) with budgetary provisions through Public Interest Litigation in Maharashtra. Prior to this work, he has served as a Research Officer in the CCJ, TISS, Mumbai, for one and a half years. He started his career by helping to rehabilitate prisoners in central prisons of Maharashtra for six years.

Sashwati Mishra has completed her MA in Social Work with specialisation in Criminology and Justice from TISS, Mumbai. She holds another degree, Joint European Masters in International Humanitarian Action-NOHA, from Univeriste Paul Cezanne Aix-Marseille III, Aix-en-Provence, France, and University of Deusto, Bilbao, Spain. She is a researcher and a trainer. Her areas of interest include governance, accountability, nomadic and denotified tribes, feminism and social justice.

K. P. Asha Mukundan did MA in Social Work with specialisation in Criminology and Correctional Administration from TISS (1998) and PhD from Mumbai University (2011).

She specialises on working with issues related to child rights and juvenile justice. She has headed the Child Rights Cell at state level and was on the panel of trainers to train juvenile justice functionaries by National Institute of Social Defence (GOI). She has been a part of several national and state-level studies. A founder Member and Project Director of RCJJ, based in Maharashtra, the project was able to create policy level impact on the juvenile justice system (JJS). She works closely with judiciary and was a part of state-level subcommittees set to monitor working of the JJS, draft standard operating procedures for Juvenile Justice Boards, amendment of Maharashtra Juvenile Justice Rules, Maharashtra Probation of Offenders Rules. She was on the Editorial Board of newsletters *Ujjwal* and *Prabodan* which published articles on children. She has published articles in journals, including *Journal of School of Social Work* and *Economic and Political Weekly*. Recipient of Endeavour Fellowship (Government of Australia, 2007), she did a study to understand the working of the JJS in New South Wales. She was also selected under Exchange Teacher Programme by the University of Gavle, under the Linnaeus Palme Programme in 2013.

Roshni Nair is an Assistant Professor and Chairperson of the CCJ, School of Social Work at TISS, Mumbai. She is presently involved in teaching, research, fieldwork and research guidance in the postgraduate degree programme, Social Work in Criminology and Justice. Her past areas of work have been with child and youth rights with an emphasis on rehabilitation of children of prisoners, youth living on the streets and runaway girls. She recently completed her PhD at TISS in social work education with a focus on fieldwork. She supervises student fieldwork in prisons, women and children's institutions and in rehabilitation settings. She teaches courses in social work methods, victimology and crime prevention, rural crimes and an online skill-based course for social work practitioners. Over 23 years of a career connected with social work, she has spent equal time being a social work, practitioner and educator. She is now keen on consolidating her experiences to work on strengthening curriculum, advocacy and research in the field of social work practice of criminology and justice. She heads a field action project of the Centre that offers individual fellowship to alumni to explore work in criminal justice themes.

Digvijoy Phukan has completed his Masters in Social Work and PhD in Social Work from the University of Delhi. He is presently working as Assistant Professor (Social Work) with Mahatma Gandhi Central University of Bihar, Motihari. Prior to this, he was a Consultant in the Advisory Team of Ernst and Young LLP. He also taught social work at the Central University of Jammu in the capacity of an Assistant Professor. He has also taught in School of Planning and Architecture. His areas of interest are community organisation, development research and criminal justice social work. He is also a University Gold Medalist and has worked extensively with the Salt Workers of Gujarat for his thesis on 'Conservation and Livelihood'. He has explored the criminalisation of communities in his thesis. He also has the experience of teaching criminal justice social work to postgraduate students. He has co-authored *Social Work Education in India: A Resource Book*.

Ilango Ponnuswami is currently Professor at the Department of Social Work and Dean of Faculty of Arts, Bharathidasan University, Tamil Nadu. With a Fellowship from the United Nations Population Fund (UNFPA) and the International Institute on Ageing, United Nations, Malta (INIA), he successfully pursued a Postgraduate Diploma in Gerontology and Geriatrics at the Institute of Gerontology, University of Malta. He also attended a short-term training course in Income Security for the Elderly in Developing Countries conducted by the INIA with a UNFPA Fellowship during May–June 1995. He was a Cairns Institute Visiting Scholar at JCU during March–May 2012. He is also a member of the Editorial Board of the *Journal of Transformative Education* published by SAGE. He has published research articles in reputed journals such as *Indian Journal of Social Work*, BOLD, *Indian Journal of Social Psychiatry*, *Indian Journal of Criminology and Criminalistics* and a few chapters in books and quite a few articles in *Social Welfare* and *Kurukshetra*—official journals published by Central Social Welfare Board and Ministry of Rural Development, respectively, Government of India. He has also published seven edited volumes. Besides, he has participated in several international ageing and social work conferences and, more recently, represented India at the BRICS Forum on Ageing in Seoul. He also attended with Full Scholarship and presented scientific papers at the International Ageing and Social Work Conferences organised by the INIA in Malta (1996), Hong Kong Council of Social Services in Hong Kong (1999), International Federation on Ageing in Montreal, Canada (1999), Asian South Pacific Bureau of Adult Education in Singapore (1999), International Association of Homes and Services for Ageing in Sydney, Australia (2003), Haggai Institute for Advanced Leadership Training in Maui, Hawaii, USA (2004), Episcopal Relief and Rehabilitation Division of the Churches in Bangkok, Thailand (2005), International Conference of ISTR, Bangkok, Thailand (2006), University of Malaya, Kuala Lumpur, Malaysia (2011), International Conference on Strength Based Social Work Practice in Social Work and Human Services, Kathmandu, Nepal (2012), and more recently, the 20th World Congress of Gerontology and Geriatrics (IAGG, 2013) and BRICS Forum on Ageing, Seoul, Republic of Korea (2013).

Venkat Pulla is a TISS alumnus and a Tata Dorabji Scholar, 1976–77. He has been the founding Head of the Social Work Discipline in the Northern Territory University (1992–95) and is currently the coordinator of Social Work Discipline at the Australian Catholic University, Brisbane. He has previously taught at the Charles Sturt and the Sunshine Coast universities in Australia. In India, he taught at the College of Social Work, Hyderabad, and offered urban development training through British aid (DFID)-funded projects for metropolitan cities in India through the Regional Centre for Urban and Environmental Studies (RCUES), Osmania University. In India, he founded the Centre for Environment Concerns in Hyderabad, as a reflective sequel to the Bhopal tragedy and initiated the first-ever written Citizen's Report on the City of Hyderabad and Its Physical Environment. In Australia, he founded the Brisbane Institute of Strengths Based Practice and the Impetus Global, Brisbane, that offer training in strengths-based strategies for human services and the corporate sector. He writes on green social work, spirituality, coping resilience and building hope. His research interests include poverty interventions, health rights and transition countries.

Vijay Raghavan has done MA in Social Work with specialisation in Criminology and Correctional Administration and PhD in Social

Work from TISS. He is associated with the CCJ, School of Social Work, TISS, since 2005. Prior to 2005, he was the Project Director (since 1993), Prayas: Social Work in Criminal Justice, an FAP of the CCJ, engaging with issues of protection of legal rights and social re-entry of criminal justice clients, with a special focus on women, children and youth. He has been involved in training of police, prison and judicial officers on issues around gender, prisoners' rights, correctional laws, anti-trafficking, and re-entry of crime-affected persons. His research interests include custodial justice and prison reforms in post-colonial societies, social work practice in criminal justice regimes, anti-human trafficking and, more recently, youth involvement in organised crime in post-industrial cities. He is associated with two other FAPs of TISS: Koshish, working on rights and social inclusion of the homeless and destitute populations since 2006, and TANDA, (Towards Advocacy, Networking and Developmental Action), working on rights and entitlements of nomadic and de-notified tribes since 2011.

Atul Pratap Singh is presently working as Assistant Professor (Senior Scale) at the Department of Social Work, Dr Bhim Rao Ambedkar College, University of Delhi. He has 20 authored/co-authored/edited/co-edited books, about 60 research papers/articles/book chapters/columns to his credit including third *Encyclopedia of Social Work in India*, journals of international and national repute/books/newspapers/magazines. He has presented more than two dozen papers in international and national seminar/conferences which have been widely appreciated for their contents and analysis. He has also acted as Convener and Co-convener in two national seminars, respectively. He has served various positions in 20 different international, national and state-level research/consultancy/quality evaluation projects which include programme evaluation, social assessment, need assessment, KAP (Knowledge, Attitude and Practices) analysis and so on. Besides, he was invited as resource person/guest speaker/visiting faculty on more than 50 occasions. He is a committed and devoted teacher as well as a researcher. He received 'Best/Meritorious Teacher Award' from Government of NCT of Delhi in 2012 and prestigious 'Jan Jagriti Samman' from renowned freelance journalists and writer's organisation 'Akhil Bhartiya

Swatantra Lekhak Manch', New Delhi, in 2013. He has also been associated with several academic, professional and social welfare and development organisations. His areas of interest include social work education and fieldwork practicum, social welfare administration, community development and social research.

Ruchi Sinha is the Associate Professor with the CCJ in the School of Social Work, TISS. She completed her MA in Social Work from TISS, Mumbai, and her MPhil/PhD from Jawaharlal Nehru University (JNU), New Delhi. She has over two decades of experience on issues of violence, conflict and peace processes, policing, corrections and correctional laws, criminology, crime and development, criminal justice policy, criminal justice social work, trafficking, child rights and protection, and juvenile justice as well as human rights. She has actively advocated at the policy level on all the issues mentioned above. She is currently focusing on effect of public policies on policing, crime and the response of the CJS to the public policy shifts. She, along with her centre colleagues, is involved with the National Research on Human Trafficking in India. She has been engaged with many initiatives including the Prime Ministers Rural Development Fellowship Scheme and RCJJ. Currently, she is a member of Chhattisgarh State Planning Commission. She constituted a sub-group on 'Children, Adolescent and Youth'. She is also part of the team involved in drafting the Maharashtra State Children's Homes Policy.

Amit Gopal Thakre is presently working as a Trained Criminologist (Consultant) in the Department of Criminology, Raksha Shakti University, Ahmedabad, Gujarat, and providing consultancy services to the Ahmedabad City Police. Prior to the present position, he served as Research Consultant at the National Human Rights Commission of India, New Delhi. He was a UGC-Junior Research Fellow at the Department of Criminology and Criminal Justice, Manonmaniam Sundaranar University (MSU), Tamil Nadu, and he is awaiting thesis defense for his research on Community Policing. He is an alumna of LNJN National Institute of Criminology and Forensic Science, New Delhi. Earlier to joining Doctoral Program as JRF in MSU, he was lecturer in Institute of Forensic Science, Nagpur University, and Guest Faculty in Bihar Judicial Academy. His research interests are crime prevention and innovative interventions.

Praveen Varghese Thomas, a Commonwealth Young Professional Fellow (2013, Chandigarh), nurtured as a Social worker (MSW) from Pondicherry Central University while holding a Bachelor's degree in English Literature. His research concerns encompass counter-culturalism, multi-dimensional exclusion faced by youth, youth development and community health. His operational area includes research, consultancy, creative writing and integration of theatre (arts) in social work and facilitation. He identifies himself as a qualitative researcher and is passionate about capturing the reality and lived experiences of young persons in urban slums, victimised by multidimensional exclusion.

Kelly-Ann Williams completed her Bachelor of Psychology (Hons) in 2014. Her honours thesis explored community attitudes towards the management of sexual offenders. She has worked with children in foster care, supporting individual challenging behaviours related to early trauma and neglect. She also worked as a Probation and Parole Case Manager for Queensland Corrective Services. She is currently pursuing her Master of Psychology (Clinical), and is conducting research on the role of social capital on mental health and well-being in North Queensland (Australia) communities.

Index